the Female Gaze

WOMEN AS VIEWERS OF POPULAR CULTURE

LORRAINE GAMMAN AND
MARGARET MARSHMENT

editors

First published by The Women's Press Ltd. 1988
A member of the Namara Group
34 Great Sutton Street. London EC1V 0DX

Reprinted 1991. 1994

Jackie Stacey's article 'An Investigation of Desire between Women
in Narrative Cinema' was first published in Screen. vol. 28. no. 1.
Winter 1987. copyright © Jackie Stacey and the Society for
Education in Film and Television. 1987

British Library Cataloguing-in-Publication Data
The Female gaze: women as viewers of popular culture.
    1. popular culture. Influence of women
    I. Gamman. Lorraine   II. Marshment. Margaret
    306'.1

ISBN 0 7043 4109 3

Printed and bound in Great Britain by
BPC Paperbacks Ltd
Aylesbury. Bucks

Contents

Acknowledgments

Thanks to all those who participated in the Popular Culture course on the ma in Women's Studies at the University of Kent. To all those at home who answered the telephone; to Jane Collins and Jane Gibb who discussed the project; to Mary Knight and Helen Clohessy who helped with clearance of copyright; to all those who attended the 'Ideas In Progress' seminars at Middlesex Polytechnic – particularly Lon Fleming, Judith Williamson, Barry Curtis, Mike Dawney and Martin King; to Gregg Elliot who inscribed New Left syntax into gaps of the female imagination; to George Barber who advised about illustrations; and to Lorraine's mother who over-fed everyone when given the opportunity. Finally, the editors would like to take responsibility for any mistakes but to dedicate all the good bits of the book to the contributors who have worked hard and patiently to achieve a female gaze at popular culture.

Grateful acknowledgment is made for permission to reproduce the advertisements and illustrations published in this volume. 'Splash it all over', photograph by Neil Mackenzie Matthews is reproduced by kind permission of Blues Ltd; 'The "new man"?' by kind permission of Mothercare; the cover of *Lace* by permission of Penguin Books Ltd; the still from *All about Eve* by permission of Twentieth Century Fox; pictures from *Cagney & Lacey* by George Barber; Jenny Seagrove as Emma Harte in a Portman/Artemis production *A Woman of Substance*, reproduced by permission.

Introduction

> 'Don't be impertinent,' said the King, 'and
> don't look at me like that!'. . .
>   'A cat may look at a king,' said Alice.[1]

Why write a book about women *looking*? At men or at each other? In most popular representations it seems that men look and women are looked at. In film, on television, in the press and in most popular narratives men are shown to be in control of the gaze, women are controlled by it. Men act; women are acted upon. This is patriarchy.

How can we change it? How can we change patriarchal relations of looking? If patriarchy informs our political regimes, our economic systems, our culture, our language, our unconscious, then it is not surprising that a male perspective is dominant in representation. How can we shift this perspective and inscribe a female gaze into the heart of our cultural life?

Smash the state; stop having relations with men; deconstruct the text; degrammaticise the sentence; return to the pre-Oedipal 'imaginary'? Radical strategies for change can be mind-blowingly apocalyptic. And while there is no denying our need for revolution, we cannot simply equate this with terrorism, and isolate ourselves from the economic, 'which determines in the last instance'.[2] This is capitalism.

Change is more often the product of a slow struggle that goes on day by day, within capitalism, and within patriarchy: to shift the balance of power and prepare the ground for radical change, or even to make more bearable the lives of those at the sharp end of these systems of oppression, we need pragmatic strategies for today as well as tomorrow. This involves, centrally, a struggle over meaning. Over who, as Humpty Dumpty said to Alice, is 'master', and over whether we want masters at all.

Popular culture is a site of struggle, where many of these meanings are determined and debated. It is not enough to dismiss popular culture as merely serving the complementary systems of capitalism and patriarchy, peddling 'false consciousness' to the duped masses. It can also be seen as a site where meanings are contested and where dominant ideologies can be disturbed. Between the market and the ideologues, the financiers and the producers, the directors and the actors, the publishers and the writers, capitalists and workers, women and men, heterosexual and homosexual, black and white, old and young – between what things mean, and how they mean, is a perpetual struggle for control.

Since the late seventies feminists have argued against any simple notion of 'false consciousness', and have suggested instead that women's experience is subordinate to the categories and codes through which it is articulated. Here, feminist appropriations of Continental Marxism have been of particular significance: the work on 'commonsense' and 'ideology' by Gramsci and Althusser, and psychoanalytic work on the acquisition of gender, have been employed by feminists to 'politicise everyday life – culture in the anthropological sense of the lived practices of a society'[3] – and to problematise the culture's definitions of femininity and masculinity.

Feminist artists too have been involved in this project: work as different as that by, say, Judy Chicago, Laura Mulvey, Jo Spence or Kathy Acker has engaged with issues around gender and its representation, and has enabled us to begin to think in new ways about the ideologies which underlie our commonsense assumptions about 'femininity' and 'art'.

As strategies of resistance, however, these radical texts do suffer from an element of pessimism: brilliant at uncovering our oppression and rewriting women into the history of creativity they have, for the most part, effectively remained 'alternative', outside the mainstream.

Our concern in this book is with a different strategy. We feel that we cannot afford to dismiss the popular by always positioning ourselves outside it. Instead, we are interested in how feminists can intervene in the mainstream to make our meanings part of 'commonsense' – or rather to convert commonsense into 'good sense'. For it is here, from popular culture – soaps, sitcoms, the tabloid press, women's magazines, mass-produced fiction, pop music, etc. – that most people in our society get their entertainment and their information. It is here that women (and men) are offered the culture's dominant definitions of themselves. It would therefore seem crucial to explore the possibilities and pitfalls of intervention in popular forms in order to find ways of making feminist meanings a part of our pleasures.

As writers, directors, producers, technicians, actors, publishers journalists, critics, teachers and students, women do participate in the production and distribution of popular forms and in the discourses surrounding them. Yet we cannot ignore the fact that the majority of women who are very visible in popular cultural life – from Barbara Cartland to Samantha Fox – can be viewed as non-feminist, not to say anti-feminist. Nevertheless, there have been enough examples of feminists entering the mainstream for us to be able to suggest that effective intervention is not impossible. From Fay Weldon to Victoria Wood, from *Stand We at Last* to *Widows*, from a 'rape issue' of *Woman's Own* to pop videos by Annie Lennox and Aretha Franklin, there is plenty of evidence that the 'Sisters Are Doing It For Themselves'.

There are problems too, of course. To start with, however much we pile up the examples (and we can), they amount to no more than a drop in the ocean of sexism that pours daily from the tabloid press, prime-time television and, of course, pornography. Men dominate overwhelmingly in the production of nearly all popular genres, and, as Anne Ross Muir points out in chapter 10 about the position of women working in the film and television industries,[4] this is not a situation that seems to have been improving. Even when a few (token?) women do manoeuvre their way in, they do not necessarily hold feminist views. Given, too, that the male-dominated institutions of production and distribution are inscribed with sexism, we cannot be surprised that the feminist presence, both behind and in front of the camera, is a minority one.

The more important question, however, is whether it is a presence at all, or whether, in order to enter the mainstream, feminism is co-opted by being harnessed to other discourses which neutralise its radical potential. This question is discussed by Maggie Anwell and Andrea Stuart, who consider what happens when 'alternative' fiction written by women (Angela Carter's 'The Company of Wolves' and Alice Walker's *The Color Purple*) becomes mainstream film. Have these 'feminist' productions identified at last a popular market for feminism which they are attempting to exploit? Or are they yet one more insidious appropriation of feminist themes?

The answer is not obvious. The speed with which advertisers, for example, pick up on feminist discourse (bras to 'liberate' us in the late sixties, the 'freedom to choose' package holidays in the eighties!) suggests not only that co-option lurks round every corner, but also that advertisers do not believe that women are necessarily as hostile to feminist ideas as the rantings of the tabloid press would have us believe. As Ann Treneman argues in chapter 11, the contradictions in this 'liberating' aspect of consumption are the premise of menstrual product advertising. Of course, advertisers are not in the business of liberating women – only of liberating their money. So if feminist ideas will sell bras and tampons, they will be co-opted for consumerism. But not even the whizz-kids of Saatchi and Saatchi have total control over polysemy: if the ad talks about 'liberation', in whatever context, liberation is still what it is talking about, not confinement, and if it can sell bras perhaps it can change lives. It can work both ways. After all, feminists have always engaged with the minutiae of language and culture – the restricting clothes, the masking make-up, the constraining ideologies - and if the language of popular media changes in our direction, then maybe we can re-appropriate it for our own purposes.

If feminism can only enter the mainstream through forms of pleasure which are ideologically implicated, this need not totally neutralise its impact. In her consideration of the treatment of women's sexuality in *Lace*, Avis Lewallen argues that, despite its politically reactionary context, this popular novel does show women in control of their own sexuality (a prime feminist demand) and thus, as Angela Carter has said, 'fucking their way into history'.[5] Our examinations of *Cagney & Lacey* and *A Woman of Substance* produce similar conclusions. Aspects of female autonomy and control have found expression in popular genres that have conventionally featured male protagonists without falling into a simple reversal of gender roles. What is being argued in these pieces is that the contradictions of capitalism and patriarchy allow space for disturbances of dominant meanings to occur in the mainstream, with results that may not be free of contradictions, but which do signify shifts in regimes of representation. And thus perhaps in commonsense notions about women.

This struggle over meaning directly relates to questions about the female gaze. Can a female perspective, which controls situations and their definitions, be produced from within the mainstream? And if it can, what would it look like? And look at?

Popular culture for women has conventionally been concerned with representations of women (the female protagonist of romance fiction, the cover-girl on women's magazines). In this respect it is both like and unlike popular culture for men: men are invited to look at women (e.g. in 'girlie' mags), and so are women (e.g. in women's mags); but obviously these invitations to look are different, and we may assume that the resulting experiences of looking are also different.

So how do women look at women? Are female looks at other women always about identification or (by analogy with male looking) objectification? Or do dynamics of fascination and difference have other, more progressive, resonances? These are questions addressed in different ways by Belinda Budge in her discussion of Joan Collins and by Jackie Stacey in her article on *All About Eve* and *Desperately Seeking Susan*. Suzanne Moore, on the other hand, looks at the 'new man' and asks what happens to the male body in representation when it is subjected to the female gaze: can it bear the kind of objectification that women's bodies have borne for so long?

The Male Gaze

These questions arise from Laura Mulvey's pioneering article, 'Visual Pleasure and Narrative Cinema',[6] but are ones that were not only absent from her discussion, but have tended to remain absent in the tradition of feminist film criticism that followed upon it. Briefly, Mulvey's thesis states that visual pleasure in mainstream Hollywood cinema derives from and reproduces a structure of male looking/ female to-be-looked-at-ness (whereby the spectator is invited to identify with a male gaze at an objectified female) which replicates the structure of unequal power relations between men and women. This pleasure, she concludes, must be disrupted in order to facilitate a feminist cinema. Mulvey's article paved the way for a great deal of interesting work on the representation of women. Unfortunately, however, the notion of a 'male gaze' as dominant in all mainstream genres has since become something of an orthodoxy.

Because this notion was grounded in psychoanalytic theory, it proved difficult, theoretically, to move outside its parameters. Cultural analysts found it difficult to criticise the use of 'blanket' terms culled from psychoanalytic discourse without entering into debates about the usefulness of psychoanalysis for film theory, for feminism, or indeed for its own project. In all these areas its use is still controversial,[7] both from outside and within psychoanalytic theory. Those of us involved in the production of this volume do not have a unified stance in relation to these controversies. What we do share is a sense of unease about the adequacy of psychoanalysis, at least as it has been appropriated in theories of representation, to analyse the complexities and contradictions evident in popular culture, or even, at times, to raise the most interesting and pertinent questions for feminism.

It was this unease and the personal experience of contradiction that gave rise to doubts about the universal validity of Laura Mulvey's description of Hollywood cinematic form. In the first place, is it true that the gaze is always male? And if it isn't – if it is merely 'dominant' - how do we analyse the exceptions? Mulvey assumes a (heterosexual) male protagonist and a (heterosexual) male spectator. What happens when the protagonist is a woman – as in *A Woman of Substance*?; or when there is a range of female looks – as in *Cagney & Lacey* or *Lace*? What happens when there is nothing for us to look at but men, whether actively forwarding the narrative as in war films or Westerns, or more obviously coded for erotic appeal as in the examples discussed by Suzanne Moore in chapter 3? What about the representation of gay relationships (not now absent from the mainstream)? And what about spectators who are not male or not heterosexual?

These are questions that should pose problems for the theory. But too often they don't. When they are discussed, they are explained in terms which seem more concerned to fit the facts to the model than the other way round. Thus, as Jackie Stacey demonstrates in chapter 8, lesbian desire can only be theorised as 'masculine'; a man represented for erotic contemplation is said to be 'feminised' (see chapter 3 for a full discussion of this point); and anything that challenges the model is repositioned within it:

> What is there to prevent [the woman] from reversing the relation and appropriating the gaze for her own pleasure? Precisely the fact that the reversal itself remains locked within the same logic. The male striptease, the gigolo – both inevitably signify the mechanism of reversal itself, constituting themselves as aberrations whose acknowledgement simply reinforces the dominant system of aligning sexual difference with a subject/object dichotomy.[8]

Many images and narratives depend for their specific meaning on the play between culturally defined 'masculine' and 'feminine' elements, and this play can shift the boundaries of the definitions themselves. The reductionism which tends to result from the application of psychoanalytic theory to cultural analysis may flatten out the specificity and polysemy of texts so that this play is, when it comes down to it, theorised as just more of the same. This is not only intellectually unsatisfying, it is politically unproductive. It allows no space for considering differences and shifts in the representation of gender which may amount to new patterns of definition with real effects on how we can visualise ourselves. These effects may, of course, be negative as well as positive, but we are not helped in coping with either by a model which does not distinguish between them. What we need is an analysis which can begin to explain in more specific ways the relationships between our pleasures and their ideological grounding, and how we might go about changing these relationships.

Not by Gender Alone

In privileging gender as the category which structures perspective, psychoanalytic criticism tends to depoliticise other power relations in our society – most notably those of class, race and generation. A feminist analysis can perhaps afford autonomy in terms of its interest in gender, but not, we would suggest, if it produces a theory which cannot relate gender inequality to other structures of social inequality.

The structuring of dominance through processes of identification and objectification in narrative fictions can be applied with equal pertinence to power relations organised on the basis of class, ethnicity or generation. Can we really assume that audiences identify on the basis of gender (or even sexual orientation) rather than on the basis of the other categories that contribute to the construction of our identities? The ideological implications of, say, audiences of working-class and/or black social identities being positioned to identify as white middle class – as Jacqui Roach and Petal Felix discuss in chapter 9 in relation to a black female gaze – are clearly as important for class and race relations as are those of women's positioning within masculine discourses for gender relations. Psychoanalysis may appeal to some feminists because it highlights gender, but it does so at the expense of theorising the subject in terms of class, race, generation – or feminism. In chapter 13, Shelagh Young's exploration of feminist discomfort about Madonna's appeal and meaning for women raises questions about the politics of power which underlie feminism. Which women are doing the looking? Who owns the female gaze? Differences between women give the lie to any claim for a single female, or even feminist, subjectivity, as Janet Lee identifies in her discussion of the market addressed by *Elle* magazine in chapter 12.

The idea for this book arose out of a course in Popular Culture on the MA in Women's Studies at the University of Kent. It grew in collaboration with students and lecturers at the Middlesex Polytechnic and workers at The Women's Press. We have written it because we want to be part of what we think is an important debate about the representation of gender in popular culture, and we hope that our contribution to that debate will stimulate further discussion and work in the field.

1
Watching the Detectives
The Enigma of the Female Gaze

Lorraine Gamman

> If they ask the people who put *Cagney &
> Lacey* together, they will tell you that the
> genesis of the show was engendered by an
> observation in Molly Haskell's book *From
> Reverence to Rape* that there are no women
> buddy movies . . . Cagney and Lacey are
> buddies – they joke, they fight both with
> each other and side by side . . . When Mary-
> Beth Lacey finds out she has a lump in her
> breast, it is Christine who overcomes her
> fearful reluctance to see a doctor. Can you
> imagine Robert Redford sharing anxiety
> about a lump in his testicle with Paul
> Newman? If we say, then, that *Cagney &
> Lacey* is the women's buddy picture, we
> also have to say that it has redefined the
> genre. Or created it . . . providing a
> shimmer in an area that the mythmaking
> apparatus has swerved so widely to avoid –
> the area of women's friendships . . .[1]

What is it about *Cagney & Lacey* that distinguishes it from other
police series, including those featuring women?

In recent years, more and more fictional police officers seem to be
dominating the screen at peak viewing times. As an entertainment
genre[2] TV cop shows function ideologically to reproduce notions of
male social authority and to legitimate contradictory aspects of police
work by securing consent for the most brutal components of the
repressive state apparatus. In dealing with issues of justice, power,
and law and order, TV cops provide a perfect visual scenario for the
trials and triumphs of the male ego as the 'acceptable' face of the
State: the fight against crime in these series is mostly fought and won
either by individual macho heroes in uniform (such as the American

street cop T. J. Hooker), or by undercover male 'crime busting' partnerships, such as Regan and Carter of *The Sweeney*, Bodie and Doyle of *The Professionals*, and their American precursors, *Starsky & Hutch*. Even the eighties' vogue for retro-chic or self-conscious and sensitive 'new men' hasn't really disturbed the formula. Today the designer detectives of *Miami Vice* dominate the action just as much as their precursors who wore flared trousers. Machismo might occasionally be reduced to ironic parody but replacing male violence with male narcissism doesn't *automatically* alter the position of women within the frame.[3] The female gaze is still marginalised, even if the viewer sometimes has the impression that the heterosexual male gaze has given way to homo-erotic imagery.

Partners in Crime

> She's watching the detectives
> Oh, it's so cute;
> She's watching the detectives
> When they shoot, shoot, shoot...[4]

Cop partnerships began to appear in abundance on the TV screen soon after the mainstream cinema 'buddy movies' of the sixties and seventies – *Midnight Cowboy* (1969), *Butch Cassidy and the Sundance Kid* (1969) and *California Split* (1974). Like buddy movies, these TV cop narratives deal with men who bolster each other in conflict and crisis, and who are defined by their personal and professional relationship to each other, rather than to individual women, or to a group. In male TV cop partnerships – as in the buddy movie – women tend to play unimportant characters (as victims of crime or vehicles of minor love interest). Female characters often intrude solely in order to supply a yardstick against which the heterosexuality of the male partnership can be measured – and secured. Male sexuality, as much as crime, seems to be at issue in most of these series. Heroes such as Starsky and Hutch, or Regan and Carter, are seen to solve crimes only after they have *proved* their masculinity – usually by 'courageously' and violently overpowering the opposition. Here, phallic power is reinforced with every blow inflicted in the 'name of the law'.

While more women have been playing police officers and detectives on the TV screen in the past two decades, they have not always convincingly reflected the changing status of women in society. Women in police/detective series are all too often represented for the sake of glamorous spectacle, rather than as the focus of significantly women-centred entertainment. Angie Dickinson, who played the lead character in *Police Woman*, or the 'gorgeous trio' who made up *Charlie's Angels* showed how it was possible to run like Olympians while wearing stiletto heels. Here, the idea of female power was equated with a fantasy of glamour (rather than violence). The potentially progressive representation of female strength is negated by the idealisation of femininity. Worse, the structural position of the invisible patriarch (the voice of Charlie, for example) as the one who finally resolves the enigma/action, displaces any positive rereading of female activity.

The character of Emma Peel in *The Avengers* represented the spirit of the active and liberated woman anticipated in the sixties. Yet even her karate chops never smudged the perfect make-up or disturbed Steed's admiring gaze at energetic sexual spectacle. Emma Peel may not have been overtly subdued by a James Bond style hero in a classic heterosexual resolution,[5] but her relationship with Steed was certainly sexual judging by the level of innuendo characteristic of their dialogue. Peel's athleticism and leather gear were vital components in a powerful representation of autonomous womanhood – but this image is not necessarily disturbing to men, partly because Peel's costume feeds into the pornographic scenario of fetishised male fantasies about women in leather,[6] and partly because the underlying narrative structure of the series conspires against her outright independence. For even in those episodes where Peel does save Steed he maintains the upper hand because he usually *knows more* about the enigma being investigated.[7]

Sadly, in the 1980s, the female half of male/female TV detective partnerships has been even less positive. Female detectives in 1987 TV series like *Hunter*, *Dempsey & Makepeace*, and *Moonlighting* are imparted less physical competence than Emma Peel in *The Avengers*. Dee Dee McCall (of *Hunter*) and Makepeace (of *Dempsey & Makepeace*) bring high fashion to the business of catching criminals. Yet URST (unresolved sexual tension), not angst about unsolved crime mysteries, would appear to be the real dynamic in such partnerships, with sexual difference exaggerated to operate almost as a masquerade of butch/femme signifiers. The door-slamming, high-kicking, gun-firing style associated with Dempsey, for example, supposedly articulates class as well as sexual difference. This butch and 'brash' American detective contrasts sharply with his British female colleague, detective Makepeace, the small, emotionally cool but fashion-conscious *femme* 'partner' who accompanies the *brute* on assignments. Cop series like *Dempsey & Makepeace* are ultimately less about crime than about providing romantic scenarios for an allegedly antagonistic pair, who are spurred on by weekly crises that demand some sort of heterosexual coupling or resolution. No wonder the 'wet gel' detective of the rival BBC series *Pulaski* can parody this over-the-top representation of masculinity without breaking the genre's other codes and conventions. While *Pulaski* may represent more than one modality of masculinity, it really doesn't challenge the overriding supremacy of the male point of view and provides little space for an independent female gaze.

'Independent' Female Cops?

Not all female cops on TV are offered as spectacle or positioned for heterosexual romance. Maggie Forbes of *The Gentle Touch* and Kate Longton of *Juliet Bravo* are usually presented as efficient in their own right, more than equal to their male counterparts in dealing with crime, and, if necessary, with recalcitrant male subordinates. These representations of 'strong' women may serve as powerful role models for female spectators, offering them pleasurable viewing and identificatory opportunities. Nevertheless, the play on sexual difference here is ultimately co-opted by the ideology of sexism: the encoding of sexism is simply more subtle, in so far as it is articulated through excessive proof of female competence, or the idea of exceptional ability.

The sub-themes of programmes which feature independent women cops tend to make much of their feminine isolation in a male world, defining them as unique, rather than introducing themes of sexual discrimination. When, for example, Maggie Forbes or Kate Longton deals successfully with men who find it hard to relate to a female boss, the episode presents this as a purely personal conflict. As a result of this *personalisation* of issues, their professional competence is overdetermined.[8] Usually resolution suggests that Kate Longton or Maggie Forbes are special cases, women who can cope in a man's world. There is no suggestion that, given the opportunity, women generally are as capable as men.

There have been occasions in *Juliet Bravo* where 'sexism through exceptional ability' appears to have been subverted. In the 1985 series, for example, Kate Longton was confronted with sexist questions when interviewed for promotion by an entirely male police board. Her angry response articulated a clear feminist perspective on sexual discrimination. This was also one of the few episodes where Kate Longton's experience of the workplace was shared and compared with that of another woman – the female constable who brought in the tea! In general, however, we get a clearer picture of the representation of women if we look beyond the central protagonists and across gender at the portrayal of *all* female characters in the series. What we find are very few professional equals who are not depicted as authoritarian prigs or rivals, and the majority of women in lower status roles are portrayed either as victims of crime or petty criminals – categories which reinforce the idea of Forbes' and Longton's singularity.

The Female Gaze?

One of the main differences in the narrative gaze of *Cagney & Lacey* is that it seems to be a product of shared female experience in the workplace. The collective dimension of female experience is articulated, together with ideas of female friendship and solidarity. Such a range of looks – often fragmented and contradictory – perhaps more importantly constitutes an overall female perspective. This shift warrants further examination for it suggests that mainstream genres can facilitate a dominant female gaze and a route whereby feminist meanings can be introduced in order to disturb the status quo. Yet the female gaze has virtually remained absent from our screens and from discussions about the representation of women by feminist critics. While many writers have considered how men look at women, few seem to have asked how women in the eighties create and view images of each other and of men. The female gaze remains an enigma because, as I shall argue, the very framework of debate reinforces assumptions which blinker the vision of change for women.

Female Friendship

> The girls want things that make common sense,
> The best for all concerned
> They don't want to have to go out of their way
> And the girls want to be with the girls . . . [9]

Stories about female friendship do turn up in mainstream cinema every so often, for instance in *Stage Door* (1937), *The Women* (1939), *Caged* (1950), *The Group* (1966), *Julia*, *Three Women* and *The Turning Point* (all 1977), *Girlfriends* (1978), and, more recently, in mild 'feminist' films like *Nine To Five* (1980).[10] But a handful of productions in the space of fifty years still amounts to a significant gap in popular culture, and one that warrants further investigation.[11] Nevertheless, one might argue that their existence does challenge Laura Mulvey's thesis about the ubiquitous male gaze of classic Hollywood cinema.[12]

On television women are more frequently shown, not as friends, but in opposition to each other, as love or business rivals (the fighting 'bitches' of *Connie* or *Dynasty*). Even in British sitcoms centred on relationships between women – from *The Liver Birds* to more recent series like *Girls on Top* (1986) and *The Refuge* (1987) – some of the comedy seems to depend on stereotypes of women as 'scatty'. American TV programmes like *The Golden Girls* and *Kate and Allie* tend to be more successful in representing female friendship as an important part of women's everyday lives; but they are unusual, and humour is once again often produced by ideas about female 'scattiness' or 'confusion'.

Cagney & Lacey

Christine Cagney and Mary-Beth Lacey are not rivals; they are partners. And they are certainly not scatty. They are an effective female 'crime busting' team of detectives operating from a New York city police precinct. Although they function in a predominantly masculine environment, and are the focus of the narrative, they are not represented as exceptional. They are one team among many, with a male boss, but with Detective-Sergeant Cagney as second in command. They receive much the same treatment and use virtually identical police methods (including, occasionally, violence) as their male colleagues. Yet the creators argue this series isn't really about the police force at all but provides a scenario for showing women as 'buddies', and, like the American newspaper series *Lou Grant*, provides a context in which humanitarian issues can be realistically dramatised.

The relationship of Cagney and Lacey is one of personal friendship as well as professional partnership, although they are shown to have distinct private lives which articulate differently with their police work. Cagney is single, a cop's daughter whose ambition is focused on her career, she has a lawyer for a lover (plus occasional 'extras') and a problem of alcoholism – both with herself and her father. Lacey is married with three children; although her salary is essential to the family's income, career comes second to family. Having two female protagonists at the centre of the narrative facilitates this comparison, which suggests that women's experience of work and family, and the relations between them, is as important as men's (an obvious aspect of social life but a 'new' concept for film and TV!).

These differences in personal circumstances and attitudes mould their distinct personalities and inform their approach to the specific issues with which they deal in their working lives. Cagney is often represented as being more militant in respect of women's rights, while Lacey is more liberal on political issues in general. This is related to their respective class positions – Cagney is more middle class, from a white Catholic family; Lacey is more working class, from a Bronx background. Despite a certain schematism in this opposition, the complex of differences represented – class, ethnicity, family, personality and attitude – locates gender within the social totality. This allows for a more multifaceted interaction with their male colleagues, whose masculinity is contextualised in terms of ethnicity (black, Polish, Jewish, etc.) but is shown to a lesser extent tied up with class, family and politics because their private lives are only sketchily drawn in.

In terms of genre *Cagney & Lacey* represents a significant shift in a mainstream form. The codes and conventions of the series are informed by a late seventies' feminism (the central characters are significantly now in their early forties), which, if somewhat diluted, nevertheless does make positive links with themes of equal rights and civil liberties. By focusing on plots which relate policing to such feminist concerns as sexual harassment, violence against women, pornography, rape, prostitution and child abuse, the series adopts a female perspective on the law and social issues and provides a coherent narrative position from which the female protagonists are able to speak. Moreover, the main narrative theme in each episode – a particular case – is often accompanied by a sub-theme concerning their private lives, which echoes or comments upon the former. An episode about an anti-abortion demonstration, for example, includes reference to Lacey's past abortion of an illegitimate child (the significance of Lacey's intervention is doubly emphasised by the fact that she is heavily pregnant at the time she makes her 'stand'). Also, one episode about a child pornographer has a sub-theme where Lacey is shown dealing with her teenage son's consumption of 'girlie' mags. In this way the public world of crime overlaps with the private lives of women, who in this case just happen to be police officers. Crime is shown as a continuum rather than as something entirely 'other' inhabited by an 'enemy' that needs to be destroyed.

Such women-centred themes do not create a problem when it comes to reformulating the questions of justice or ethics which inform other TV cop series. But the fact that Cagney and Lacey are women does disrupt the mechanism of signification associated with the genre. This applies to the genre's treatment of sexuality, as well as law and order. Thus, while those characters outside the police context who supply the 'love interest' – Lacey's husband, Cagney's lovers – work on one level as narrative pivots to confirm the protagonists' heterosexuality (as in male buddy genres), there are significant differences in their characterisation. Lacey's husband, Harve, and Cagney's lawyer lover are three-dimensional characters, rather than the cardboard 'girl-friends' familiar from other police series. Harve's problems as an unemployed construction worker, with responsibility for housework and childcare, and his feelings of exclusion from Mary-Beth's working life, were represented from his point of view as well as hers. In other words, he isn't just a problem for *her* (imagine this happening the other way round in a male buddy series!). Similarly, Cagney's boyfriend is occasionally seen to have his own problems in their relationship. Although his part is often no more significant than walking through the squad room in the usual designer suit in order to accompany Cagney on a date, he is depicted as having a mind of his own – and sometimes he even speaks it. This is in stark contrast to the literally dumb and stereotypical female love interest which is *de rigueur* in this genre. Perhaps the main difference compared with *Starsky & Hutch* is that members of the opposite sex are allowed to relate to each other as working colleagues rather than as primarily sexual beings.

The Female Gaze as Mockery of Machismo

Isbecki, the squad-room macho bore, is one character we see trying to penetrate Cagney's and Lacey's professionalism and to reposition them in traditional female gender roles. But Isbecki's character is a conscious narrative device employed to illustrate sexism in the workplace, and is subverted through a gaze which articulates *mockery of machismo*. Mockery as a narrative strategy is an interesting phenomenon, as it appears capable of expressing a coherent, if not controlling, female gaze as well as effecting a fissure in the representation of power itself.

The 'female gaze' in *Cagney & Lacey* stems mainly from the point of view of the central female characters themselves, who articulate it via witty put-downs of male aspirations for total control. But in dismantling a masculinised notion of power, they don't automatically assume what in Lacanian theory has been described as the position of the 'Father'. On the contrary, they distance themselves from mastery.

This factor is precisely what enables their male colleagues, who neither share nor support Isbecki's approach, to follow their lead and identify with the humour underlying their mockery. Cagney and Lacey don't invert power relations, claiming total mastery for themselves, but instead subtly displace such relations. As mentioned earlier, they do this through laughter generated by mockery. The playfulness of their gaze invites their co-workers, and us, to join in the fun. Because no one is ultimately in control in this game, everyone can play. The female gaze can literally throw itself within the frame and outside it to whoever is clever enough to catch it. In this sense, then, it can be said that the female gaze cohabits the space occupied by men, rather than being entirely divorced from it. Further, it does not alienate 'bystanders' (as displays of emotion might) but begins to negotiate hierarchies of discourse about 'masculinity' and 'femininity' within the narrative itself. This is far more sophisticated than the strategy associated with Mae West; Cagney and Lacey do not simply reverse roles with men by adopting sexually explicit innuendo that positions men as passive.

The above strategy underlying the representation of the female gaze in *Cagney & Lacey* hints at why there is a feminist sub-text in a series primarily about law and order. Although Cagney and Lacey do the same job as their male colleagues, they are not the same as them. Their presence alters the dynamics of the squad room, not only because they are different from men but because their 'difference' does not simply translate into 'otherness': Cagney and Lacey are not simply passive objects; they 'speak' female desire. *They look back*. These central characters maintain autonomy and independent initiative throughout the series. They do this by pointing out to colleagues (and viewers) in a witty and amusing way why the male gaze is sexist. Acerbic wit complements the pace of action located in a fast-talking metropolitan environment, and operates to destabilise and problematise 'common-sense' notions about sexual difference that exist in the squad room.

Women and Power: Subversive Strategies

The value of undermining or destabilising the status of gender is recognised in the writing of Julia Kristeva, who has discussed the positive implication of strategies of resistance that subvert those gender identities which define 'woman' as marginal in a male-dominated world. In *About Chinese Women* Kristeva argues that women cannot simply exchange roles with men because thought and representation in the 'phallocratic order' are constructed in the context of a linguistic binarism that always equates masculine with hard/active and feminine with soft/passive. Yet Kristeva acknowledges that 'we cannot gain access to the temporal scene, i.e. to political affairs, *except by* identifying with the values considered to be masculine (dominance, superego, the endorsed communicative word that institutes stable social exchange)'.[13] So, she suggests, when women are represented as powerful, or assume power, this doesn't inevitably alter the representation of power. For she says, 'Power cares nothing about sexual difference, women as well as men can lend their bodies to its mask . . . let others have rulership; there is nothing a woman can do with it. Her role is to say to power "that's not it, that isn't enough".'[14]

Kristeva therefore suggests women should reject trying to assume power. Instead, she argues they should engage with a 'revolution' in language, one which 'refuses all roles' and which, by returning to the ungendered pre-Oedipal moment of the formation of the subject in language, recognises 'the unspoken in speech, even revolutionary speech'. This strategy is actualised, Kristeva suggests, 'by calling attention at all times to whatever remains unsatisfied, repressed, new, eccentric, incomprehensible, disturbing to the *status quo*.'[15]

There are obvious limitations to 'perpetual anarchy' or 'self dispersal' as forms of political organisation, or to seeing *Cagney & Lacey* in quite these terms. But I would speculate that some of the series' strategies in relation to gender – the mockery of Isbecki's macho power base, for instance – might be explained in Kristevan fashion, as a strategy which 'refuses' any simple role or subject position, particularly as Cagney's and Lacey's laughter and mockery here disrupt rather than assume dominance.

Yet orthodox readings of Kristevan ideas about a 'revolution' in language don't usually provide us with a pragmatic model of how to go about disturbing everyday representations of gender in the mainstream. Certainly, the destabilising of the 'language' of popular narrative conventions and the encoding of feminist meaning through *mise-en-scène* seem to offer a far more practical route for feminist intervention than releasing the 'pre-Oedipal' repressed. Where *Cagney & Lacey* is subversive within mainstream conventions – utilising mockery to disrupt the male gaze – it appears to adopt much simpler strategies than those derived from psychoanalytic criticism. They are more in line perhaps with Brecht's idea of 'cheerful and militant learning'.

It is probably an overstatement to say that *Cagney & Lacey* is 'Brechtian', but I am trying to express my overall doubts about the usefulness of employing psychoanalysis for the study of representation. While I enjoy the metaphor of feminist film critics, as 'detectives' adopting the 'Morelli method'[16] in order to find clues or identify symptoms of a return to 'infantile sexuality', or 'hatred of the Mother', I believe the alliance of Conan Doyle and Freud offers little to feminist demands for change. At a time when we need more theoretical work which helps to clarify how we might bring about political shifts in society, exponents of Lacanian criticism, with some notable exceptions, seem only to offer repetitive accounts of the acquisition of gender. These explanations are often of negative rather than positive value. For as Elizabeth Wilson points out, 'the last thing feminists need is a theory which teaches them only to marvel anew at the constant re-creation of the subjective reality of subordination and which reasserts male domination more surely than ever before within theoretical discourse!'[17]

Essentialism and the Female Gaze?

At least Kristeva's analysis of the relation of the gendered subject to operations of power in society does oblige us to challenge the *essentialism* and *relativism* of radical feminist texts.[18] Arguably, material explanations about the acquisition of gender have been one of the most significant contributions of psychoanalysis to feminism. From Mary Daly to Dale Spender, women have been posited as endowed with innate moral superiority; 'female wisdom' or the 'female gaze' is construed as a product of biology – as a 'gift' of nature – rather than as the conditioning of culture. Yet this radical feminist framework is implicitly patronising: it often dismisses those women who are not feminists as 'suffering' from noxious and poisonous 'gases' of 'patriarchy',[19] without really developing an adequate theoretical analysis of the complex operations of ideology underlying 'commonsense'.

Obviously, the female gaze is not produced simply because women are behind the camera or because the main characters are women. I hope my earlier comments on *Charlie's Angels* demonstrate how the female gaze can be a mask for a male point of view. So how can TV programmes like *Cagney & Lacey* be regarded as progressive or feminist when the female gaze is articulated in the context of masculinist ideologies like law and order and individualism? Is the female gaze a 'con' here too? Or is it only available to us in, as it were, the negative – through strategies like mockery, which disrupt the male gaze? Or are there perhaps moments in the text when the female gaze is really dominant? Let's hear first from the counsel for the prosecution:

> *Cagney & Lacey* is proving very popular with many feminists. So WHY? . . . *Cagney & Lacey* serves to glorify the police force. It may represent a different approach to other TV cops but the exercise remains the same.[20]

With all its patriarchal and authoritarian associations, law enforcement seems an unlikely site for 'feminist intervention'. After all, the main images we have seen of 'feminism' in the British news media over the past few years have been Greenham women or miners' wives being forcibly removed from nuclear bases or picket lines by the police. So how come, all of a sudden, 'feminists' have joined the fictional force? The attraction of law enforcement as a site for positive representations of women derives, not from any great love of the police force or a consensus that women are more ethical or less aggressive and destructive than men, but from the fact that such scenarios permit focus on female *activity* rather than on female *sexuality*.

In spite of the levels of co-option discussed with reference to programmes like *Juliet Bravo* and *The Gentle Touch*, these series do feature independent female cops as strong central characters, and this is itself an important ideological shift in terms of mainstream images. Such characterisation does not reduce female activity to familial roles (as girlfriends, wives, mothers and daughters), but acknowledges other social identities of women in the workplace – which inevitably involve class positions in social hierarchies. Even though Cagney and Lacey do not have the more conventional trappings of material success associated with the characters of Alexis or Sable in *Dynasty* or *The Colbys*, they are shown as autonomous.

Representations of women with access to power – especially power unrelated to conspicuous consumption or ideologies of 'romance' – are quite uncommon in the mainstream. Positioning female characters as detectives in roles which show them 'thinking' and pursuing 'knowledge' without overdetermined reference to their physical competence or conventional 'attractiveness' is unusual because – as Raymond Williams, of all people, has explained – this is the 'type of plain straightforward and honest character (particularly in formulas that depend on excitement, movement and conflict) . . . who gets written out very often'.[21] Nevertheless, there are levels of co-option in the representation of Cagney and Lacey as detectives. Their clothes might not seem to be obvious signifiers of power, like those 'authoritative' tailored jackets worn by Mrs Thatcher or the padded shoulders associated with *film noir* heroines like Mildred Pierce. But the fluffy jumpers associated with Cagney and the attention to hairstyle and make-up suggest that the creators have been careful to avoid any simple role reversals which position women as 'female men'. These detectives are shown as active, assertive and yet still 'feminine'. Naturally there are problems underlying this 'careful' strategy. The image of Cagney and Lacey has been described as 'sugar coated' by some feminist critics who feel the series hasn't been able to disturb the fictional construct 'woman' or move beyond ideas about heterosexual monogamy.

Intervention or Co-option of Feminism?

How can *Cagney & Lacey* be defined as a radical text which disturbs dominant notions of gender, when BBC presenters virtually dismiss the series as one which has heroines 'fighting crime the feminine way'? Worse, Cagney and Lacey are frequently (if not invariably) portrayed more like probation officers or social workers, 'caring' for victims of the system, than like law enforcers. Granted, the person with the most powerful job in the series (the district attorney) is played by a black woman, and the series has dealt with the issue of racism in the squad room. But the symbol of justice epitomised by the characters of Cagney and Lacey is still white and often 'matronising' – even though, unlike the symbol of British justice, the eyes of the law in *Cagney & Lacey* are not completely blind to difference: to its credit the series has often adopted a narrative strategy which privileges the point of view of oppressed minorities. Yet the bottom line of *Cagney & Lacey* is frequently about 'individual choice' – even when tackling such issues as racism or sexism. At the very time when all involved with the series were collectively campaigning to prevent *Cagney & Lacey* being shown in South Africa, an episode called 'The Marathon' took a soft-focus look at apartheid and discussed 'individual choice' – a disappointingly weak message given that it is one of the few series that occasionally has a black director participating in production (Georg Standford Brown).

The apartheid episode is not the only disappointment in a series that otherwise disturbs dominant stereotypes. *Cagney & Lacey* hasn't extended the right of 'individual choice' to lesbians, despite its concern with issues about gender and sexuality. While male homosexuals have appeared (Cagney's neighbour is gay) and male homosexuality has been discussed, lesbianism seems to be the 'repressed' of the series. Is this a strategic absence? It seems likely. Meg Forster, who played Cagney in the first feature-length episode, was considered 'too butch' by CBS and the creators seem to have contacted Sharon Gless soon afterwards to persuade her to take the part, as a more 'glamorous' contrast with Tyne Daly.[22] Despite the homo-erotic imagery implicit in some of the scenes where these characters almost 'flirt' with each other, there is clearly a heterosexual presumption underlying the representation of the female gaze in this series.

The Feminist Voice

If images of 'femininity' compromise the narrative of *Cagney & Lacey*, the feminist 'voice' of the series gives us more cause for optimism. The nasal tones and working-class Bronx accent of Lacey are frequently employed to challenge the more reactionary views spoken through Cagney. In the episode 'Waste Deep', for example, Lacey persuades Cagney to take seriously the evidence of a female 'greenpeace' campaigner who has discovered that a toy company has been illegally dumping toxic waste. Here, the female 'voice' of the narrative is posited as more significant than the image; for the greenpeace campaigner is certainly not represented as glamorous spectacle. Moreover sound is a feature requiring consideration in theoretical terms. The soundtrack has frequently been ignored by theorists like Christian Metz, who seems concerned only to divide up individual frames of film into visual 'syntagms' or other linguistic categories.[23] Similarly Laura Mulvey overlooks the soundtrack when arguing about the male gaze of classic narrative cinema, and in so doing negates the important semantic implication of women's voices on the screen.[24]

The soundtrack is obviously important in *Cagney & Lacey*, perhaps because television images are smaller and hence less overwhelming than those in the cinema. As John Ellis has pointed out, 'TV demonstrates a displacement of the invocatory drive of scopophilia [the love of looking] to the closest relation of the invocatory drives, that of Hearing'.[25] This is an interesting point because the female perspective of *Cagney & Lacey* is not only articulated via images on the screen, but is embedded in general philosophies about meaning *spoken* through the central female protagonists. Also, ideologies of masculinity connected with the police force are subverted by ideas about 'truth' spoken by the central characters. Cagney and Lacey may derive power from the symbolic and literal 'law of the father' (the institution of male social authority represented by police ID badges that dominate the presentation of the characters in the opening 'trailer'), but as characters, they are shown to have access to a 'truth' which is more relevant and appropriate than traditional male authority. Cagney's and Lacey's experience of the contradictions of being female is drawn upon in cases dealing with sexual violence, rape and incest. This experience is shown to lead to a fairer concept of justice than that normally found in the squad room.

So What's New About Female Detectives?

Although this chapter has been primarily concerned with the possibilities and implications of the female gaze in a police series, there is clearly interaction between the private and the public space, between the crime 'enigma' and the actual investigation going on as we watch the detectives. We hear Cagney and Lacey talking 'outside' the investigation, when they are supposed to be at their most 'workaday' (in the 'Jane', in the car), nearly as often as we watch them following up leads within the 'underworld'. The nuances of this shift of emphasis between the 'social' and the 'private' eye, from the respectable to the 'underbelly' of society, are important because they are characteristic of the bulk of detective fiction. Novels by Raymond Chandler, and thrillers by new feminist detective writers like Mary Wings,[26] are usually based on *two* stories. As Todorov explains in 'The Typology of Detective Fiction': 'the first – the story of the crime – tells "what really happened". Whereas the second, the story of the investigation, explains how the reader (or the narrator) came to know about it.'[27]

As in most written detective fiction, the second story – the one about the investigation – frames all the visual action of *Cagney & Lacey*. Yet the narrative does not simply reflect the omnipotent viewpoint of the police force. On the contrary, we witness a deflection of the single scrutinising gaze associated with nineteenth-century fiction or Hollywood cinema; as in, say, *Hill Street Blues*, we find the kind of multiple narrative structure (i.e. we follow action through the eyes of many different characters) typical of soap opera. Indeed, each episode of *Cagney & Lacey* is told from the point of view of a multiplicity of voices, together with fragmented and frequently interrupted 'looks'. As John Ellis has pointed out, this is because TV facilitates the 'glance' rather than the omnipotent gaze of the cinema.[28]

The 'glances' between Cagney and Lacey themselves certainly have a feminist implication, and within them we find several subjectivities about everyday life. As well as juxtaposing Mary-Beth's married life with Cagney's single status, other contradictory ideas about women's roles are introduced into the script. So there isn't, and there is unlikely to be, any single or omnipotent female gaze in the series. The different lifestyles of officers, victims and perpetrators of crime are closely scrutinised. The consequent precarious balance is frequently so contradictory and recalcitrant to resolution within individual episodes that characters are forced either to decide not to make the attempt or to acknowledge that their own ideas about truth are not shared. It is almost as if the narrative focus and stress on the 'plurality of cultures' identified by Craig Owens[29] has been recognised by such scripts, which play on the idea that the female gaze can be viewed from more than one subject position.

Cagney & Lacey certainly doesn't presume that there is one 'feminine' way of looking at the world, if only because episodes frequently deal with conflicting and contradictory ideas about women. Moreover, the series makes sophisticated and self-conscious use of parody in order to challenge ideas about realism. In one episode, for example, when an exaggeratedly glamorous 'gun in bra' TV cop arrives to observe the 'real' activity of police officers, the narrative cleverly sets the hyper-reality of the actress playing the TV cop against Cagney and Lacey's 'real' experience – a dizzying use of textual self-referentiality partly achieved through mockery of the lecherous squad-room gaze at the TV actress. Yet Cagney's and Lacey's problematising of roles, and their refusal to play them the way they are often superficially represented, forces upon the viewer the realisation that femininity is always intertwined with its own reflection: that there is no single reality simply awaiting its 'accurate' representation.

The Fantasy of Realism

While *Cagney & Lacey* can be compared to the classic realist text, which has been defined as positioning the spectator outside the realm of 'contradiction' and therefore outside of 'production', its use of parody makes it quite different. Further, because TV series continue week after week, they do not effect the kind of 'closure' characteristic of novels or Hollywood cinema. Thus the visual work of film and TV described above, which employs parody and which plays around with conventions, offers potentially exciting strategies to feminist writers and film-makers. Such works suggest that new meanings can be produced within existing genres without resorting to the sort of marginal positions advocated by Kristeva. The mixing of genres, the merging of fiction and non-fiction, pastiche and parody, could well be used by feminists to 'subvert' dominant meanings about women in popular culture and to create pleasure, surprise and interest in feminism. It seems a great pity that at the moment it is advertisers who are using these techniques to greatest effect.

Clearly, there are economic reasons for this, but also some feminist film-makers have argued against 'intervention' in the mainstream, suggesting that only 'tendentious' texts have revolutionary potential, and that these alone will help wrest socially constructed phenomena from that stamp of familiarity which protects them from our grasp.[30] Laura Mulvey's suggestion that the avant-garde is a more suitable site for radical intervention is derived from her belief that mainstream cinema is so structured by the male gaze that it is unable to accommodate images of women without fetishism. Thus, she argues, the first blow for feminist film-making practice would be 'to free the look of the camera into its materiality in time and space and the look of the audience into dialectics of passionate detachment.'[31] She advocates the 'destruction' of all the old pleasures associated with Hollywood, but never explains why women who are not feminists should want to engage in this process in the first place. This strategy seems unacceptably puritanical to me, because, although Mulvey discusses desire, she appears, albeit unwittingly, to force discussion on to Mary Whitehouse's ground: certain pleasures are to be repressed in favour of (feminist) morality.

Mulvey's views are a little out of focus in the eighties, when mainstream genres like *Hill Street Blues* use the sort of multiple narrative techniques that ten years ago were restricted to independent film-making. Mainstream advertising and television are currently pioneering new film forms and techniques which would previously have been termed avant-garde.[32] Nevertheless Mulvey's arguments, formulated in a Lacanian psychoanalytic framework which she has since modified,[33] have been taken very seriously by British feminist film critics, who continue to read images of *strong* women in terms of 'phallic replacement'. Hence, we must ask just how useful is psychoanalysis for feminist discussions of representation. Can it be employed, as Mulvey suggests, as 'a radical political weapon'? Or does the phallocentric bias of the theory undermine our discourse to the extent that it *forces* us to discuss strong women in the negative? Moreover, how useful is the theory for studying female spectatorship if it cannot adequately formulate the significance of the active female experience except in terms that assume a masculine position in language, 'always to some extent . . . restless in its transvestite clothes'?[34] As mentioned above, Mulvey has since criticised the binarism of her earlier work, but hasn't really shifted her position on Freudian theory or offered any new ideas about the way women view popular culture.[35] This situation seems doubly unfortunate to me because the Freudian/Lacanian framework of Mulvey's research not only fails to conceptualise female sexuality adequately, but also doesn't allow conceptualisation of how other dynamics of identity – such as race, class and generation – may well affect how viewers of the visual media identify with protagonists.

Female Spectatorship and Feminist Strategy

One of the reasons I chose to examine *Cagney & Lacey* in the first place was that this series does seem to address an absence in popular culture. Presumably it is popular with women because the female gaze of the series at the protagonists provides opportunities for female spectatorship not often available on television. For example, the female gaze as mockery of machismo offers spectators the possibility of identifying with the pleasures of activity without the sort of mastery or voyeurism associated with the male gaze position of classic Hollywood cinema. What is more, the series has a peak viewing slot, a steady nine million viewers in Britain, and a British fan club that floods the BBC switchboard with telephone calls and pressures the network into taking the series seriously. How many feminist productions can boast similar support?

Yet, despite its success with women viewers, in the UK as well as in the USA, despite the fact that it was created by feminist script writers, Barbara Avedon and Barbara Corday, and that women are involved in the production process, neither the programme's makers, nor the actresses who play the lead characters, will 'own' the feminist content of the episodes. When interviewed on the Terry Wogan show in 1986, Sharon Gless, the actress who plays Cagney, said the programme was 'humanist' and that she didn't want the series to be considered 'feminist' as this was 'limiting'. My subsequent correspondence with Orion Productions, USA, who produce the programme, and with the British *Cagney & Lacey* Appreciation of the Series Society (CLASS) provoked similar reponses. The Club Secretary of CLASS wrote in 1986 in reply to my enquiries: 'we do not wish to be involved in discussing our views on feminism. We maintain a neutral position on this . . .' It is clear that the current distaste for the label 'feminist' is not merely symptomatic of an as yet unformed feminist consciousness, but, as Janice Winship has pointed out, is more likely 'a sign that the *style* of sixties and seventies feminism is inappropriate to what's happening for some women in the eighties'.[36]

Why is it, as Janet Lee asks (see chapter 12), that sales of magazines like *Cosmopolitan* and *Elle* are so much greater than those of *Spare Rib*? If the answer is related to Thatcherism, we need to analyse the Thatcherite co-option of feminism, not just bemoan it. If there are questions about style to be considered, then we need to not just dismiss them, but ask how they relate to feminist strategy.

I am not suggesting that intervention in popular culture, either as practitioners or as students, will necessarily make feminism popular all of a sudden, or that the liberal feminism associated with *Cagney & Lacey* is a revolutionary force! We know that the media does not work like a massive hypodermic needle injecting audiences with new ideas. On the contrary, most media effects research indicates that it operates predominantly to reinforce existing ideas and ideologies underlying 'common sense', rather than directly determining what viewers think.[37] If this is the case, can we ever disturb negative common sense about feminism or change it to 'good sense'? Gramsci's ideas about transformist and expansive 'hegemony'[38] are very relevant here. Perhaps we can *negotiate* the status quo to take account of women looking, on and off the screen, providing a less narrow range of stereotypes than currently exists in the mainstream. Perhaps by participation, as well as by deconstruction, we can present new images within conventional formats. It is in this respect that *Cagney & Lacey*, for all its contradictions, offers us one model of how to inscribe a female gaze and represent ideas about female friendship and solidarity currently absent from the mainstream. Of course, there are limits to the female gaze, particularly if we are to avoid simple reversals and a perpetuation of the idea that there should be one monolithic view about feminism, rather than a 'plurality of cultures'.[39] But there are possibilities too, and we should keep them in focus, even if this means arguing against feminist 'orthodoxy' and challenging the discursive practice of monolithic theories which culminate in effect to create a blind spot to the female gaze.

Most of this chapter was completed as part of an MA thesis on *The Female Gaze* written in 1986 at the University of Kent. However, I particularly want to acknowledge the writing and teaching of Claire Johnston (formerly of Middlesex Polytechnic) who died in 1987.

2
Substantial Women

Margaret Marshment

Why can't a woman be more like a man?
My Fair Lady

She was the only one man enough to stand
for the leadership.

Lord Pannell on Margaret Thatcher[1]

When Margaret Thatcher was dubbed 'the only man in the Cabinet' it may not have been clear who was being insulted more: she for her lack of femininity, or the other Cabinet members for their lack of masculinity. The joke rests on the commonsense assumption[2] that there is something unnatural and reprehensible in a woman being like a man, so that even as the gap between the natural and the cultural is exposed, it is closed by claiming that there is something freakish about anyone whose nature does not conform to the cultural definition. Femininity is an essential attribute for a woman. Not quite as essential as masculinity for a man, however. For the insult is not directed evenly at Thatcher and her Cabinet members: their failure is an unequivocally moral one – they are not 'real' men, not worthy of leadership. By comparison, she is worthy of leadership, because she is a 'real' man. But she pays a high price for this accolade: she sacrifices, according to the joke, her identity as a woman.

This inequality of insult suggests a dilemma for feminists: should we aim to appropriate the definitions and qualities assigned to men, in an attempt to prove women's ability to participate equally at all levels of society? Or should we concentrate on presenting a re-evaluation of existing definitions of femininity? Either strategy lays us open to reappropriation through stereotyping, or to validation of masculinist values.

A third possibility would be to attempt to create a new regime of representation which might redefine, or even abolish, gender boundaries and structures. This strategy, necessitating a disruption of conventional modes and genres of representation, would seem to belong primarily to the avant-garde and is one that has been recommended and practised by feminist critics and artists. Laura Mulvey sees this as the only way to counter the inherent sexism of mainstream Hollywood film practices.[3] But, valuable as this strategy is, its impact is likely to be limited, at least in the short term, to a very restricted élite audience. To deny even the possibility of effective feminist intervention in mainstream forms sounds suspiciously like a counsel of defeat. In addition, it is Mulvey's avowed project to destroy the ideologically grounded pleasures of popular forms. That this has a puritan ring about it may matter less than the implied abandonment of attempts to ground our pleasures in opposition to sexism rather than in complicity with it. And finally, there is evidence that a radicalisation of form does not automatically bring in its wake a radical content, and that the polysemy championed by post-modernist critics may be as open to co-option by the dominant ideology as are popular forms of realism.[4]

In relation to popular mainstream forms we are likely to find two main strategies of challenge to sexist representation of gender: first, those aiming to show how much more like men women really are, in comparison with sexist stereotyping of women as different and inferior; and second, those which defy masculinist criteria, representing masculine behaviour and characteristics negatively, and feminine ones positively. It must be recognised, of course, that while some instances of such challenge will be the product of conscious feminist intervention, many will be more in the order of responses to the market, fashion, shifts in the genre and so on. After all, we do not need to assume a deliberate intent to be sexist on the part of producers of works which depend upon, and conform to, the dominant ideological positions on gender.

Because women's oppression is overdetermined ideologically, in our creative and critical work we need to use a multiplicity of approaches in challenging sexism. At a global level this is easy to say, and perhaps easy to agree with; but particular instances give rise to contradictions and conflicts which are not so simply dealt with. The analysis of individual works often reveals that there is an ideological price to pay for each glimmer of 'progress', and we may have reason to wonder whether it's worth it. For example, if a woman is represented as being 'more like a man' – competent, intellectual, brave, strong, rich, powerful, or whatever – this positive representation is one that holds up conventionally defined masculinity as a model of the *human*. Here there is no criticism of masculinity as it is defined and practised, nor of the social structures and values within which it is embodied. On the other hand, if women are represented within the categories of conventional femininity, then there is no critique of that definition of femininity. This may be because the stereotype is relatively positive in the first place – like idealisations of motherhood or of female beauty. But even when it involves a redefinition of the importance of domestic work, for instance, or the positive values of passivity, the stereotypical association of women with these activities or characteristics remains unchallenged.

This may be too stark a posing of the problem, given that any particular example could involve a complexity allowing for a dialectic between stereotypes and challenges to them, between so-called masculinity and so-called femininity, etc. However, it is doubtful whether any one work could deal with the range of women's oppression in ways that are unambiguously progressive on all counts (certainly no one characterisation could) – even supposing that all readers would agree on what does and does not constitute a progressive feminist element. The arguments within the women's movement over, for example, Judy Chicago's 'The Dinner Party' or the decoration of the fence at Greenham, should demonstrate that this is rarely likely.[5] The task confronting us, therefore, is to be critical of cultural developments in the representation of women without dismissing every instance of partial co-option merely as evidence of the omnipotence of sexism, or celebrating every shift as the beginning of its end.

Women of Substance

In recent years there has developed a popular genre of women's fiction, in blockbuster form, which focuses on a female protagonist who is wealthy and powerful. These works usually appear initially in print, but in many cases have been adapted for television. Barbara Bradford Taylor's *A Woman of Substance* is typical of the genre, which also includes such works as its sequel *Hold the Dream*, Shirley Conran's *Lace*, Jeffrey Archer's *Prodigal Daughter*, *Sins* by Judith Gould and novels by Judith Krantz, Danielle Steel, and other, mostly American, mostly women authors.

The 'women of substance' at the centre of these novels are not significant only because they occupy the central position in the narrative – this is true of the heroines of other feminine forms, such as romance and family-saga fiction. They are significant also because this centrality is at the same time a controlling position which is both inscribed in the point of view and is embodied in a strong woman character who, as the subject of the narrative, is active in forwarding the story.[6] These are stories of (often spectacular) success in the public world of commerce, industry, finance and even politics, in which the heroine heads a business empire which she owns and controls in her own right. This is not the feminine underside of history, but the history we 'know' with women on top.[7]

The first effect of a protagonist who is a strong successful female is clearly a challenge to the dominant ideological construction of wealth and power as a masculine monopoly, and to femininity as passivity and dependence. The women protagonists of these fictions are rich in their own right, initiate and control the events of the narrative, and exercise power over the other characters Their fictional biographies are centred around their work and their wealth, and while their personal, emotional and domestic lives are inevitably treated, these are narratively subordinate to their public careers. This is clearly also a challenge to the ideological relegation of women to the private sphere.

To effect these ideological challenges is inevitably to represent women in roles and images conventionally associated with men. This is not merely an unfortunate or avoidable consequence of the genre's strategy; it is central to it. The ideological interpretation of men's real economic and political power relative to that of women is one that naturalises it, claiming it as inevitable and correct. As such it enters into our definitions of men and women: real men are rich and powerful, real women are young and beautiful. These definitions form the lever for our fantasies: men dream of wealth and power, women dream of the beauty that will win a man with wealth and power. Mills and Boon sell over 200 million books a year organised around this latter, female fantasy. The women of substance blockbusters are organised around a different fantasy for women: the dream of wealth and power in their own hands.

This can only be successful as a popular fantasy if it is located firmly within the dominant ideological representations of wealth and power as they concern men. To start with, this means contextualising the main woman character, and the narrative, within a structure of inequality: wealth and power only have meaning in relation to poverty and impotence. Accordingly, the world of women of substance blockbusters highlights inequality, so that the reversed gender role of the woman who conquers the heights of the economy can be celebrated by the fiction: to prove her equality with men she must be represented as fulfilling a role identical to that of a successful man within the same hierarchical structure.

The narrative interest is focused on the heroine's success. The plots can be broadly summarised as falling into two kinds: the 'rags-to-riches' story, of a young woman who begins in poverty and rises through determination and hard work to great riches and power; and the 'heiress' story in which a young woman inherits wealth and position which by dint of hard work and talent she improves upon. *A Woman of Substance* falls into the first category; its sequel, *Hold the Dream*, into the second. *Sins* is a 'rags-to-riches' plot, and so is *Lace*, although three of its five protagonists begin with rather more advantages in terms of class and connections than most women. *The Prodigal Daughter*, which pursues the story of Archer's famous blockbuster *Kane and Abel* through to the next generation, is the story of a woman who, while inheriting great wealth, nevertheless has to fend for herself in business, and after she has achieved greater wealth, through both work and inheritance, aims for and achieves the presidency of the United States.

Were these works to be critical of that hierarchical structure which facilitates the existence of wealth and power, the female protagonists at their centre would also be subject to criticism, and hence constitute negative representations of powerful independent women, which would be no challenge to sexist ideology in this respect. For it is in the nature of stereotypes that they are contradictory: while ideology claims that women cannot be powerful and independent, it also claims that when women *are* powerful and independent they are evil: from Medea to Lady Macbeth, from fairy-tale stepmothers to *film noir* heroines, the history of representation has a strong undercurrent of women who are bad and strong. Occasionally, the evil is more ambiguous, the heroine more tragic, as with historical figures like Cleopatra or Mary Queen of Scots.

It is therefore not in itself a challenge to sexist ideology for a woman to be represented as powerful: only to be represented as positively and successfully powerful. This is not to say, of course, that such challenges have not existed, both in fiction and history, although I would suggest that they are rarer in fiction, and that the historical examples have forced an accommodation within the ideology (which has often been successful in reinterpreting them, however). Effective challenges might be categorised as queens, heroines and stars. Queens are usually hereditary rulers, like Boadicea, Elizabeth I or Christina of Sweden, who, while proving themselves more than equal to their male counterparts, have achieved renown through hierarchical structures and have been 'explained' by reference to their aristocratic inheritance: blood is stronger than sex. Heroines are more usually self-made achievers who, through exceptional circumstances or character, have been saviours and helpers, like Joan of Arc, Florence Nightingale, or Mother Theresa; and some of these have been feminised as ministrants rather than fighters. Stars are a more recent phenomenon, and have characteristically been represented as victims whose womanhood was sacrificed to stardom, like Monroe or Callas. All three categories share an ideological stress on the exceptional nature of the individual woman and on validating the structures within which she succeeds: to be critical of royalty while celebrating a queen, or of the star system while celebrating a diva, requires a complexity of vision which ideology seeks to gloss over.

Thus, one cannot claim that the contemporary fictional 'women of substance' are a unique phenomenon in the representation of women. But I would argue both that they are a specific articulation of challenges to feminine stereotypes, unusual in fiction, and that they have contradictory implications for feminism and how its values are entering popular culture. They share with the three categories a validation of systems of inequality and of exceptional achievers within them; not only are the hierarchical inequalities of the capitalist system unquestioned, but success within it is claimed to be a 'good thing'. Successful heroines ike Emma Harte (*A Woman of Substance*) and Helene Junot (*Sins*) are presented as deserving their success and suffering minimal, if any, loss of personal happiness or character defect as the price of it. They are all defined as unambiguously good women. It is important, however, that this 'goodness' is not conventially feminine passivity or self-sacrifice, but is seen in terms of autonomy, energy and self-interested achievement.

The woman of substance is a successful capitalist. She demonstrates the virtues of the work ethic for the individual and capitalism's claim that within its system individuals can achieve anything they aim for if they work hard enough. In fiction such individualists have most often been men from the working class, or (especially in America) immigrants, like Archer's Kane and Abel. As a more recently identified 'disadvantaged' section of society, women are now to be seen taking their place in fiction as the exemplars of class mobility that is supposed to exist within, and justify, 'democratic' capitalism. To fulfil this role the ideology of log-cabin-to-White-House remains intact around the heroine, both to reproduce the democratic myth and to redefine woman as a full citizen of that mythic democracy. If the former mythical reproduction is unequivocally ideological, the latter is nevertheless a progressive element consonant with certain feminist aims, albeit of a liberal hue, more in line with the values of American magazines like *Ms.* or *Working Woman* than with radical or socialist feminisms.

And since it is the logic of liberal feminism, as of liberal anti-racism, that women should be represented 'fairly' throughout the hierarchy - i.e. in proportion to their numbers in the general population – and should be permitted to prove equality with men in terms of competence and their right to its rewards, the hierarchies themselves are not rejected: merely the dominance of men at the top of them. Socialist feminism has been rightly critical of this position, arguing that, even when the individual is successful (which is, in practice, only possible for a tiny minority), the underlying injustices of the hierarchy as such remain unchallenged; new and greater divisions are created between women based on differences in their wealth and power; and the values of patriarchy, far from being questioned, are further reinforced by women adopting them.

What is less frequently remarked are the pitfalls in the more radical strategy of challenging the hierarchy and its values, at least in respect of representation. The problem here is, first, that if women are never shown occupying conventionally masculine roles, these roles remain exclusively masculine. It may be that, politically, we are quite happy to leave violence, tyranny, individualism, etc. to men, and to pursue peace, justice and sisterhood. However, masculinity also has positive aspects, as viewed both by society and by feminist standards: intelligence, courage, strength, independence, resourcefulness, perseverance, wit, for example. Women of substance often possess these qualities in abundance. They may also possess less admirable masculine qualities, such as excessive ambition, ruthlessness, individualism. But significantly they never use physical violence against their enemies, though it is often used against them; they are astute and ruthless business women, but never 'dishonest'; they are 'fair' employers (whatever that means within capitalism); and have full emotional lives, with lovers, family and friends. In certain respects, then, they constitute a combination of positive qualities culturally defined across gender boundaries. The question is, of course, whether this particular combination can be regarded as a relatively progressive fantasy model for women, or whether it constitutes a co-option of feminist aims and values to a politically regressive message.

The celebration of female success is signified through the plethora of luxury consumer goods which these heroines come to enjoy: couture clothes, country mansions, city penthouses, chauffeur driven cars, swimming pools and private jets. These are described in loving detail – no critique of consumerism here! And this despite the fact that the rags-to-riches plot may devote up to half the narrative to the period of the heroine's life spent in poverty and struggle. Her success leaves this behind, rather than constituting a comment upon it.

No Cinderella She

I shall take as a paradigm of recent fictional women of substance the heroine of Barbara Bradford Taylor's *Woman of Substance*, Emma Harte. Both it and its sequel, *Hold the Dream*, were bestsellers, were adapted for television and shown twice, at prime time.

Emma Harte begins life as the daughter of an impoverished mill worker, and ends it as the owner of a multinational capitalist empire. Hers is a rags-to-riches story with a vengeance. But Emma is no Cinderella: far from waiting for a prince, she declares war on the class of princes, in the person of Edwin Fairley, the son of the mill owner who declines to marry her when she is pregnant with his child, and dedicates her life to accumulating wealth and power for herself in order to destroy his wealth and power – an ambition which she more than fulfils.

Emma has the conventional entrepreneurial qualities: ambition, hard work, determination, ruthlessness, intelligence, initiative, imagination. As a fictional character she possesses the qualities claimed as essential to success by those of her real life counterparts interviewed by Leah Hertz in her study of female entrepreneurs, *The Business Amazons*: hard work, tenacity, motivation.[8] In addition, she is beautiful, talented and possessed of impeccably good taste. While the former qualities are used to account for her success, and do so adequately, the latter are more relevant to justifying it. Indeed, if they seem at best superfluous to explaining her career, they are essential to securing her femininity and her moral right to a higher class position than she started out with.

An entrepreneur in food and clothes hardly needs to be a super cook and seamstress, but Emma is. Nor does she need to be beautiful, but she is. Emma is a superwoman in more senses than one. Clearly she is represented as an exceptional person: her success is exceptional by any standards. And it is success in a man's world, proving her superiority to the majority of men, and certainly to all the male characters in the novel. As such she may be seen as a positive role model for women, a point of identification with a power position for women readers/viewers. In this respect she may perform for women the function within the narrative that Mulvey claims the male protagonist performs for men readers/viewers in masculine genres:

the pleasure of identifying with 'a more perfect, more complete, more powerful ideal ego', who is positioned in control of the world of the narrative.[9]

There may, however, be difficulties for women in making this identification in a culture which defines femininity in terms of passivity, gentleness and powerlessness, and has available negative stereotypes for women who transgress this definition – bitch, virago, etc. – in other words, non-feminine women. So Emma is feminine too: she is a superwoman according to ideological definitions of woman. Her physical beauty ensures her sexual attractiveness to men. Her good taste in clothes, furnishings, etc. not only explains her success as a retailer; it also ensures that her sexual attractiveness takes a form associated with middle-class wives, which is perhaps less threatening to women readers than that of the sex symbol or the siren. As played by Jenny Seagrove in the television adaptation, she has the healthy girlish beauty of the 'good' girl destined to marry the hero. In this respect Emma Harte differs both from more traditional images of the 'career woman' and from most of her fictional counterparts, especially American ones, who combine a more glamorously coded sexuality with entrepreneurial power, along the lines of Helene Junot as played by Joan Collins in *Sins*.

Because her talents are not only the 'masculine' ones of entrepreneurial success, but also the 'feminine' ones of cooking and dressmaking, which constitute the realm of her initial business enterprises, her femininity can be confirmed while offering a point of identification for women readers/viewers with her commercial success, since this can be seen as an extension of domesticity into business.[10] Many of the better known women entrepreneurs in our society share this feminine sphere of operations (e.g. Laura Ashley, Debbie Moore of Pineapple Studios, Helena Rubinstein, Coco Chanel, etc.). According to Hertz, and to Goffee and Scase,[11] this point is not true of women entrepreneurs in general, but, like Mrs Thatcher's housekeeping metaphors, women are given a purchase on the public world through this link with the domestic and/or decorative.

Strong Looks

Some of the contradictions surrounding the representation of women in terms of the femininity of their physical appearance or interests are suggested in Susan Butler's review of Mapplethorpe's *Lady*, a book of photographs of Lisa Lyon, the body builder:

At the most immediate level, the insistence on legitimising a connection between femininity and physical strength seems implicitly a victory, a liberation: women can now look and be both strong and glamorous. But a new imperative may arise from this, for the cataloguing of Lyon in an exhaustive variety of glamorous guises seems to add a corollary message to women, 'You can only have permission to be this strong if you can also look this beautiful.'[12]

Translating Lyon's physical strength into the woman of substance's social strength, this observation could apply equally to her: you can only be this successful if you are this feminine. As Butler continues:

. . . the appeal of Lisa's looks and Mapplethorpe's skill in photographing them effectively gives Lyon the freedom to get away with a kind of experimentation less conventionally attractive women would find more difficult to carry off. Yet a positive counter-argument is plausible here as well: that Lyon's attractiveness helps to create greater acceptability for the idea of physical strength in women generally, and therefore paves the way for women less obviously endowed with a conventional brand of good looks to feel freer to develop their bodies as they wish.[13]

Women of substance are also conventionally beautiful and attractive to men. They are all white (with the marginal exception of the character played by Diahann Carroll in *Dynasty*), and while they do age in the course of the narrative without losing their attractiveness (something not to be undervalued), their sexual desirability remains associated with youth, and more especially with that purchasable commodity, glamour.[14] So they too carry the danger of co-option into male criteria for female acceptability – they are only allowed to be successful because they are attractive to men. In addition, their success may come to be culturally defined as part of their attraction, thus adding to the imperatives loaded upon women in male definitions of their sexuality. Yet, like Lyon, in the process they may be paving the way for other women to view professional success as compatible with femininity. Butler cites the 'super-strength represented by women Olympic shotputters' as a 'deterrent' to many women to pursue sports and physical development.[15] In this context, the image of Lisa Lyon may represent a degree of progress in the representation of women. Similarly, I would argue that, *in context*, so does an Emma Harte. Compare her determined activity with the prissy, if 'spirited', passivity of a Mills and Boon heroine, or the glamorous masochism of the women in *Dallas*; or consider this pontification upon executive women written little more than twenty years ago:

> Women themselves know it is not simple to hold on to their femininity mid the fierce rivalries present at each rung of the executive ladder. Too many, in their striving for executive position, sublimate their sexual and maternal instincts. Therefore it is not startling to learn that a survey of the private-life status of women listed in *Who's Who* shows 40 per cent to be unwed – just as many are married but childless. This leaves but a fifth of the total who have escaped 'the serious price of fame'.[16]

No questioning of the social and ideological pressures that produce this conflict between success and femininity; and no exploration of that twenty per cent who resolved it. Instead, the book concentrates on case studies of neurotic women destroyed by the 'masochism' or 'sadism' that underlies their ambition, who can only be saved by renouncing it in favour of husband and children. The fictional women of substance pay no such 'serious price of fame': they combine success and femininity, and as such constitute a possibly positive role model for women. Although, just as the image of a physically strong woman is embedded within the values of a male-defined competitive sport, so the image of an Emma Harte is embedded within those of patriarchal capitalism.

Another respect in which this combination may be seen as a challenge to sexism concerns the tendency to refuse to take seriously women who are conventionally beautiful. A tendency not absent from feminism, of course. Because cultural definitions of beauty have excluded a majority of women, most of us don't feel we suffer from being too beautiful, and the problems of those who do seem comparable to those of poor little rich girls. But from film stars to schoolgirls women are punished as well as rewarded for their looks,[17] and this affects all of us – and not only when we tone down our make-up for an interview, or leave it off for a feminist conference: if femininity and seriousness are mutually exclusive categories, then we will always be denied one or the other, and the curvaceous blonde running a business may be as much a test case as a pathfinder.

The point may be clearer if we compare characters like Emma Harte and Helene Junot with that of Bea, the doctor in the television series *Tenko*. Bea was a professional woman in late middle age; competent, intelligent, sensitive, caring and angry; slightly gauche, and more than slightly butch; a woman-orientated woman, who was represented with absolute seriousness as a complex, positive character: one of the most satisfying and moving representations of womanhood in a popular form. The women of substance seem flimsy floozies by comparison. But there was something the character of Bea couldn't do: she couldn't challenge sexism's divorce of the feminine from the human, because Bea wasn't, according to conventional definitions, a feminine woman. The women of substance *can* do this, because they take a conventional femininity and re-articulate it to a kind of power that has to be taken seriously.

Family Business

And Emma Harte is definitely to be taken seriously. The weight of the volume (868 pages), with its ponderous prose, and Emma's (or rather Jenny Seagrove's) face staring determinedly at us from the white background of the cover, suggests her substantiality compared to those lightweight misses whose fates are sealed in 189 pages, melting into the arms of craggy males, who adorn the covers of Rose of Romance products. Nor does she suggest the long-suffering mum of a family saga: here's a woman who knew how to get what she wanted – not a whole lot of fun perhaps, but the decent sensible sort of woman our mothers wanted us to be, smartly turned out with her permed hair and fur coat. The sort of woman we might have been but for . . . well, but for femininity? Or but for feminism?

Emma's fictional biography is focused on her career as a business woman. Her initial success is due entirely to her own determination and hard work. From her wages as a worker in a clothing factory and a woollen mill, together with extra money earned from dressmaking in her 'spare' time, she saves enough to rent and stock a small dress shop; then again by dint of working so hard that her friends worry about her health, she saves from the profits to buy another shop, then a third, and finally a department store. As a young pregnant girl she is helped by her equally poor friend, Blackie, and his friend (and later wife) Laura, with accommodation and emotional support. She is also befriended by the family of her employers in the small clothing factory. But she receives no financial assistance until she has enough capital of her own to propose business deals which are mutually beneficial. She marries her landlord, Joe, when she is already running two shops and about to rent premises for a third. This marriage is financially beneficial to her: she is able to buy, and then sell at a profit, the properties she rents from Joe to finance her department store, and to use his capital to set up other businesses. When he is killed in the First World War, she inherits all his substantial property and is thus established as a rich woman. Thereafter, her commercial empire expands through a combination of investment, enterprise, continued hard work and a massive inheritance from her long-term lover, Paul. (A second husband is an economic liability, who has to be maintained and finally bought off.)

In so far as her personal life serves her commercial life, Emma's career would not seem implausible: her increasing business successes bring her increasingly into touch with other successful people. She is self-made because her initial capital is the result solely of her own efforts, not the product of luck or someone else's generosity, and its growth depends on her continued diligence. A model of Thatcherite initiative, indeed – and a model of feminist self-determination too?

Straight Sex

But her private life is also important. As in other genres which replace the conventional masculine hero with a feminine one (e.g. police series – as discussed in chapter 1), the gender of the protagonist permits, or dictates, treatment of the interaction of public and personal life – something evident in the case of really substantial women (think how much more we know about Denis, Mark and Carol than about any other British Prime Minister's family). *A Woman of Substance* also has a sub-plot which traces the heroine's relationships with men and children.

Emma's relationships with men are many and unorthodox, and are all related to her business career. The most consistent is her relationship with Blackie, the Irish navvy whose career follows a parallel, if lesser, trajectory of success to building and architectural entrepreneur. This relationship is one which outlasts her romantic and sexual liaisons, so that he occupies a sort of consort role to her grandmotherly matriarch until his death. Her husbands are Joe, whom she marries for 'protection' after Gerald Fairley's attempted rape; and Arthur, whom she marries because, as she says in the television version, 'a woman in my position needs a husband as much as she needs a butler'. She does not love, or have a successful sexual relationship with, either of them. Then there is her business collaborator, David, whom she loves but relinquishes, in an excess of sense over sensibility, because his Jewish mother would oppose a 'mixed' marriage. The other men she loves, but does not marry, are Edwin Fairley, whose betrayal motivates her to succeed in business, and Paul, whom she cannot marry because of that melodramatic standby, the alcoholic Catholic wife, although she lives with him happily for fourteen years until his death. In Emma's personal career then, love and marriage do not overlap.

Neither do marriage and motherhood. Her five children are born of four different men: one from her first lover, three from her two husbands, and one from her last lover. This disruption of the traditional yoking of love, marriage and motherhood is arguably as radical an alternative for women as their relegation to a subordinate part of her life.

Not that the disruption is of Emma's seeking. The affair with Paul, although it is only an episode in a long life, is important in establishing Emma as a 'normal' woman: it has many of the hallmarks of a Mills and Boon romance (with him all 'sheathed strength', 'potent virility' and 'hoarse commands'); it is the sole relationship that takes priority, even temporarily, over her career; the only one in which Emma is sexually fulfilled, and that produces a loyal and loving child. Sex and love are not permitted to part company, and sex is always heterosexual.

Of the women contributing to Rowland's collection *Women Who Do and Women Who Don't Join the Women's Movement*, those who 'don't' were mostly politically active, apparently independent women.[18] Their main quarrel with feminism seemed to lie, not in feminism's complaints about sexual discrimination, nor in its claims on behalf of women's abilities, but in the feminist critique of the family: they wished not only to retain the family they valued, but to strengthen its influence in society. This may then be extended to a generalised political conservatism. A participant in the annual Conservative Younger Women's Conference in November 1987 was quoted in the *Guardian* as explaining her position thus: 'I don't agree with the way the party presents all its issues but I agree with the philosophy of Conservatism. I believe in family.'[19]

Emma Harte, like the other fictional women of substance, lives an unorthodox family life, but does not reject its principles: she is a (serially) monogamous, devoted mother, whose failure to achieve the 'normal' family of the cornflake ads is presented more as part of the imperfect pattern of life than a personal shortcoming. Readers/viewers are therefore not required to accept a critique of the family, while simultaneously being permitted to enjoy a lifestyle transgressive of it. Another instance of not being a feminist, but . . .

Vengeance is Mine

One respect in which the women of substance might be said to be employing masculine strategies is in their preoccupation with revenge. In part, this supplies a morally respectable motive for their ambition: they do not want wealth and power for their own sake, but in order to avenge themselves or their family. The lioness motif, maybe. Or, less acceptably, the woman wronged. Underlying Emma Harte's ambition is a desire for revenge; her friends worry about the quality of her ambition; she herself renounces her vendetta in her old age in order to enable her granddaughter to marry her old enemy's grandson. Yet none of this amounts to a condemnation of either her ambition or its fulfilment. Indeed, the narrative pleasures also allow for our delight in her destruction of those whose class and gender enabled them, with apparent impunity, to seduce and abandon her, cause the deaths of her mother and her father, and attempt to rape her. Helene Junot (*Sins*) is likewise bent on revenge – against the Nazi officer who tortured, and sent to their deaths, her mother and sisters during the German occupation of France. First she uses her profits as a rich man's mistress to track him down, and then her power as a tycoon to force him to live in fear. When they are children it is her eldest brother, Edmond, who shoots the soldiers who torture their mother; but when they are adults, it is she who takes the initiative, with Edmond performing a secondary role as her confidant and adviser.

Vengefulness is, with reason, an unfashionable quality: it is un-Christian and antisocial. But, as Brecht pointed out, in an unjust society it is the privileged who define morality, and the oppressed may need to redefine it.[20] And this may apply to revenge. Christianity has a long history of preaching humility to the poor, to black slaves, to women. Frantz Fanon claimed the liberating role of violence in colonial struggle: it destroyed the mystique of invulnerability surrounding the coloniser and restored to the colonised a sense of their own pride and power, which colonialism had denied them.[21] The immense dangers in this position are only too clear; yet it is not simply a matter of the oppressed aping the oppressor. For Emma Harte there are no social mechanisms available to secure justice for herself and her family – quite the reverse, for her society would tend to punish rather than avenge a girl who 'got herself' pregnant. For Helene Junot there might have been recourse to a 'war crimes' court, but she chooses to use this as a threat, rather than pursue it directly. This is what she does in the television version, which shows the legal process as corruptible: the former Nazi is released some time after conviction. In neither book are the political implications spelled out; they are narrativised as the biographies of exceptional women. However, this would not preclude women readers/viewers deriving a little healthy satisfaction from seeing their own sex get their own back for once.

Emma Harte's revenge is complete: the Fairley family is bankrupted; she buys their business and demolishes their home, and she achieves this herself. But she then occupies their former position of privilege. There is no irony in this substitution; no comment on the injustices of class and gender power which necessitated her revenge in the first place. *Sins* can use the culture's knowledge, and acceptance, of Nazi Germany as evil to contextualise Helene Junot's revenge against one of its servants. There is no challenge in this to the reader's assumptions of the political ethics involved. Nor does Helene complete the destruction of her enemy by her own efforts: he is destroyed by another of her enemies, his co-conspirator in a plot against the heroine. Nevertheless, in so far as both novels involve a revenge plot, it is with a woman at its centre, refusing the role of victim, initiating and executing her own revenge. In this she uses the masculine tools of power and money, but not those of physical violence. These are 'heroines', not female heroes.

Not Just a Pretty Face

Like her other fictional counterparts, Emma Harte may be said to combine conventional characteristics of both masculine and feminine heroes. The question is whether this feminisation of entrepreneurial power constitutes a positive element in the social construction of femininity, or whether it represents a co-option of feminist claims and aspirations of which we should merely be critical. Beatrix Campbell's analysis of Margaret Thatcher's transformation of Tory tradition and femininity is pertinent here:

> She is a model neither of traditional femininity nor feminism, but something else altogether – she embodies female power which unites patriarchal and feminine discourses. She has brought qualities of ruggedness and ruthlessness to femininity which perhaps only men hadn't noticed before in women. She has not feminised politics, however, but she has offered feminine endorsment to patriarchal power and principle.[22]

It is tempting to accept this as applying to Emma Harte and company too. Certainly these heroines are rugged and ruthless in a way that is both patriarchal and feminine. This is presumably their appeal. They are neither feminist, nor traditionally feminine: in the 1980s neither traditional femininity nor feminism is quite acceptable as a self-definition for many women. ('I'm not a feminist but . . .' suggests this unease.) Feminism has exposed too many injustices and insults to women, in practice and in ideology, for traditional femininity to have maintained its hold on commonsense knowledge among women about women. But the virulence of media images of feminists has successfully defined them as undesirable extremists. In the kind of welding evident in Thatcher's image, and in those of blockbuster heroines, lies one solution to the dilemma.

The blockbuster heroines are super-successful liberal feminists, claiming equal rights with male heroes in terms of wealth, power and individual autonomy. In order to appropriate male privilege, socially and symbolically, they must be shown as possessing that privilege. And if this excludes the possibility of their being socialists or sisters, is there any point in complaining that they aren't? Can we imagine these feminine millionaires renouncing their fortunes to work in a refuge? Turning their empires into co-operatives? Or forsaking their men to live in a lesbian commune? What would happen to their status as popular fantasy if they did? And wouldn't they then be in danger of negating those very claims they had made on women's behalf? Women don't want wealth, they'd say, they give it away. They can't handle power. Successful women can't get a man. No, it seems we can't have everything, not in a single text, at any rate.

But are we really so desperate that we must look to these elegant entrepreneurs for hope? Well, yes we are: sample a week's worth of the tabloid press or prime-time TV, with their representations of women as simpering sex objects, if you don't believe me. A woman who knows where she's going is a breath of fresh air in that context.

But then, read an article about unemployed black kids in the inner cities, or watch a programme about the neglect of old people in our private homes in Kent. What have 'substantial women' to do with them? The answer is, of course, only too much. The problem being that Mrs Thatcher isn't just a text (though she is that too). We can be tolerant of Alexis Dexter, or Emma Harte, or Helene Junot, for all their limitations, because we also have Victoria Wood and Hazel O'Connor and *Brookside* (who have their own limitations). Taken together they constitute a multifaceted challenge to sexism. A kind of pluralism is necessary in cultural analysis, because texts don't rule alone. But Prime Ministers, these days, do.

3
Here's Looking at You, Kid!

Suzanne Moore

> All I want is a room with a view
> a sight worth seeing
> a vision of you
> All I want is a room with a view
>
> All I want is 20-20 vision
> a total portrait
> with no omissions
> All I want is vision of you
>
> If you can
> Picture this . . .
>
> D. Harry/C. Stein/J. Destri, 'Picture This'
> (for Blondie)

Virginia Woolf may have needed a room of her own, but by the late seventies Debbie Harry was asking for a 'room with a view', 'a sight worth seeing', '20-20 vision'. That particular object of desire was turning the tables – she was singing about watching and wanting, about looking at *her* object of desire.

Shortly afterwards, Richard Gere was taking a very long time to get dressed in *American Gigolo*, the camera lingering over his body in a way normally reserved for female flesh. The ritual of getting dressed, the pampering and preening of the male body became a mechanism by which movies from *Mean Streets* to *Saturday Night Fever* could effectively relocate the cinematic gaze within the strict confines of narrative structure. Standing in front of the mirror, masculinity could legitimately be displayed. Looking hot meant looking cool, looking sharp meant looking hard. Dressing to kill might mean just that – even goody goody Michael Jackson is panting and pouting to show us that underneath he's really *bad*.

By 1986, however, you no longer needed the excuse of getting ready to go out to show half-naked men: you could show them getting *un*dressed. Nick Kamen's determined unbuttoning of his flies in the launderette was enough to make him an instant success – in a neat bit of role reversal, Madonna had soon whisked him away, and written and produced his hit single.

Something had happened. After years of women complaining about the objectification of their bodies, we find ourselves confronted with the male body on display: cut up, close up and oh! so tastefully lit. For some time now such images of men have been quietly slipping into the mainstream via films, videos and – above all – advertising, selling us everything from jeans to make-up and baby clothes. Yes, by 1987 even Terence Conran had 'sussed' it – Mothercare's spring catalogue featured, instead of the usual blonde mother and toddler, a New Man – naked to the waist with, not one, but two bouncing babies. It now seemed to be less a case of taking the toys from the boys than of getting yourself a 'toyboy'.

This new breed of images of masculinity would not have been possible without two decades of gay and feminist politics which advocated the idea that sexuality is socially constructed rather than god-given and immutable. Hence femininity and masculinity are processes in a state of constant negotiation, not static categories from which there is no escape. Out of this flux steps the image of the New Man (many would argue that he exists only as an image): he is tough but tender, masculine but sensitive – he can cry, cuddle babies and best of all buy cosmetics. He is not afraid to be seen caring but mostly he cares about how he looks. So how do you represent such a man? Well, what's so interesting is that many of these images are culled in both form and technique from a long tradition of softcore homo-erotica, and yet are they being aimed at, and consumed by, women as well as men. Moreover I want to suggest that they appeal to women precisely because they offer the possibility of an *active female gaze*.

As theory lopes in its ungainly way behind what is actually happening I could find little explanation for this phenomenon. When I sought material on how women look at men, I discovered, instead, a strange absence. There is plenty on how men look at women; some on how men look at men; and just a little bit on how women look at other women. But to suggest that women actually look at men's bodies is apparently to stumble into a theoretical minefield which holds sacred the idea that in the dominant media the look is always already structured as male.

But in the end the way that we regard a body of theory is much the same as we regard real bodies. We can disavow the things we don't like, fetishise the bits we do, make do with what is familiar while fantasising about something altogether different . . .

A hard man is good to find?

Such writing as there is on the male body tends to offer a reiteration of its stereotyped portrayal: the Stallone-type hard man, the glorified man machine, the celebration of emotional inarticulacy:

> This brings up the question of how it is not to be looked at with the eye of desire. This is precisely the look that the masculine body positively denies, as though it were saying 'Whatever else, not that!' The hardness and the tension of the body strives to present it as wholly masculine, to exclude all curves and hollows and be straight lines and flat planes. It would really like to be a cubist painting. Or whatever. But above all not desirable to other men because it is definitely not soft and feminine; hairy if need be, but not smooth; bone and muscle, not flesh and blood. The masculine body seeks to be Rimbaud not Rambo.[1]

Certainly many representations of men would substantiate this argument, as Antony Easthope illustrates, but the key point is to do with the suppression of homosexual desire between men. This suppression, which according to Freud forms one of the foundations of our society, is precisely what renders the cultural representation of masculinity so limited. But its consequences work in contradictory ways. Rosalind Coward suggests that because the male body is not seen as desirable, men remain in control of desire and the activity of looking. Yet this is not without its price: such male dominance is dependent on the sublimation of narcissism (the self as desirable), and the accompanying lack of satisfactory representations of masculinity results in men feeling alienated from their own bodies.[2] So, ironically, as Coward goes on to say:

> One of the major consequences of men's refusal to be the desired sex, however, is that even women have difficulty in finding them attractive. There's a sort of failure of will at the heart of heterosexual desire.[3]

Things have changed in the few years since Coward's piece was written. Although Rambo still rules in some quarters, competing images of masculinity are coming to the fore which *do* show men as desirable. Such images do not suppress desire between men and so their narcissistic elements are made explicit. These images offer the possibility of being looked at with the 'eye of desire', whether it is a male or a female eye. Their capacity to disturb lies in their appeal to both men and women.

The following passage is from an article in the free London magazine *Girl about Town*:

> For a lot of people last year's Levis 501s campaign came as a revelation – or should that read revolution. Gone were the product shots, naff jingles and predictable copy lines – instead we had fetish, flesh and fulsome torsos. Those jeans, that flesh, that man. Hey wait a minute . . . yes, but it's true, even for us blokes Levis was one hell of a shock.[4]

The Levis 501s advertising campaign was one of the most successful ever, managing to connect Levis to a nostalgic longing for a simpler time – 'What a wonderful world it would be . . .' and putting fifties style over sixties songs (the lyrics are indeed fitting – 'Don't know much about history'!).[5] But when the camera focused on the leather belt sliding off, the assured unbuttoning of the flies, or James Mardle easing himself into the bath, a different kind of longing altogether was evoked.

This wasn't the first time, of course, that the male body was represented as an object of desire – from the silent movie stars to *Smash Hits* there is a long if uneasy history of male pin-ups. What was different was that, in a mainstream context, here was a male body coded, in Mulvey's apt but awkward phrase, for its 'to-be-looked-at-ness'.[6] The usual mechanisms that signal erotic spectacle had crossed gender boundaries. 'Nowadays, the half-naked body you see on TV ads making tasteful love to a bottle of scent won't necessarily be a woman's body.'[7]

As it becomes more problematic to show naked women in advertisements, so naked men come to the fore. The Grey Flannel aftershave ads are a typical example. Shot in grainy black and white, they feature a man, again nude. He looks, not at us, but sideways out of the frame. The picture is cut off at crotch level presumably to leave the rest to our imagination. Again this ad is aimed at women as well as men – and with reason, since it is still women who buy the majority of men's clothes and cosmetics.

And it's not just the advertisers: it's also the people who produce calendars, cards and posters. As the art director of the Athena chain said in an interview in *City Limits*:

> The public want pictures of half-naked men – but all done in the best

possible taste! We've played down the macho thing, the men are more passive, there's nothing aggressive.[8]

So alongside all the predictable calendars full of pictures of semi-clad females, 1986 saw the introduction of calendars called *Blues Boy* by Neil Mackenzie Matthews; we also had *Select Men* and *Cindy Palamanos Men*. All three in the same tasteful but suggestive style that could be sold to both men and women. In fact the 1988 *Blues Boy* calendar moves further into the field of multi-purpose sexuality: 'On the reverse of every languid, soft-focus Blues Boy pose is a Blues Girl in exactly the same setting. So depending on which way you hang/swing it gives you a choice of two calendars.'[9] Skilful marketing or a real indication of the blurring of gender boundaries?

What *is* clear, however, is that in both the still and the moving image the camera lens is zooming in on male flesh. In *Top Gun*, where the camera moved effortlessly between cockpit and locker room; or in the American soaps, where it cuts from boardroom to bedroom to catch Jeff/Bobby/Dex just getting out of the shower . . .

> I will give you my finest hour
> the one I spent
> watching you shower
> I will give you my finest hour
>
> All I want is a photo in my wallet
> a small remembrance
> of something more solid
> All I want is a picture of you
>
> D. Harry/C. Stein/J. Destri, 'Picture This'
> (for Blondie)

The Finest Hour?

The finest hour of what has become known as *Screen* theory can't really explain the production or the consumption of the kind of images that I have mentioned. They are certainly not coming from a political avant-garde but are emerging within popular culture as a result of the renegotiations over masculinity brought about by radical political discourses. Obviously, such shifts are precarious and contradictory, yet perhaps they offer the female spectator a different position from those which Jackie Stacey neatly summarises in chapter 8 as 'masculinisation, masochism or marginality'.

Dwelling as they have on woman as object of the gaze, many of the theories associated with *Screen* have been vital in understanding the relations of power involved in relations of looking. Paradoxically, however, such theory has also contributed to the repression of the female gaze. For repression is about power too, and as Mary Ann Doane comments: 'In theories of repression there is no sense of the productiveness or positivity of power.'[10]

Likewise there is no sense of the productivity of resistance: to say that women *can* and *do* look actively and erotically at images of men and other women disrupts the stifling categories of a theory which assumes that such a look is somehow always bound to be male.

The appropriation and rereading of certain genres and films by gay subculture as 'camp', the wresting of subversive meanings from popular heterosexual discourses such as Hollywood melodramas, is a way of deliciously disturbing the 'true' story. While homosexuality itself may be repressed, *camp* empowers a gay sensibility that can creatively outmanoeuvre the preferred or dominant meanings of a text. 'Camp sees everything in quotation marks,' writes Susan Sontag.[11] For women this kind of creativity seems to be almost a by-product of the whole process of socialisation. Not only are they surrounded by representations of female sexuality through which they must somehow find pleasure; they live both with the 'power of the image' and an acute awareness of its artificiality. Socially, they are expected to be the 'carers', which involves having to be extremely attentive to visual codes and clues. Indeed looking after babies or small children is skill largely based on being intimately aware of how another body behaves or looks.

It is well documented that women tend to be able to name slight visual discriminations in colour, for instance.[12] Advertisers aim their more obscure 'lifestyle' ads at women, who are able to pick up minute visual details with great ease. Campaigns aimed at women sometimes deliberately play upon the ability of women to decode the visual clues that signal class and status, such as furniture or interior design. These ads work by making the spectator feel part of a world to which she aspires, using her knowledge to affirm her right to it. Other products, aiming for a wide market, may underplay anything which can be identified with a particular socio-economic group so as not to exclude potential consumers. Avon, for example, use mostly outdoor shots of flowery fields in their catalogues, which are presumably not thought have particular class or status connotations.

In some ways, then, the very cultural context that weaves the relations of looking into the fabric of power makes it easier for us to unpick it. Nancy Henley's research, for instance,[13] shows that women listen more, look more and are more attentive than men in face-to-face interaction. In public situations, by contrast, men stare at women to assert male dominance, while women look away. But when discussing the way that women look at images or representations of men, we cannot locate them easily in either the private or public sphere. Images on advertising hoardings or in magazines can be looked at privately in the sense that they are always 'just an image' and not a real person who requires a response. Yet on the other hand our access to many images is in and through public space – going to see a film, for instance, involves being part of an assumed audience.

Yet film theory which is primarily about the 'gaze' of the cinema cannot be *simply* mapped on to other media. As John Ellis points out, 'TV is more about the look, and the glance and sound' than the overwhelming cinematic gaze.[14] Video, which puts control of the image within the hands of the viewer, may involve altogether different relations of looking. Clearly, flicking through a magazine is different from staring at a huge poster while waiting for a train, which is different again from replaying a favourite old film on video.

Recognising the contradictions between public and private contexts in which these images are viewed, as well as the differences between the images themselves, means that we cannot be satisfied with a theory premised on a unified spectator sitting alone in a darkened cinema, luxuriously free of the constraints of race or class, history and other texts. This idealisation is attractive because we could so much more easily talk about the 'female gaze' as though it were an attribute of anatomy – the rational retina, the iris free of ideology . . . All men could then be offered a choice of operations – straightforward castration or the removal of their phallic cataracts!

What I'm talking about, of course, is *essentialism*, that most emotionally satisfying, but politically crippling, of all discourses. Basically the argument suggests that women *see* things differently – whether it is a landscape or a teacup (see for instance the work of Judy Chicago) – and therefore a female eye behind the camera would automatically produce a different perspective! In some respects this argument runs parallel to the 'unified masculine model' (Stacey) proposed by Laura Mulvey, who returned to Freud via Lacan because here was a theory which stressed the importance of the visual for the formation of the ego.

Briefly put, in Mulvey's terms there are two types of visual pleasure on offer in Hollywood films. One revolves around an active, objectifying look that requires a distance between the viewer and the object on screen. This is the voyeuristic or fetishistic look. The other involves identification with the screen image and so depends precisely on the dissolution of the distance between screen and spectator. Both these processes, Mulvey argues, are structured through the narrative in such a way that the spectator identifies with the male hero and with his objectification of the female. Femininity as spectacle is encoded into the operations of mainstream cinema so that only a radical and deconstructive film practice could disrupt these pleasures. This argument has been tremendously influential and important in getting beyond a simple 'images of women' type of film criticism. Yet because her argument produces only a masculine spectator position, she is forced in a later article on *Duel in the Sun* to assert that pleasure for the female spectator must involve a type of psychic transvestism. A temporary masculinisation is the only way that Mulvey can offer active pleasure for the woman viewer. But the pleasure offered to women by theorists such as Mulvey is linked only with 'enjoying the freedom of action and control over the diegetic world that identification with a hero provides.'[15]

The possibility of the male as erotic object doesn't really exist, because according to D. N. Rodowick:

> Mulvey conceives the look to be essentially active in its aims, identification with the male protagonist is only considered from a point of view which associates it with a sense of omnipotence, of assuming control of the narrative. She makes no differentiation between identification and object choice in which sexual aims may be directed towards the male figure . . .[16]

This arises because, although Mulvey speaks of female sexuality as an oscillation between an active but regressive masculinity and a passive femininity, the terms active and passive remain static. Freud himself noted but never really overcame the confusion that occurs when active/passive becomes automatically mapped on to masculine/feminine:

> 'Masculine' and 'feminine' are used sometimes in the sense of activity and passivity, sometimes in a biological, and sometimes, again, in a sociological sense. The first of these three meanings is the essential one and the most serviceable in psychoanalysis. When, for instance, libido was described . . . as being 'masculine', the word was being used in this sense, for an instinct is always active even when it has a passive aim in view.[17]

Though Freud ends up by saying that there is no such thing as pure masculinity or femininity and that we are all bisexual, it seems that the force of history overwhelmed him into naturalising the descriptions of gender which psychoanalysis in fact undermined. Why do active and passive need to be translated into the terms of masculine and feminine? This is a socially constructed convention that, as Stephen Heath points out,[18] has no place in a theory of the subject that is radical precisely in its insistence on the cultural determinations of so-called gendered behaviour.

While Freud discusses the need for the ego to fantasise itself in an active manner, Mulvey maps this on to a cultural masculinity, thus dramatically limiting the options of the female spectator. In contrast, recent work on fantasy and identification by writers such as Elizabeth Cowie[19] points to a far more complex process in which identification may occur with the activity itself, not simply with the subject/object of the representation. According to John Ellis, there are shifting identifications between the images on screen and the varying positions, both active and passive, offered within the narrative. 'Identification is therefore multiple and fractured, a sense of seeing the constituent parts of the spectator's own psyche paraded before her or him.'[20]

So, given the complex and contradictory nature of identification, and the difference between sexual aim and object choice described by Rodowick, we cannot simply assume that gender is coterminous with a predetermined subject position within the text. Preferred readings may not always be preferred . . .

I only have eyes for you

Woman as erotic spectacle brings both pleasure and pain. The anxiety induced by seeing the image of woman supposedly reminds the male spectator of the threat of castration and is therefore displaced by the fetishisation of the image. Through this process, Mulvey argues, the image of woman is once more made perfect or visually complete. In traditional Hollywood genres, such as the historical epic, or the Western, there are also moments when the male body is on display, where male spectacle takes over from narrative. This also causes anxiety, which, according to Stephen Neale,[21] is dispelled through sadism – the body is wounded or punished in aggressive fight scenes and ritualised gun battles. Alternatively, as in films such as *American Gigolo* or *Saturday Night Fever*, punishment may be meted out through the narrative itself. Both these films show the problems inherent in the male body becoming an object of desire.

Yet the overt sexualisation of the black male body in the media unsettles such a line of thought – for it seems that if a body is coded racially as 'other', then in some cases it may be legitimately fetishised. The sublime mixture of fear and desire that such images produce may in fact be at the very heart of fetishisation. Unfortunately the reduction of people to bodies, of complex histories to animal physicalities, is also at the core of racism.

So how do the more contemporary images that I mentioned at the beginning of this essay fit into this scheme of things? The answer is that they don't. What seems to be happening is that now we are seeing the male body coded precisely as erotic spectacle but *without* the accompanying narrative violence. Does this offer women a voyeuristic, even fetishistic look? I'm afraid not, girls. Mark Finch writes in an otherwise interesting article on *Dynasty*:

> Women are not trained to objectify bodies as men are, which implies that *Dynasty*'s codification of men along a *Playgirl/Cosmopolitan* discourse enables a gay erotic gaze through the relay of the women's look.[22]

Now I'm not suggesting that the gay male gaze is not being facilitated by programmes like *Dynasty*, but because so many of the images in question are appropriated or influenced by homo-erotic genres anyway, I want to argue the opposite: *that the codification of men via male gay discourse enables a female erotic gaze*.

Explicitly sexual representations of men have always troubled dominant ideas of masculinity, because male power is so tied to looking rather than to being looked at. In a discussion of male pin-ups, Richard Dyer describes the disturbance caused by presenting men as passive, and the frantic need to disavow any notion of passivity. Identifying the hysterically phallic symbolism surrounding publicity shots of stars such as Bogart, he writes of the totally excessive quality of much male imagery:

> The clenched fists, the bulging muscles, the hardened jaws, the proliferation of phallic symbols – they are all striving after what can hardly ever be achieved, the embodiment of phallic mystique.[23]

You have only to see a Stallone film or a video of any Heavy Metal band to recognise the truth of this. Indeed, Sylvester Stallone crams every available signifier of masculinity into each frame of his films – which turn into a kind of grotesque masquerade of manhood, but one that is none the less highly popular.

Some macho men, however, flirt with this very ambiguity – Schwarzenegger (body builder turned film-maker), for example, ostensibly from the same school as Stallone, consistently loads his films with self-conscious references to his manliness, which results in a camp sub-text that sends up the whole ridiculous enterprise. Clint Eastwood, in a seemingly paranoid mood in 1971, made two very interesting films about what it was to be the object of female desire. In *Play Misty for Me* he is pursued by a woman who is murderously obsessed with him, while in *The Beguiled* he plays a soldier wounded in the American Civil War who takes refuge in a girls' school – it ends up with the women sawing his leg off to keep him there. What the loss of a limb signifies depends upon how seriously you take your Freud (or Clint's fear of women).

The striking thing about contemporary images of men is that at least some of them seem to acknowledge and even embrace a passivity that was once symbolically outlawed. The feel is softer, their gaze un-threatening. Many of the ads use black and white photography or moody lighting which connotes that this is just an image – thus a distance can be created between the image and the viewer so that the image may be fetishised precisely as an image. This distance provides the space for the spectator to insert her/himself into the fantasy scenario evoked by many of these representations as the male is marked out as an erotic object.

The Look of Love

In the first Levis 501s ad we are offered the secret vantage point of observing a man in the midst of his beauty routine – he doesn't know that we are watching his narcissistic pampering. When he glances at the picture of the girl, his narcissism is momentarily contained – the pleasure in his body is for someone else and yet as the camera focuses on the water covering his crotch and he gets into the bath, the auto-erotic aspects of the image win out. Water, though often associated with female sexuality, has long been used in homo-erotic imagery to signify male orgasm. Just think of all those gushing sounds in Frankie Goes to Hollywood's *Relax* and think of the reason why the record was banned!

'Splash it all over' seems to be a recurring theme – from the post-coital blues boy to George Michael of Wham. The male body displayed for enjoyment allows women to look actively and powerfully at these private rituals. For a change they are responsible for their own voyeurism and their own desire. In the Nick Kamen ad the relay of looks between the people sitting in the launderette sets him up as object of the gaze – so we too can look. If, in the past, erotic images of men's bodies carried with them the threat of male homosexuality and therefore had to be rendered powerless in some way by being feminised or wounded (the agony is the ecstasy), it now seems possible to represent the male body as a pleasurable object on condition that this pleasure can be contained within a narcissistic/auto-erotic discourse.

The slippage into and from homo-erotica is of course inevitable. Unsurprisingly, many of the kinds of images I have mentioned have been discussed from a gay male perspective (see for instance the work of Mark Finch mentioned earlier and of Frank Mort[24]), which tends to underestimate the pleasure that women may derive from such images. Thus Mark Finch can write about *Dynasty*:

> It seems to me that the pleasure for female spectators is in seeing men treated like women, rather than the pleasure of seeing nudity itself: a textual equality to match representations of strong women.[25]

On the contrary homo-erotic representation, far from excluding the female gaze *may actively invite it*. What's more, as many shrewd business men have realised, it sells to young girls. When Simon Napier-Bell first saw Wham on *Top of the Pops* he immediately picked up on the homo-erotic tension between the two boys and saw it as a marketable phenomenon. Many people puzzled over what Andrew Ridgeley's role was – he didn't write, play instruments or sing – but the combination of him and George Michael provided visual points of entry into many permutations of fantasy. Many of Wham's publicity shots play with classic homo-erotic traditions (George Michael looking ecstatic in the shower, etc.), for it is in this space that men can be presented as desirable. The use of Ridgeley is a kind of third term that breaks down the binarism of either identification with the image or the controlling look of voyeurism. What we have here is a far more complicated scenario, one which allows fluid relations of activity and passivity across multiple identifications.

This more mobile concept of desire, which emphasises its productivity, is to be found in Jacqueline Rose's comments on Freud's 1919 essay 'A child is being beaten':

> For what the fantasy of the female patients reveals is the difficulty

and structuration of feminine sexuality across contradictions in subject/object positions and areas of the body – the desire of the woman is indeed not a 'clear message' . . . The essay demonstrates that male and female cannot be assimilated to active and passive and that there is always a potential split between the sexual object and the sexual aim, between subject and object of desire. What it could be said to reveal is the splitting of subjectivity in the process of being held to a sexual representation (male or female), a representation without which it has no place (behind each fantasy lies another which simply commutes a restricted number of terms).[26]

So although fantasy may only operate with a restricted number of terms, it can endlessly and creatively rework them. What many of these new images of men do is to leave a gap for the female spectator to occupy, a position sometimes within the frame of the picture, sometimes outside it; sometimes active, sometimes passive. Whereas images of women are fetishised as a disavowal of phallic absence, what seems to be going on here is the disavowal of phallic presence – these men are not presented as all-powerful but as objects of pleasure and desire. They undermine the symbolism of the phallus. As Luce Irigaray writes:

> When the penis itself becomes a means of pleasure, and indeed a means of pleasure among men, the phallus loses its power. Pleasure, so it is said, should be left to women, those creatures so unfit for the seriousness of symbolic rules.[27]

Yet Irigaray would be unlikely to endorse my view that women can take pleasure in the kinds of images that I have been describing, for she suggests that female eroticism is linked to *touch* rather than *sight*. She regards the realm of the visual in our culture as intrinsically problematic for women, in that the process of looking always requires a split between subject and object. The transformation of the object of the gaze into the object of desire which is premised on a difference – a splitting – is therefore regarded as an essentially masculine activity. Women whose auto-erotic pleasure is in closeness, sameness – in what Doane calls 'over-identification' – are unable to distance themselves from images in the way that men are. According to the theory, in terms of visual discourse it becomes impossible for women to become subjects of their own desire.

To escape the ultimate sin of objectification (why is it in itself so terrible?) Irigaray retreats into the world of transcendent orgasmic bliss where subject melts into object and where difference dissolves, arguing that touch is the 'true' feminine sense. In a culture where the power of visual images assumes ever greater importance in our lives, this seems to me to be taking the position of the child who shuts her eyes believing that no one can see *her* any more. Touch may be a peculiarly female sense but then so might smell for that matter – and where would that leave us?

While it is crucial to treat women's pleasure as distinct from men's, we must avoid discussing both as though they were fixed outside social conditions. For surely as social conditions change, so do our pleasures. A simple explanation for the proliferation of these new images of men may be found in more liberal attitudes to homosexuality. As homosexual discourse has become public, what was once hidden has become more explicit.

Accompanying these changes there have also been shifts in attitudes to female sexuality. In the 1970s magazines such as *Playgirl* were launched, on the assumption that women could move from being sexually passive to being sexually active by behaving like imitation men and devouring pictures of naked models in ludicrous poses with ridiculous captions. As Margaret Walters writes, 'Such magazines are trying to reduce a woman's feelings to a formula before she knows what they are or might be.'[28] The laughter occasioned by projects such as *Viva* and *Playgirl* compensated for their failure to provide us with anything remotely erotic. If a distance between the viewer and the image is a prerequisite of pleasurable looking, it seems that in this case the gulf was so wide that it could not be filled by any amount of cheap talk about the 'liberated woman'. Ironically, part of these magazines' commercial failure was the fact that advertisers did not want to place their ads on the same page as pictures of naked men!

You're so vain

> One eye in the mirror as you watched yourself
> go by . . .
>
> Carly Simon

As representations of male homosexual desire become incorporated into the mainstream, they disturb the suffocating dualism of the theory which provides little pleasure for women. Yet is all this to our benefit? Well, like many of the shifts thrown up via the marketplace, I think it works in contradictory ways. So far I have sketched out what I see as potentially positive for women, i.e. an erotic and pleasurable look. Yet not surprisingly what these representations allow, which has so long been repressed, is the 'coming out' of male narcissism. A few years ago, at a press conference in London, Schwarzenegger suggested the boom in male body building was connected to feminism: 'For years men looked at women. Now women are looking back at men.'[29] However, it's not that simple, for, as Walters suggests, 'the male body builder is less concerned with women than with his mirror.'[30]

This would appear to be reinforced by men-focused ads and new men's magazines, such as *Arena*, which promote a kind of 'Look, don't touch' sensibility whereby sexuality becomes a self-conscious status symbol. The idea of smooth sexual autonomy, rather than the messy world of relationships, is the one that sells all those 'personal adornment' products. We're talking strictly *market* penetration here. Listen to Tony Hodges, managing director of the agency that handled the Grey Flannel campaign, speaking about the 'New Man':

> The individual at the heart of this brand is in his early twenties, is discovering himself – discovering what women discovered years ago – that the mirror is perhaps more important than the other person.[31]

Frank Mort suggests that there is positive potential in men becoming self-conscious in so far as it leads to the realisation that they *can* change, rather than thinking of masculinity as an unalterable norm. Yet such superficial changes, so skilfully utilised by the advertisers, will remain precisely at the level of *image* unless they are tied to parallel social changes in male attitudes – unless men are convinced that they need, and want, to change. Caring has to mean more than caring about how one looks. Two decades of feminist demands that men should be more sensitive must surely result in something more than men with sensitive skin?

So are we to welcome this upsurge of male narcissism as a 'good thing'? Or is it just another way of excluding women? Now that men can look good and be emotional, are women expendable? Or are we just trying to pull a homosexual discourse into a heterosexual space?

Such questions arise out of contradictory cultural processes; on one hand culture promotes gay imagery and style in order to target young men as consumers, and on the other, the political climate is increasingly repressive and anti-gay. So although in some contexts the male body is being legitimated as an object of desire, explicit portrayals of the male genitals are still forbidden. An erect penis is still what makes hard porn 'hard'. The right is ever more frantic to preserve its phallic mystique – the erect penis is still supposed to be an object of mystery rather than a bit of a disappointment – so we get uproar at the hint of a Derek Jarman film and a BBC spokesman announcing that there will never be 'an erection at the BBC' (to which someone wittily replied that there would still be lots of cock-ups – and the rest of us thought: just a bunch of pricks . . .).

The fear experienced by men of women's Medusa-like stare, which petrifies everything in sight, is in reality a fear that the female gaze will soften everything in its path. Yet this softening has *already* been achieved in many of these new representations of men and such a mythology may actually obscure what is different or disturbing about the female gaze. If a female gaze exists it does not simply replicate a monolithic and masculinised stare, but instead involves a whole variety of looks and glances – an interplay of possibilities.

> We read a text (of pleasure) the way a fly buzzes around a room: with sudden, deceptively decisive turns, fervent and futile . . .[32]

Not for us the singular and silent view of the fly on the wall, instead we must insist, like Barthes' fly buzzing around the room, that our ways of seeing are myriad, our pleasures plural.

Here's looking at you, kid . . .

The Color Purple:
In Defence of Happy Endings

Andrea Stuart

The Color Purple is a rare example of a work which has effected a
feminist intervention in popular culture in two essential ways. The
book, an alternative novel turned bestseller, is an instance of direct
intervention, where a woman writer has created a text featuring
progressive representations of women, which has enjoyed a huge
popular readership. The film of the same name illustrates feminism's
more indirect, yet in this case powerful, influence on popular genres,
in having engaged the active interest of a male director who turned it
into a box office success, with, of course, subsequent spiralling sales
for the book of the film.

For Steven Spielberg is not just any old director. Responsible for
five of the ten biggest box office hits of all time, including *ET*, *Raiders
of the Lost Ark* and *Close Encounters of the Third Kind*, Spielberg has
an almost uncanny instinct for a commercial product. Everything he
touches, it seems, turns to gold. His work had not previously been
characterised by a particular interest in women. On the contrary, his
was a traditionally masculine vision, involving SF plots, intricate
special effects and a minimum of human complexity in the creation of
character – which makes his interest in *The Color Purple* all the more
significant. It is perhaps a measure of the real impact feminism can
have on popular culture, as opposed to tabloid sneers and feminist
pessimism, that Spielberg was not only willing to accommodate Alice
Walker's woman-centred vision, but correctly predicted its popular
(i.e. financial) success.

The Book of the Film

Alice Walker's novel *The Color Purple* represents a vision which is
very specifically that of a black woman. The book addresses the
difficulties of women's position within the black community in the
United States, and in so doing engages with all those oppressive forces
which have conspired to create imprisoning stereotypes of black

women – stereotypes which black women writers need to resist in order to begin to tell the truth about themselves. In order to forge a positive identity for black women, this means taking issue, not only with the assumptions and institutions of white male culture, but also with the oppositional cultures of white feminism and black male writing.

Walker sets the women at the centre of her novel within the hierarchies of oppression of class, race and gender. Black women, as has often been noted, are oppressed by all three of these power structures. Significantly, however, she focuses on a specific aspect of power relations within the black community itself – the exploitation of black women by black men. This has long been a taboo subject for black women. For obvious reasons, discussion of power and its abuse between black people has been regarded as a betrayal of racial solidarity in that it presents white people with negative images of black people to fuel their racism. Yet ironically, the negative descriptions of black women in the works of some black male writers have passed largely unremarked, and have certainly not been interpreted as a treachery against the race.

It is in addressing these suppressed issues that Alice Walker defines her own territory as a black woman writer. And it is essential to understand the context of silence within which she writes, and the complexity of the debate she addresses, in order to appreciate *The Color Purple* as a progressive, and often radical, tale.

The very existence of *The Color Purple* as a popular cultural product, in the United States, Britain and elsewhere, challenges the near invisibility of black women in mainstream culture. The almost bloody-minded survival of its black heroine, Celie, can serve as a metaphor for the book itself in its representation of the defiance inherent in black women writing at all: 'I'm pore, I'm black, I may be ugly and can't cook . . . But I'm here.'[1]

The novel tells the story of Celie, who by the age of twenty has been repeatedly raped by the man she knows as her father, forcibly separated from the two children she bears as a result, and then married off to Mr., a widowed farmer. Mr. is more interested in Celie's 'prettier' sister Nettie, but settles for Celie, despite her being 'spoiled', because he needs someone to take care of his children. He abuses her physically and verbally, humiliates her publicly, and is responsible for her decades-long separation from her much-loved sister Nettie.

Celie's experience is unspeakable – in more than one sense. In the everyday sense of the word, what she suffers is appalling. More literally, because she is without formal education, she is illiterate, and because she is schooled in self-denial and submission, she cannot speak up for herself – an act which requires self-possession and confidence. In addition, she is silenced for much the same reason as the author herself might have been silenced: because the atrocities she suffers are committed against her by the very men the mythology of family and community claim are her protectors, to whom she owes her loyalty – her father and her husband. The historical link between accusations of inter-racial rape and the lynching of black men makes any suggestion of sexual abuse within the black family a particularly taboo area, as Walker explores in a different context in her short story, 'Advancing Luna – and Ida B. Wells'.[2]

But Celie does not remain a victim. Through her own determination, and with the support and love of others in the community – namely, black women – she finds the self-esteem and contentment she deserves. Celie's capacity to survive exploitation and abuse, as well as her existence on pages of her 'own' authorship, are evidence that black women, however oppressed, are not only worth the paper we are written on, but worthy of attention and, above all, of *respect*.

The characters in *The Color Purple* are socially located within a fairly affluent peasant community. The effect of this relative affluence is twofold. First it allows Walker to counter the image of black people as one homogeneous, lumpen, classless mass: a stereotype as firmly cherished on the left as it is on the right, and a longstanding source of annoyance to black people. Second, Walker creates characters who *own* things – houses, cars, stores, land – and have done for generations (like Mr., who inherits his home from his father). They are for the most part self-employed, or employed by each other, or (in one memorable case) the employer of a white man. So white people - vicious, tedious and comic when they do intrude – are peripheral to the action of the novel. By focusing on the black community itself, rather than on its position in white society, Walker is able to concentrate on the dynamic of its own power relations, especially those between women and men.

This is very different from the focus on the power(less) relationship of the black community to white American society which characterises the works of classic black male authors like Richard Wright and Ralph Ellison. Their greatest talent lay in their ability to depict the brutality of racist oppression and its traumatic effects on black Americans. Their work is, at least in part, aimed at explaining the 'black condition' to white people: an appeal for justice, addressed to white society in its own 'good' English. A couple of decades on, black female writers like Toni Morrison, Sonia Sanchez, Ntozake Shange and, of course, Alice Walker herself, have shifted their focus and address their work to a black – even a black female – readership. Their interest is not in explaining or justifying themselves to anyone, but, as Morrison put it, in 'talking to the tribe'. Their work aims to empower the black community to act for themselves, to recognise their own worth, their own history, their own reality. Essential to this purpose is the need to counter both the myth of homogeneity in the black community and the self-hatred experienced by black people – a self-hatred revealed, for example, in Wright's *Black Boy*, where he laments the '. . . strange absence of real kindness in Negroes, how unstable was our tenderness, how lacking in genuine passion we were, how void of great hope, how tired our joy, how bare our traditions.'[3]

This self-hatred is a form of internalised oppression which is easily as dangerous to the black community as oppression from without. We may therefore regard as subversive the aim of contemporary black women writers to present the black community as a semi-autonomous social totality, with its own dynamics of power, and its own potential for psychological and social wholeness. Perhaps more subversive than the deceptively radical white-hot rage of their male predecessors.

In these earlier representations of the black American community, the focus is firmly on the black *man*. It is men who suffer the dehumanising effects of racism; it is men who deserve better at the hands of whites. Black women's role in this scenario tends to oscillate between that of pathetic burden on the one hand, and that of threat to the black man's masculinity on the other: they are, in short, the embodiment of the sublimated hatred of black men for their blackness. Even white women, as complex symbols of that which is hated but desired, desired but forbidden, are sometimes portrayed with more human reality.

In *The Color Purple* it is women who constitute the focus of the representation of the black community, with men relegated to the periphery of female consciousness. Rather like the weather, men are part of women's (usually) hostile environment, a perennial force to be dealt with daily, but not the centre of their emotional existence. Mostly troublesome, sometimes cruel, occasionally endearing, men are never the source of emotional sustenance or long-term happiness for women. Celie, for instance, does not expect emotional support from Mr., so his failure to provide it cannot hurt her: he can only really hurt her (as he does) by separating her from her sister. Similarly, she does not care that her lover, Shug, returns home with a husband. She cares only that Shug is back with her: the existence of a husband is irrelevant to what is important – the relationship between the two women. Even Shug, who enjoys sexual relationships with men (including Mr.), finds her emotional centre with a woman:

> 'I know how you feel about men . . . But I don't feel that way . . . I would never be fool enough to take any of them seriously . . . But some men can be lots of fun.'[4]

The story of Celie is one of a black woman empowered to reject the role of passive victim and become active agent in her own life, through her relationships with other women: sister, lover, daughter-in-law and friends.

In this there is a message to all women – black and white: to look at the reality of their relationships with each other, and with men, and, by acknowledging where their real emotional sustenance is located, to discover its empowering force for themselves and each other. It is a message to be found in other contemporary black women novelists: Toni Morrison, for example, magnificently explores the transformative power of women's love for each other in her novel *Sula*. It can, perhaps, be compared with Adrienne Rich's concept of the 'lesbian continuum', the bonding between women at all levels from sexual passion to neighbourliness.[5] Like Rich, Walker and Morrison challenge the centrality of men to society, to culture and to women, inviting us to redefine ourselves as this centre, with a female perspective on the men, culture, and society.

If the representation of black women has been bad, the depiction of our sexuality has been even worse. Walker seizes our sexuality back from those black male writers who have abused it, and from white popular culture, which has denied or exploited it. Instead of depicting it as our service to black men, in Celie's love for Shug it becomes a symbol of the autonomy of black women's sexuality. Celie's sexuality is not used as a metaphor of radical oppression, in the way that Ralph Ellison uses father/daughter incest in *Invisible Man*,[6] where it is treated as a comic interlude that represents how the black community becomes the recipient of white people's displaced sexual anxiety and transgressive desire. Walker, like Morrison in *The Bluest Eye*, or Maya Angelou in *I Know Why the Caged Bird Sings*, reclaims the horror of incest from the victim's point of view and the terrible emotional damage it causes her. But she also shows how our sexuality can be used, not to oppress us, but to liberate us, in developing and expressing a shared sense of identity.

Many of the characteristics of the generation of black American women writers to which Walker belongs are evident in the works of their female literary predecessors. The influence of Zora Neale Hurston on Walker's own work is an outstanding example of the continuity of this tradition. Hurston was brought up in one of the few all-black towns that existed in the USA around the turn of the century. This environment sheltered her from the direct experience of racial prejudice that scarred some of her contemporaries. As a result, in her essay 'How it Feels to be Colored Me' she describes herself as being coloured, 'but not tragically colored'.[7] She seems not to have preceived being black as a problem, and therefore did not present it as such. The representation of the black community in her work as semi-autonomous and psychologically whole supplied a model for writers like Walker and her contemporaries.[8]

Hurston also perhaps provided the model for the oral tradition which informs Walker's novel. *The Color Purple* is written as letters from the down-trodden, inarticulate Celie, addressed to God. She writes to 'God' because there is no one else to whom she can tell her story. 'You'd better not never tell nobody but God,' threatens her father. Silenced by the taboos surrounding her oppression, and by her own lack of education and assertiveness, she speaks, 'silently', in her own idiosyncratic but peculiarly expressive grammar. Like Hurston's language, which was dismissed by one critic as 'comical nigger dialect', Celie's is 'uneducated', but rich with the vitality and impact of the spoken word.

An oral tradition has often been crucially important to oppressed peoples. Excluded from the established culture by lack of formal education, poverty and illiteracy, they have been denied a written heritage of their own. The spoken tradition has therefore provided an alternative medium for creating their own literature, history and protest. It is no wonder that Walker and many of her contemporaries have resisted attempts to 'upgrade' or dismiss the language and forms of black oral culture, but have instead drawn upon it in the creation of their own, written, works.

It is also from the oral tradition that the folk tales which supplied the model for many of Hurston's stories originated. And in a peculiar way *The Color Purple* is itself a folk tale. It certainly isn't a realist novel in the ordinary sense, so it is irrelevant to criticise it, as one reviewer did, for 'evading the real implications of [the characters'] lives'.[9] Rather, it draws upon a tradition like that of the Uncle Remus stories so popular with black American children, which advocate tolerance, patience, perseverance and cunning for the underdog's survival; and upon religious parables, whose messages of moral optimism mean so much to an oppressed community. *The Color Purple* is a morally inspiring tale about an underdog who not only survives but triumphs, designed to explore in the process responses to oppression which are philosophically and psychologically positive strategies for survival.

The oft-repeated accusation that Walker's novel is too full of happy coincidences and/or 'wishy-washy' spiritualism is evidence of how this text has been undervalued as a result of a failure to understand it on its own terms. The implication of such criticism is that Walker does not herself understand the logical conclusions of her own characters' suffering. This is surely rather insulting. Alice Walker has depicted the grim reality of the black experience, with all its tragically horrifying consequences, in many of her earlier books. In *The Third Life of Grange Copeland*,[10] for instance, she dissects the prevalent notion of black masculinity and reveals its devastating effects on black women and children. Many of the stories in *In Love and Trouble* make equally painful reading.[11] If the author of these works chooses to end *The Color Purple* happily, she presumably knows what she's doing.

The happy coincidences with which Celie's story concludes – the appearance of her long-lost children, the discovery that the man who raped her as a child was not her biological father, the return of her beloved sister – can be read as an improbable fairy-tale ending. In a sense, of course, it is. But it can be read as something other than a failure of the realist imagination. Folk tales and fairy tales tradi-tionally reward the heroine/hero at the end, often in an excessive way (great wealth, marriage to the prince, sainthood). Celie's reward at the end of *The Color Purple* may seem equally excessive (at least by the criteria of the realist novel). But, in the manner of a folk-tale protagonist, she has earned it through her own subversive efforts; and, like the heroine of a morality tale, she deserves it. Seen within the context of the oral culture of American blacks, the happy ending is that of the folk tale or parable, and as such entirely appropriate in form and content.

For this is not just an optimistic book, but an optimistically didactic one. Black women must learn to respect themselves, it says, to be respected; learn to speak for themselves to be listened to; speak up for themselves to be recognised. They must not internalise oppression by responding with self-hatred and submission. They can, and must, look to themselves, and to those who can give them the support they need in this struggle – that is, other black women – and draw sustenance from them. Then they will realise that they have strength in community and can give as well as receive. Then they will find each other as sisters, discover that their past was worse than had been admitted, but not as bad as they'd feared (Celie's children are the product of rape, but not of incest), and thus forge their own future in autonomy and freedom. This would be a cruel message without the happy ending.

Despite the atrocities she suffers, Celie has the courage to speak of them. In giving voice to the unspeakable, she discovers that it can be spoken. She defies the taboos and thereby deprives them of their power to destroy her. In speaking to God she discovers herself and her own strength, because 'God' is not another powerful and potentially hostile force – 'God' is everything that lives:

> God is inside you and inside everybody else. You come into the world with God. But only them that search for it inside find it. And sometimes it just manifest itself even if you not looking, or don't know what you looking for . . . It ain't a picture show. It ain't something you can look at apart from anything else, including yourself. I believe God is everything, say Shug. Everything that is or ever was or ever will be. And when you can feel that, and be happy to feel that, you've found it.[12]

Celie learns to 'chase that old white man out of [her] head'[13] and recognise her own 'divine' humanity – her own capacity for joy, freedom, control, autonomy and love. She learns to notice 'the color purple in a field',[14] so that she can no longer dismiss her life as merely the sum of her oppression or accept suffering as her destiny. Here too is a message for black women generally – indeed for all oppressed people. Celie's redefinition of the meaning of her life is one that rescues oppressed people from the negative implications of their status as victims by pointing to ways of transcending it, without minimising either the intensity of their oppression or the difficulties of resistance.

This also gives her the strength to forgive. The capacity to forgive is much emphasised in black women's novels. It cannot, in *The Color Purple* at least, be read as a sentimental spirituality which aims to transcend the political, or as an act of Christian charity for the benefit of the individual's immortal soul. Rather, it is an essential mechanism in the black woman's liberation, which allows her both to free herself from the self-destructive emotions of hatred and bitterness, and to shift her emotional focus back where it belongs – into the black community. For it is Mr. and his son Harpo who are forgiven; white people are not so much forgiven as excommunicated from consciousness.

The Film of the Book

Spielberg's film, for all its differences from the book, is essentially faithful to this part of Alice Walker's vision; surprisingly perhaps, in view of the history of black people's place in mainstream cinema. Contrary to popular belief, black films have not automatically been box office poison: from *Showboat* to *Shaft*, directors have realised their financial potential. But all too often this has meant the perpetuation of stereotyped images of the black community. As late as the 1980s, a film like *Cotton Club* can relegate black people to subsidiary roles in a story about Harlem in the 1920s!

The Color Purple is a very different proposition. Spielberg's film is set in a disturbingly beautiful South. The visual medium of film is exploited to depict a geographical beauty at which the printed page can only hint. This led to accusations that the director was glamorising poverty – which, while not without substance, is nevertheless a revealing criticism. Most people's image of the American South is as clichéd as their image of poverty itself. Poverty is commonly identified with the media of its representation – the grey and grainy texture of old black and white films, newspaper photographs and socio-realist documentaries, associated with bleak urban landscapes and cramped dark conditions. These images, often chosen to reinforce our perceptions of the harshness of the conditions themselves, have come to represent the reality of the lives of oppressed people. This is how we often envisage black life in the South: the lush scenery, the sun and the space belong to our image of the rich white antebellum South of *Gone with the Wind*, with its colonial mansions and Southern belles.

Yet it is in this extravagant landscape of dazzling colours that Spielberg sets the black characters of his film. This was not an image of oppression we could readily recognise, or feel comfortable with, because our image was perhaps a specifically urban one, where poverty and oppression are incompatible with beauty in the environment – something which, in industrial societies, has come to be a class privilege, to be purchased in leafy suburbs and on exotic holidays. But rural poverty, as in the South depicted by Walker, and as it exists in so much of the Third World today, is experienced in a context of often stunning tropical beauty, where an aesthetic of nature is not the sole prerogative of the rich. The film of *The Color Purple*, even more than the book, forces us to re-examine our preconceptions about the colour of poverty and facilitates an association between black people and their environment as beautiful (very different from grimy ghettoes or plantation shacks), which not only contributes to a more positive image of black life, but is also one that tells a different truth about us.

But then the community depicted in the film, as in the book, is not one mired in hopeless penury: these are people with a degree of economic self-sufficiency, relatively free from face-to-face racist oppression. In the book, however, the white society, if not a direct presence in day-to-day living, is still the omnipresent context of the black community – a constant 'miracle of affliction',[15] which, through its exploitation and abuse, reverberates throughout the black community and ultimately influences its own dynamic of relationships. This context gives the lie to white assumptions that being 'nice' to black people is all that is needed to abolish racism. On the contrary, being 'nice' is neither effective in the face of the ubiquity of such hierarchical structures of oppression, nor important to black people, whose emotional concerns are not focused on white people but on each other.

In representing the financial and emotional self-sufficiency of the black community, Spielberg reproduces this positive aspect of Walker's portrayal. But in almost entirely removing white society from the film's frame of vision, he renders invisible the pervasive power of racism and thus throws the power structure of the black community itself out of 'sync'. Taken out of the context of white racism, the black men in the film can only appear as monsters acting out individual ego problems, rather than as victims themselves, taking refuge in notions of masculinity which involve visiting their oppression on those weaker than themselves: black women and children.

The one occasion on which white racism is seen to intrude directly into this community affects a woman. The story of Sofia, the straight-talking wife of Mr.'s son Harpo, is closer to the kind of black realism we are familiar with in depicting the cruelty visited upon black people when they defy the petty rules of a white racist society. Sofia's failure to show the 'appropriate' politeness to a white woman in the street is 'punished' with imprisonment, servitude in the mayor's household, years of separation from her children, and physical disability.

Instrumental in Sofia's fate is the only white character in the film, the mayor's wife. She is represented as a stereotype of middle-class women: incompetent, dependent and hysterical. While the book portrays her behaviour in the context of her own oppression as a woman in a male-dominated society, the film presents her in isolation, making her nothing less than ridiculous. This not only carelessly reproduces an insulting sexist stereotype, but, in using it to represent white society, individualises the socio-political reality of racism, reducing it to a callous but ridiculous character trait, from which white audiences (especially the men among them) can easily distance themselves and from which black people would seem to have little to fear. The result is that, while Sofia's suffering can be read as demonstrating the omnipresent threat posed to black people by the distant power of white society, because its immediate agent is this caricature of a white woman, it appears to have a random, unpredictable quality quite separate from the normal organisation of power. The result is effectively to remove from view the culpability of white society as such, and especially of white men, just as their image is removed from the view of the camera.

The representation of black women is altogether more laudable. This is where the film really comes into its own. It presents a world seen entirely from a black female perspective, with sexism an integral part of its subject matter. Walker's vision of women living in an emotionally female world is reproduced for a mass audience, carrying a message about women's needs and priorities which undermines one of the most basic assumptions of sexism – that men are what is important to women. Just as the focus on the black community undermines white assumptions about their importance to black people, so the focus on the women within that community implies that, contrary to ideologies of romantic love and companionate marriage, men are not really the emotional focus of women's lives. Spielberg reinforces visually Walker's point that when women stop defining themselves in terms of their relationships with men they are more likely to discover their own source of happiness. Women are quite literally foregrounded in the film, with their perspective on events the dominant one. Even scenes between men are witnessed by a woman character (usually Celie) and often framed by her vision of them, as when Celie is seen observing conversations between her father and Mr. or between Mr. and his father through the window. Spielberg subverts the conventional male gaze at the female performer in the scene where Shug sings 'Sister' as a love song to Celie in a bar full of admiring men. And the final scene (marred by a frankly comic excess of emotion) nevertheless begins with a powerful shot of the three women emerging from Celie's house, where they all live, on to the balcony, down the steps, to welcome Nettie – their husbands all in the background, at the edges of the screen.

As the protagonist, Celie remains the pivotal point of the film's narrative, although she relinquishes her camera-like perspective on the action to the camera itself. This may be largely due to the inability of film as a medium to reproduce a novelistic perspective, since it cannot avoid positioning us to look at Celie as well as to look with her. Nevertheless, Whoopi Goldberg is quite wonderful (as is Desreta Jackson, who plays Celie as a child). Though she is virtually silent for most of the film, except for her voice-over, Goldberg's marvellous facial expressions and gawky movements speak volumes. Her eyes imply a delicious, albeit repressed, sense of humour, along with a wistfulness and steely doggedness that is irresistible in its suggestion of the rich complexity of consciousness that is the truth behind the stereotype of oppressed black womanhood. As an actress, Goldberg has a rare ability to appear sometimes ugly (as Celie believes herself to be), mostly just plain, and at other times, breathtakingly beautiful. Spielberg's decision to cast her in the role was a brave and astute one. A more conventionally and consistently 'pretty' actress would more readily have invited the audience's sympathy: instead, we are required to work at it, forced in the process to reassess our assumptions about the role of physical beauty in how women are treated (something visual representations rarely do): to ask not only why beauty should be so important for a woman, but also whether it is, as we so often assume, a physical gift or, as seems to be true of Celie, a state of mind.

It is in this respect that Shug, played by Margaret Avery, was a serious piece of miscasting. It seems that Spielberg was playing it safe here, and in so doing has undermined the quality of his translation of Walker's vision on to film. The Shug of the novel is black, nappy-headed and raunchy. In fact, the only appreciable difference between her and Celie lies in how she perceives herself and is therefore perceived by others. Margaret Avery is more like an *Ebony* model – honey-coloured, slim, elegant and sophisticated. When Mr.'s father asks him what he sees in Shug, he can find no reply:

> Old Mr. _____ say to Mr. _____, Just what is it bout this Shug
> Avery anyway, he say. She black as tar, she nappy headed . . . Mr.
> _____ turn his head slow, watch his daddy drink. Then say, real sad,
> You ain't got it in you to understand, he say. I love Shug Avery.
> Always have, always will.[16]

Mr.'s incomprehension at his weakness for a woman who transgresses all his expectations – that she should be faithful, dependent and subservient – and who doesn't even conform to the then black community's own racial hierarchies of beauty by having 'good' hair or 'yellow' skin – reveals for once his own vulnerability. But in the film the answer is only too obvious to the audience: Shug as played by

Margaret Avery is every aspirational black man's dream. The Shug of the book has an altogether more elusive appeal. In reinforcing the stereotype of conventional beauty as the source of women's power, the film completely fails to understand Walker's very important point about the relationship between women's strength and their beauty. Shug is more beautiful than Celie, not because she was naturally endowed with more beautiful physical features, but because she possesses a confident sense of her own identity. She is beautiful because she is strong, not the other way round. Accordingly, Celie too can be beautiful if she learns to be strong; as she does. Walker's message here is profound: the only way for women to counter men's power over them is for women to have a strong sense of their own worth. In this respect the book empowers women, irrespective of their 'looks', to use their individual 'sass' and their shared love for each other to acquire a sense of dignity. This message is considerably weakened in the film.

By contrast, the casting and performance of Oprah Winfrey as Sofia is a masterstroke of characterisation, which captures Walker's meaning perfectly. In 'real life' Oprah Winfrey is a glamorous talk-show host on American television. But nothing of this glamour is apparent in the Sofia of the film: a large powerhouse of a woman, whose ability to survive disaster with a glint in her eye symbolises for Celie (and for us) an instinctive fearlessness in the face of the brutalities of sexism and racism. When Celie finally defies Mr. and announces her decision to leave with Shug, Sofia, with her blind eye and prematurely grey hair, is present at the dinner table – a grim reminder of the price of defiance and a measure of Celie's courage.

For the most part Spielberg avoids the problematic arena of black sexuality. This has long been a source of anxiety for white film-makers: so many racial fears and fantasies have been invested in it. No doubt attracted by a contemporary Cinderella story as offering box office appeal, Spielberg found himself dealing with rape, incest and illegitimacy in a black family, a forced marriage, and a lesbian love affair between two black women. No doubt this was good box office too; but it also raised the spectre of accusations of racism, sexism and voyeurism. Whatever the reason, the film's approach is cautious. The incestuous rape of Celie is only spoken by her in voice-over, not shown; in its place is a graphic and noisy birth scene which conveys the sense of Celie's pain and outrage. The only sexual encounter shown is the emotionless 'humping' that Celie endures from Mr., which, seen from her point of view, constitutes a bleak comment on women's experience of sex and marriage.

The sexual dimension of the love between Celie and Shug is only delicately, ambiguously, suggested. Neither visually nor verbally is it ever made explicit in the film. Should we regard this as an evasion motivated by homophobia, an unacknowledged racism or just plain old discomfort? Many black women would have been uncomfortable with the explicit portrayal of black lesbian love by a white male director for a predominantly heterosexist and racist audience. So perhaps we should be relieved that we were not called upon to confront it. The film does manage to capture some of the intimacy of the relationship between Celie and Shug and its importance in Celie's story of self-discovery. Maybe explicit inclusion of its sexual dimension would have clouded this point. But to omit it inevitably meant also omitting the passion and intensity between the two women, which sex symbolises.

The novel's spirituality, which, as we have seen, tends towards a form of pantheism, is seriously misinterpreted in the film. The politically subversive implications of love's redemptive power in Celie's self-realisation is translated into a pseudo-Christian individualism whereby the 'worthy' individual gets her just reward. Spielberg takes this to its most banal extreme in the reconciliation scene between the community's wayward woman (Shug) and its devout patriarch (her preacher father). This resembles nothing short of a cross between *The Wiz* and a revival meeting, and is easily the most irritating scene in the whole film, disillusioning those of us who thought that, for once, we were to be spared another black musical!

Spielberg's avowed intention in making *The Color Purple* was to explore his 'adult side'. He wanted to make a film about 'people' – not another movie where the plot required an oversimplification of character. But the film suggests that it was the life-enhancing message of Walker's work that attracted him, rather than an understanding of the nuances of her text. What the film fails to convey is the cool delicacy of the book's style which qualifies the starkness, and indeed extravagance, of the human misery depicted. Instead, this is worked into tragedy and melodrama, until we feel manipulated by an excess of emotional appeal. Where Walker uses Celie as narrator of the experiences of an entire community, the movie – perhaps predictably in line with conventional film practice and its need for a star – focuses on her as an individual, relating to other individuals (although this does maintain her female point of view). The overall result is that the film is sensational where the book is subtle. Despite this, which might be seen as Spielberg's co-option of Walker's vision, it is arguable that it was a sensationalism worth putting up with in view of what it does manage to achieve.

Perhaps the most serious limitation of a film like *The Color Purple* is that it has to operate in a vacuum. There are so few films about black people, with black lead characters, and a virtually all-black cast, which take black people seriously, that any such film must bear an immense burden. No single film can be expected to do justice to everyone in the black community (of even the United States, let alone those of Britain, the West Indies, etc.), or present the diversity, complexity and, indeed, contradictions of the black experience. Since no film can be all things to all people, even if Spielberg had created a work perfect in its own terms, it was doomed to at least partial failure.

If a mainstream film about the black community is unusual, then one about a black woman's experience is virtually unique. This intensifies the problem of the film's isolation, which is further exacerbated once the film's audience moves outside the black American community. The gulf between black and white American perceptions is paralleled by the gulf between American and British perceptions once this book/film crosses the Atlantic. At a basic level, the book/film has the universal appeal of its optimistic message. Beyond that it speaks particularly to the black community and women. For black people in Britain the debates on race, and the very language of black activism, have to some extent been appropriated from the black American tradition, so, despite historical and geographical differences, we share some of the same problems and some of the same responses to those problems. To a lesser extent, perhaps, something similar can be said of feminism within both communities and both countries.

Despite its imperfections, *The Color Purple* was, and is, a very important film for black people. We cannot afford to dismiss it with quite the impunity displayed by some critics, simply because it *is* such a rarity. The film is also a rarity in that it remains true, however partially and however inadvertently, to a book which takes women so seriously, focuses on their experience and perspective, and has such a powerful anti-sexist message in its visual and emotional marginalisation of men. For both these reasons, black women have reason to take the film seriously, and, with whatever reservations, to welcome its presence in high street cinemas and video shops.

At least it has proved that a film about black women can make money. Regardless of the motives of decision makers in the film industry, if anti-racism and anti-sexism can make as much money as racism and sexism, this has to be regarded as basically in our interests as black feminists, and as deriving ultimately from our work in attempting to counter racism and sexism in society.

Hopefully, the commercial success of the film *The Color Purple* will encourage more films about black people, and more films about women. Because it is only when we have more varied, indeed just more, images in the mainstream that negative, reductive stereotypes can begin to be effectively challenged. And it is only when we participate in the creation of these images ourselves that we can expect to see our reflections in the mirror of popular culture.

Lolita Meets the Werewolf:
The Company of Wolves

Maggie Anwell

> A bold and imaginative excursion into the
> sexual awakening of a young girl – from the
> writer of *The Company of Wolves*.

> From the press release for the film *The
> Magic Toyshop*

'Typical Carter territory', according to the *Guardian* film critic; 'a
kind of fairy story about growing up which is at once chaste and
knowing, ambiguous and straightforward'.[1] Another review talks of
'recognisable Carter ingredients: the critique of patriarchy, the
genesis of female sexuality, the fascination with the themes of
children's literature and with the fantastic, the taste for the
grotesque'.[2]

Do such comments suggest that Angela Carter has created a new
space within popular culture for this area of female experience to be
expressed? Is this the territory which Elaine Showalter urges feminists
to explore as 'the newly visible world of female culture'?[3] Certainly the
writing of Angela Carter, with its explorations of myths, taboos, rites
of initiation and of passage, challenges patriarchal views of femininity.
But is this challenge sustained in the transfer of her work to the screen
in mainstream cinema?

Any examination of her short story 'The Company of Wolves' and the
subsequent film of the same name must confront a familiar dilemma
for feminist artists: how can feminism engage with the mainstream of
popular culture without having our ideas and fantasies reduced and
manipulated – even travestied – by the underlying market forces?

'Isn't she a little, well, vulgar?'[4]

In the reception of her writing, even sympathetic critics have at times
portrayed Angela Carter as the inheritor of the 'infected sentence',[5]
the happy outlet for the feverish outpourings of the female

imagination; a writer in the Gothic, Romantic tradition of women writers, 'erotic, exotic and bizarre'[6] and open to the charge of keeping alive 'that superstition which debilitates the mind.'[7] She is without doubt a determined fantasist, and fantasy, which seems to employ linguistic and imaginative excess, and moves uncomfortably close to the borders of insanity, has always had a mixed critical reception, by virtue of its capacity to subvert the stability of realism in order to describe alien psychic states and at the same time to give voice to censored female eroticism. But fantasy, suggests Mary Jacobus, can be seen as a textual strategy for escaping realist images of repressed female experience; it offers the possibility of a fictional transformation of material reality, and affirmation of women's ability to 'speak female desire as multiplicity, joyousness, pleasure, *jouissance – la mère qui jouit*.'[8]

Angela Carter's 'territory' of dreams, surrealism and ambiguity makes a conscious use of fantasy to articulate a female gaze, which, with its 'bold and disciplined imagination and its power to perceive symbols'[9] disturbs the everyday assumptions of patriarchy.

In this analysis of her retelling of the fairy story of Little Red Riding Hood, I shall aim to show how the transformation of Perrault's faltering, passive figure into the 'strong-minded child' is crucial to the reclamation of the story. Perrault's version was itself a falsification of the dynamics of the original folk tale, which offers an image of a girl who has to use wit and cunning to escape her fate, whereas Perrault's girl has to wait passively to be rescued. This enforces the patriarchal view that girls should accept their narrow sphere of action. The central character in the film version is another matter, and the reasons for the evident change of emphasis here lead us back to the feminist dilemma referred to above.

The Wise Maiden

Close examination of Carter's short story reminds us that her original gaze at Red Riding Hood was not an 'obvious' feminist reclamation of a fairy story. Carter's heroine is undoubtedly the Wise Maiden cited by Propp in *Morphology of the Folktale*, who is able to outwit the villain by appearing to go along with his pretence until the truth is revealed, at which point she takes control of the action, insisting on her right to do as she thinks fit. Perrault's heroine, by contrast, gives no such indication of will or self-generated desire.

This change from passive victim to active protagonist is clearly a crucial textual strategy, and a feminist retelling might well be expected to follow Roald Dahl's assertion-trained Red Riding Hood in his *Revolting Rhymes*, who, at the critical moment, reacts in accordance with her Women's Self-defence Manual:

> Her eyelid droops, her eyelid flickers,
> She pulls a pistol from her knickers.[10]

Female victim becomes female aggressor and beats the wolf at his own game. But this kind of mechanical retelling is just that: an obvious reversal of plot convention, dealing only with a realist analogy. A radical retelling must delve deeper than a simple manipulation of the familiar plot.

Carter's heroine is firmly within the folk tradition: she is the specially favoured youngest; she actively seeks her adventure; she has the wit, courage and cunning to save her skin. She understands the game more subtly than the wolf, who talks of death when she knows that his appetite can be assuaged in other ways. She acquiesces in the burning of her old clothes, for she knows that she won't be returning as the same person. She is apparently philosophical about her grandmother's fate – what's dead is dead and life must go on. She escapes her own fate as victim by asserting her own desires – for this little Red Riding Hood throws in her lot with the Big Bad Wolf.

The Strong-Minded Child

Nothing could be further from the picture of female resistance in Roald Dahl's gun-toting heroine, who meets male aggression head on, than this willing acceptance of the wolf's advances. It is, indeed, an enigmatic ending, and if it is seen as a moral fable in the Perrault vein, then its message can only be that willing acceptance of male aggression is the best way to guarantee survival – hardly a message to gladden the hearts of women angered by the constraints put upon their freedom by aggressive masculine sexuality.

But it is in the form of the retelling, in the complexity of the inner world of the protagonist, that the story achieves its radical potential, and transcends this superficial reading – which is disturbingly present nevertheless.

Let us examine the depiction of this 'strong-minded child':

> Her breasts have just begun to swell; her hair is like lint, so fair it hardly makes a shadow on her pale forehead; her cheeks are an emblematic scarlet and white and she has just started her woman's

bleeding, the clock inside her that will strike, henceforward, once a month.[11]

With astonishing economy the girl is placed at the crossroads of female experience, when the vulnerability of childhood has to accommodate the visible signs of the unavoidable future. We are told that 'children do not stay young for long in this savage country', as if the gentle transition from childhood to adulthood is an unaffordable luxury. To survive one needs a strategy for dealing with the dangerous, hostile world; sentiment is of no use. And yet, 'she has been too much loved ever to feel scared.'[12] More than this, she has been indulged – her mother cannot deny her and her grandmother has knitted her the red shawl. A sense of one's own power to deal with the danger is essential if one is to keep one's nerve. She sets off on her adventure with an unquenchable confidence and a pleasure in her own independence. She is already constituted as a whole person, and most important of all is the power of her virginity:

> ... the invisible pentacle ... She is an unbroken egg; she is a sealed vessel; she has inside her a magic space the entrance to which is shut tight with a plug of membrane; she is a closed system; she does not know how to shiver.[13]

It is not new, this image of the power of virginity – a state set apart from the common lot, and in Christian folklore a prerequisite for female redemption. But this virgin is resolutely pagan; she has no intention of retaining her virginity once it is no longer useful to her. It is discarded then like the clothes which she will not need again. What *is* new in the description is the physical image of internal space, which of its essence can only be experienced by women. This is a theme which Angela Carter had explored at length in her novel *The Passion of New Eve*, in which the central male character's sense of physical self is transformed when he is given a womb.

Pleasure or Appeasement?

The route to willing renunciation of this closed space is carefully laid out. It is not merely to appease the aggressor that she offers herself, but also to please herself. She had 'never seen such a fine fellow before'.[14] She takes pleasure in his company, and in his desire for her:

What would you like? she asked disingenuously.

A kiss.

Commonplaces of a rustic seduction; she lowered her eyes and blushed.[15]

Significantly, the grandmother's vision of the werewolf is very different from the girl's perception of him as a handsome hunter. The first thing the grandmother sees is the redness of the eyes of a beast of prey – 'devastating eyes red as a wound', then 'his feral muzzle' as 'sharp as a knife'.[16] Where is the charming smile? His hunter's disguise is quickly removed, showing that his hair is thick with lice – he is less fastidious than the peasants of the village. It is the grandmother who first sees his naked sexuality, but a sexuality that can have no interaction with her age. He takes off his clothing only to transform himself into a carnivore, and she can do nothing to appease or placate him.

As the girl enters, she senses a difference – not one centred on her perception of the werewolf, but in her heightened awareness of the room around her: no indentation on the pillow, a closed Bible and the tick of the clock which affects her like the crack of a whip. She realises what has happened to her grandmother, and that she herself is 'in danger of death'.[17] The girl who set out with such confidence ('she is a closed system; she does not know how to shiver') now shivers as she contemplates her fate. But the image is ambiguous: she fears the blood that she must spill, but will it be her lifeblood or the sign of her discarded virginity?

The dialogue between the girl and the wolf is written with the resonances of the original fairy tale and the tension of a plot reaching its fruition. It begins with the familiar hypnotic ritual, but then stops as she challenges him to tell her the truth – the truth she already knows from the evidence of her grandmother's hair in the hearth. His answer is evasive: 'There's nobody here but we two, my darling.' She abandons this line of questioning and, as if accepting his implied claim that they are now bound together, she asks: 'Who has come to sing us carols', and, as she looks at the wolves, she refutes their image as beasts of terror: 'It is very cold, poor things, she said; no wonder they howl so.'[18]

Her interpretation of their demented howling as distress turns the tide: her death is now no longer inevitable, which suggests that her sympathetic innocence can indeed transform their natures. She trusts her own judgment and ceases to be afraid. Now she voluntarily sheds her clothes, including her shawl, 'the colour of sacrifices, the colour of her menses'.[19] As the werewolf gives the standard reply, 'All the better to eat you with', she bursts out laughing. She knows far better than he that she is 'nobody's meat'.[20] She has discarded the role of sacrificial victim along with her shawl, and is clear in her acceptance of her own sexuality. We may note that this is not an aggressive 'masculinised' sexuality: she is neither Justine, martyred by passive acceptance of her fate, nor Juliet, equating sexuality with violence.[21] Instead, we are left with an image of her successful negotiation:

> See! sweet and sound she sleeps in granny's bed, between the paws of the tender wolf.[22]

Desire in Danger

It is this pivotal image of the girl confident of her own desire for sexual experience that the film cannot handle. In the screen version the moment of strength and humour outlined above becomes a desperate and unconvincing attack with a gun found behind a curtain. The heroine does not even succeed in her own defence, since she manages only to wound the wolf. This is enough, however, to facilitate the plot mechanism whereby she weeps to see his wounds and strokes him in a well-worn image of Victorian sentimentality involving animals and children. The disturbing image of the girl asleep in the arms of the wolf is gone: in the film the girl metamorphoses into a wolf and they escape together into the forest. This image is not so much disturbing as mystifying. Has she become a she-wolf from choice or necessity? Is wolfishness no more than a symbol of simple animal physicality? In many folk tales metamorphosis of this kind is a common strategy for survival, but that is hardly the same thing as a free expression of female desire.

It is this coy reluctance of the film to allow an image of successful sexual initiation which is so much at variance with the impact of the story. Little Red Riding Hood is no longer the strong-minded child at the crossroads of experience. Our first view of her, indeed, is an image of adolescence firmly fixed as the object of the male gaze, the successor to Pretty Baby and Lolita.

Here is how the pre-publicity synopsis describes the opening sequence:

> Rosaleen's dream is fuelled by her fertile adolescent mind. As she sleeps, she experiences a succession of lurid, sensual, violent and extraordinary events . . . revealing to her the dual persona of the werewolf.[23]

Just how clearly the image is presented to a voyeuristic gaze is shown in this paragraph from a review of the film:

> She lies, in a sweaty, half-swooning sleep. On the young girl's pillow lies a discarded magazine (*My Weekly*, the cover story, 'The Shattered Dream'). Her cheeks are daubed with rouge, her mouth smeared with lipstick.[24]

It is possible to find the image of the dream in Carter's story: the half-closed door of the subconscious through which our desires seep. The story, with its subversion of the familiar and its structure of story-telling within a story, suggests an ambiguity and plurality of interpretations which reminds us of our own capacity to dream. We can all create a world which closely resembles the one we assume to be real, but which contains the improbable, the ludicrous and the overtly frightening images which our minds have repressed from our conscious experience. Not only does the material world shift its laws; we experience our own capacity for abnormal behaviour.

Rosemary Jackson suggests that this 'avowal of uncertainty as to the nature of the real' is central to understanding the profound nature of fantasy as a *genre*.[25] In the screen version, however, the use of the dreamer as an introductory image offers the viewer an object to gaze at, rather than to identify with. We remain fixed spectators, viewing the violence of her adolescent fantasies (which incidentally include a new element – the dislike of an elder sister is the 'initial disruption which states the film's problematic')[26] resolved at the end by the interruption of her dream by a 'real' pack of wolves. She is not free to dream, still less to act out her desires.

Perhaps it is inevitable that the use of what the director of the film calls the 'portmanteau device' of the dream would encourage critics to offer psychological commentary redolent of the kind of prescriptive notions of how individuals are constituted which so offends many feminists. We are back in the traditional view of the febrile fantasy of the female imagination – an imagination which in this instance has fixed on the 'dual persona' of the werewolf.

Nipples Like Poison Fruit

The object of the girl's gaze is a highly equivocal image. It is not enough to explain the scenario as a straightforward expression of sexual attraction made manifest, for the depiction of the nature of the werewolf is too horrifically detailed for us to assume that he was really quite a nice chap when you got to know him.

In the story the uneasy ending is additionally the breaking of a taboo on bestiality as the girl is found with the wolf. The film compromises, as we have seen, by restricting the expression of sexuality and by the girl's metamorphosis into a she-wolf. But even in the text of the story the image of the starved, lice-ridden, red-eyed predator with nipples like poison fruit and a tendency to slaver is incontrovertibly sinister and repugnant, albeit a little pathetic. All that remains is appetite and, disturbingly, aggression. In a culture where women are often confronted by male violence, the suggestion that our desires are self-destructive is hard to accept – the recalcitrant female psyche with a vengeance.

But if, as Jackson suggests, many fantasies of dualism are dramatisations of the struggle between the libido and the ego, and if, therefore, we analyse the story as an attempt to recover repressed desire, then the outcome of the relationship between the wolf (repressed desire) and the girl (ego) is critical. In the Perrault version the wolf is killed and the girl is allowed to continue as before. The message here is that repressed desire must never be allowed to gain the upper hand – not, at any rate, in women. In Carter's 'The Company of Wolves' the girl asleep safely in the arms of the wolf, who is now 'tender', is indeed an image of healing, in which the ego is able to face the strength of desire without losing the ability to control its less pleasurable aspects. As the girl negotiates an understanding with the wolf, the howling of the wolves and the raging of the blizzard die down: 'All silent, all still'.[27] The external world registers that boundaries which would have left the individual resistant to new experience and growth have crumbled.

According to this interpretation, it obviously makes no sense for the girl to transform herself into a wolf, for in that case the ego has disappeared and there is merely a duplication of the symbol for repressed desire. Moreover, the absence of any clear resolution renders the film's dénouement unsatisfying, which, far from being an open-ended refusal of closure, is merely confusing.

Metamorphosis versus Animatronics

In order to appeal to investors, any film proposal within mainstream cinema must obviously be able to demonstrate that it is assured of the requisite audience. An important element in this is often an ability to show that it belongs to a form of previously proven popularity. We have already seen how the advertising for *The Company of Wolves* alluded to the Pretty Baby/Lolita style of movie; and the attractions of the werewolf genre are well established.

In his review article on *The Company of Wolves*, Michael Open argues that the transformation motif integral to the werewolf is a potential inscribed in the very nature of film:

> The idea of physical transformation – or transformation in appearance – is absolutely rooted in the cinema . . . for the very process of cinematography whereby still images are brought to life by small changes in them through our persistence of vision shows the cinema to be the art of transformation. The werewolf movie is therefore a particularly apt subject.[28]

The film's producer, Stephen Woolley, admits that it set out to achieve notoriety with its 'literal' transformations of man into wolf, by means of 'animatronics'. Its makers went to great lengths in exploring the technical problems of musculature and skeletal structure: 'To plot the effects of the huntsman's transformation into a werewolf, we tried to base it on Leonardo's drawings, especially the chest and neck.'[29]

It emerges that it was the special effects that necessitated the extended budget and which were also the deciding factor in securing financial backers. Stephen Woolley may claim that they did not wish to 'throw a bucket of blood' at the audience, but the startling transformations certainly won the film a sizeable audience. Neil Jordan, the film's director, confessed that these special effects and the consequent technical requirements exerted tremendous pressure on the way the film was directed. But what did these transformations offer as an exploration of the concept of a dual persona?

Richard Coombs, reviewing the film in *International Film Review*, remarks that the 'graphic transformations . . . can be also a self-defeating literalness.'[30] The mechanical details of the transformation attempt to hold the imaginative concept within the bounds of a deadening kind of realism. Like the partial substitution of the dreaming girl for the folk heroine, the film exchanges an overelaborate cinematographic process for a finely drawn imaginative concept. Given that the film must find a way of representing thought processes through externally defined images, these animatronics convey little of the story's troubling ambiguities about the possibility of violence within the self. The blood and violence of the transformations are linked to sexuality in a way that recalls the standard horror movie, in which the girl is seen as victim – no room for the confident folk heroine successfully expressing her desire.

The Struggle to Speak Female Desire

The reluctance to allow a positive image of the girl's sexuality in such a violent film is what is most fundamentally at variance with the impact and meaning of the story. It may go some way to explaining why Angela Carter remarked that the writer has only a small part to play in the making of a film and that she 'didn't do much of the dialogue'. But she rejects the view that the film had no subversive message:

> I would hotly deny that the movie was a piece of escapism. If you gave me five minutes, I would be able to construct an absolutely foolproof argument that it was about the deep roots of our sexual beings. The Thatcherite censorship certainly found it subtly offensive. They couldn't put their finger on it, but they knew that something was wrong.[31]

Could it be that they disliked the gratuitous violence of the physical man/wolf transformations? Or the association of violence with apparently self-destructive sexuality?

The girl in the story experiences the conflict between the censors in her own community and the understanding of her own desires. The language is the language of passion and of sensuous pleasure:

> The firelight shone through the edges of her skin; now she was clothed only in her untouched integument of flesh. This dazzling, naked she combed out her hair with her fingers.[32]

That she survives intact is an imaginative resolution, a leap into the possibilities of human behaviour, and a statement of belief in the 'subjugation of aggressive, repressive and exploitative instincts to the sensuous assuasive energy of the life instincts'.[33] The disturbing truth lies in the inescapable realisation that the constructed reality of the story's context is very far removed from reality in the known world.

Angela Carter offers us through her writing an immensely rich store of pleasure. Through her sure control she is able to assert, and then to disturb, interrogate and challenge our female gaze. How demanding it would be to offer a feminist film version of her work, and how rewarding. Is it too much to hope for?

6
Lace: Pornography for Women?

Avis Lewallen

Current blockbuster novels such as *Lace, A Woman of Substance, Hollywood Wives, Mistral's Daughter,* and a host of others which flood on to the market daily, it seems, comprise a genre variously described as 'shopping and fucking', or more euphemistically 'hoarding and humping'. Jane McLoughlin in a *Guardian* article describes them as '... second generation Mills & Boon, a kind of consumer's guide to the best beds in town.'[1] Well, they are 'second generation' romance novels in terms of moving the heroine from adolescent sexual expectation into adult sexual exploration, but they are not really a development of Mills and Boon in terms of style, structure or content. What they do have in common with the 'bodice ripper' sub-genre of romantic fiction, however, is an increase in sexual explicitness.[2]

I would like to look at the way female sexuality is being expressed in blockbusters in the context of current ideas about the representation of women. Is it possible to see within these often politically conservative, capitalist tracts, full of the ideologies of individualism, self-reliance and material wealth, a more liberated expression of female sexuality? If these texts can be classified as 'soft porn', what position is being offered to the female reader? Do they merely contribute to the further objectification of women within our misogynist society, inculcating male power, or do they offer a form of representation that facilitates the female gaze?

Romance, Sex and Liberation

Romance fiction has been described as a form of sexual foreplay that can function simultaneously as an expression and a containment of female desire, the fulfilment of which we imagine takes place in the nuptials promised at the close of the story. Ann Barr Snitow, developing an argument put forward by Peter Parisi, contends that these romances are essentially pornographic.[3] They return the reader to a position of 'pre-marital hopefulness', where the morality of a strictly secular world is upheld, but where sexual desire is acknowledged and articulated so that every look and touch becomes an expression of thinly disguised sexual sublimation. The heroine wants sex, but only within the marriage bed, and thus these romances illustrate women's lack of social and psychological freedom to express their sexuality. Sexuality must be anchored to an emotional attachment that will ensure, through marriage, material security. Given the double standard applied to male and female sexuality, and the material exigencies connected to the possibility of motherhood, it could be said, however, that this fiction reflects what is in fact a social reality for women as much as it promotes it.

In the early days of the Women's Liberation Movement there was the so-called 'sexual revolution', whereby women claimed the right to the same sexual freedoms as men. A number of novels in the late sixties and early seventies, such as Erica Jong's *Fear of Flying* (1974), were associated with this claim because of their explicit treatment of women's sexuality. In *The Sadeian Woman* Angela Carter claims that the essence of de Sade's philosophy, which she, with qualifications, endorses, is that women can 'fuck their way into history'.[4] But other feminists were arguing that there were dangers for women in a 'sexual revolution' within the structure of patriarchy, which could well make them vulnerable to even greater exploitation than the old sexual double standard; that women were simply more available to be fucked by men, rather than assuming an active sexuality based on their own desires.[5]

In more recent years women writers concerned with feminist issues have tended to move away from what could loosely be described as 'social realism' (what was written in the late sixties and early seventies) to more experimental work, such as that of Kathy Acker.[6] Or they have undertaken more general analyses of sexuality and gender, particularly in the genre of science fiction, as in the work of writers like Marge Piercy or Joanna Russ.[7] As heterosexual sex became problematic, a subject of debate, and even division, within the women's movement, so its representation in literature seemed equally problematic. Explicit representation of sex tended to be reserved for lesbian sex, which had every reason to welcome a space for public expression. The (hetero)sexual explicitness of 'bodice rippers' and blockbusters, as an effect of feminism, seems more in the nature of a hangover from the days of sexual liberation: feminist writers have become much more circumspect about the liberating possibilities of overt sexual expression in fictional form.

Commodity Sex

Fiction by, about and for women that shows women capable of achieving social, economic and sexual satisfaction is now extremely popular. From a feminist perspective these are contradictory texts: on the one hand, the capitalist ideology that pervades them largely ignores, on a manifest level at least, issues of class, race and gender; but on the other, they problematise and prioritise active sexuality for women in ways that might be regarded as a challenge to the exclusively male gaze of patriarchal structures.

The genre differs radically from 'bodice rippers', which are very definitely located within the world of romance. If a 'bodice ripper' heroine is raped, or seduced, this will be converted by the narrative into marital love-making and the rapist/seducer into a husband. In this sense they may be seen as masochistic fantasies whereby the heroine's sexuality is always represented as a passive response to active male desire. In blockbusters, by comparison, the heroines not only wilfully indulge in pre- and extra-marital sex, they sometimes eschew marriage altogether in favour of a career, and certainly do not view it as an end to their ambitions. They do seek the transcendental orgasm that will indicate they have found 'true love', but marriage is not a prerequisite for this. Heterosexual fulfilment is defined as the ultimate goal; neither lesbianism nor celibacy are considered viable alternatives. But within this context, sexual happiness is not as automatic as simply going to bed with a man: it must be achieved, much in the way that material success is, through hard work.

Sexually active, even aggressive, heroines have been around for some time in popular fiction for women. The current blockbuster genre can be seen as having developed from the kind of fiction written by Jacqueline Susann, whose *Valley of the Dolls* caused a sensation when it was published in 1966 as a sort of female version of a Harold Robbins, and which (together with her other novels) continues to sell well at mass market outlets. One important difference in current blockbuster fiction is its far greater degree of sexual explicitness.

Consumer Soap?

Generally speaking, blockbusters are structured like soap operas, and have proved easily adaptable into television 'mini-series'. They are always written in the third person, with an emphasis on dialogue and action rather than on character introspection. There is, indeed, often no central character or plot; instead, we move between the lives of several major characters, from interior to interior, as in soaps, with multiple plots running continuously. We are not, in this case, invited to identify with one character, although, whether there is a single protagonist or several, the point of identification is always with a woman character. In addition, these novels are often structured around a group of women characters who provide a support network for each other, like the friends in *Lace* or the generations of women in *Mistral's Daughter*. Unlike soaps, novels have to end, but even this is circumvented in *Lace*, which leaves one plot line unresolved, to be taken up in the sequel, *Lace II*.

In so far as these blockbusters are celebrations of capitalist values, with the heroines advancing from humble beginnings to positions of great wealth and power, Jane McLoughlin is right to call them 'consumer guides'. Expensive commodities and designer names drip through the pages as indicators of the heroines' increasing wealth and success. (For an entertaining analysis of this consumer aspect see Angela Carter's short article on the work of Judith Krantz.)[8] They could also function as social guides, so full are they of useful tips on how to conduct yourself in difficult situations or upmarket company.

Sexbusters

Lace, by Shirley Conran, is a useful example of the genre's treatment of sexuality, since a substantial part of its narrative subject matter is directly concerned with sexuality and related topics: from loss of virginity, sexual desire, sexual satisfaction and frigidity, to prostitution, rape, adultery, lesbianism and transvestism. It also deals with pornography, alcoholism, plastic surgery, childbirth, miscarriage and abortion, and makes more than passing reference to 'women's lib'. In fact, *Lace* is almost a mini-encyclopaedia of female sexuality. The novel opens with a detailed description of an abortion and closes neatly with a description of a birth. The ideological implications of this structure are readily apparent.

Adolescent and adult sex are explicitly detailed in *Lace*, with incest constituting an underlying plot enigma, although significantly this is the only sexual relationship not graphically described. Pregnancy and motherhood are important mostly when they cause problems, such as miscarriage or post-natal depression, or when, of course, they are needed to create plot tensions of various sorts. Otherwise, much as in soap opera, children hardly feature until they are old enough to have sexual relationships of their own. (This is not the main reason for their absence in soaps, of course, where it is probably due more to the problems of child actors.) Motherhood is always portrayed as secondary to a career, which female characters rightly expect, and usually attain. The wealth that derives from their success neatly disposes of the problem of childcare, because they can afford to pay someone else to do it.

Sexual satisfaction is represented as equivalent to a career: a commodity which women have the right to, but which has to be worked for. Orgasm is not shown as a biological function that will merely manifest itself at the right moment but something that is learned and acquired – a kind of social skill – much in the same way as one can learn the proper use of words like *chauffeur* or *chic*, an essential part of the vocabulary of anyone intending to be successful.

Sexual Initiation

The main body of the narrative of *Lace* is told retrospectively, as we trace the lives of four women and one of their daughters, Lili. Three of them, Pagan and Kate, who are English, and Maxine, who is French, meet at a Swiss finishing school just after the Second World War. The fourth, an American called Judy, is studying in the same town at a language school, but, unlike the others, who are middle class, has to support herself by working simultaneously as a waitress. It is only later that the other three come to realise the value of the Protestant work ethic expressed through Judy's determination to succeed.

Aged between 15 and 17, they are sexually naïve, not only in terms of men, but also of themselves: 'None of them had explored, felt or seen the area between their legs. None of them had heard of masturbation or knew that they had already experienced it . . .'[9] Unaware of their own bodies, their willingness to lose their virginity is not motivated by physical desire so much as by the need to get over the social 'hurdle' required to become a 'real woman'. From their adolescent point of view, this necessitates 'falling in love' – something they discover is as overrated as sex:

> Kate felt bewildered, indignant, disbelieving. She couldn't breathe because of his weight on top of her. With a hoarse grunt François stiffened and shivered, his grip hardening painfully on her breasts. Then he collapsed on top of her and Kate felt a stickiness trickling over her collarbone and down her neck. She knew what it was and she didn't dare move in case some of the stuff got in the wrong

place. She was terrified . . . it hadn't been romantic and wonderful, it had been messy and uncomfortable . . .'[10]

The morality of romantic fiction is subjected to questioning: 'She had gone All the Way because she was in love with him. Or was it the reverse? She wished she knew.'[11]

Pagan and Judy suffer rape as their initial sexual experience. Pagan, having heroically placed herself in a vulnerable situation to help her friend, is drugged and raped by the school's driver: this is 'revolting, but not painful,'[12] – an unusually matter-of-fact approach for a woman writer of popular fiction. The rape of Judy is less straight-forward, in the sense that the implication in the text is that she is partly responsible for it ('contributory negligence' as the courts might say). This issue is discussed early in the narrative by the authorial voice:

It was strange that not one of the girls queried the sexual double standard. They accepted that a boy could be driven uncontrollably mad by passion, but it never crossed their minds that it was understandable if a girl felt the same way. They accepted that setting the sexual limit was the responsibility of the girl, not the boy; it was *her* job to control *his* lust . . .[13] (original emphases)

Yet a few pages later, the same voice says:

It never occurred to any of them that the power they had raised in the man was not only passion but, if thwarted, the power to rape or kill. The reactions of a frustrated man had never been explained to any of them.[14]

The juxtaposition of these two passages illustrates the very sexual double standard that the first passage criticises. If women really could set sexual limits and control male 'lust', then presumably neither rape nor death could result from 'thwarted' male passion.

The rape of Judy, not described till the end of the book, is a case of thwarted male passion. Abdullah rapes Judy because Pagan has refused to have sex with him, so she is in effect the victim of the control exercised by Pagan. Neither suffer any long-lasting mental or emotional damage; the rapes are more important as plot elements (a blackmailing scheme in Pagan's case, the enigma of parenthood in Judy's) than in terms of character. While this neglects the real issues of male sexual violence against women, it is worth noting that the lack of sensationalism attached to it downplays the notions of violation and virginal purity. The characters are not destined to become lifelong victims in any physical, psychological or emotional sense: they have the resources to recover. And virginity is less a state possessed of magical properties, the violation of which has to be traumatic, than a barrier to womanhood. Female purity is not the issue.

'The Marital Chippolata'

Despite the deficiencies of these sexual initiations, we are not presented with an eruption of onanism or lesbianism in the school. The girls continue in their belief that the key to sexual pleasure is penile penetration. This remains true even though as adults they experience between them a range of sexual identities, with sexual dis/satisfaction high on the agenda of narrative concern.

Pagan marries a stolid banker, Robert, who dutifully 'stabs' at her with the 'marital chippolata', and, confused by his accusations of frigidity, she seeks confirmation of her libido with her tennis coach. By this time she has discovered her clitoris, and 'can masturbate to a climax in five minutes,' which, rather prosaically, she checks with an egg timer.[15] Her marital failure, however, results in alcoholism and divorce, from which she eventually recovers with Judy's help, to find happiness with a scientist whose fund-raiser she becomes, but whose sexuality is later marred by illness.

Kate, apparently locked in a pattern of falling for the wrong men, is convinced she is frigid until she meets Tom, a sympathetic and understanding lover who knows she fakes orgasm. As always, ultimate sexual satisfaction is vaginal:

> And suddenly, through the mist of sleepiness, Kate realised that it was going to happen. It felt exactly as she had read it felt like. Soft, intense waves rather than her excitingly violent, direct clitoral orgasm. It was unmistakably different and it was undoubtedly happening. Kate felt fecund, indescribably female, an earth mother. She felt happy, she felt at last a complete woman.[16]

Despite such emphasis on orgasm exercising maternal feelings, much attention is also paid to female pleasure in terms of clitoral satisfaction:

> She woke to feel his lips on her small secret slit, his tongue gently caressing the pale pink seed pearl, his face against the delicate folds that surrounded it. Pink upon pink, soft, sucking flesh; swirling, exquisite oblivion, falling into a caressing sea.[17]

(Marine metaphors tend to dominate in these descriptive passages.)

Lest there be an impression that women are always acted upon rather than giving pleasure, we do have descriptions of female sexual activity, such as Kate performing fellatio on Tom:

> He felt her warmth, the soft stroking touch of her hand on his manhood, then her lips were sucking, soft as a sea anemone, then more insistently. He felt her tongue searching, reaching, sliding, slipping, sucking until Tom could think of nothing except the scratching fingernails on his inner thighs, that sure insistent mouth, the mounting quickening pressure of her lips upon him until, with a groan, his pent-up force was spent. Kate, who never knew whether to swallow, spit or dribble, tasted the oddly pungent, acrid almond odour . . .[18]

The switch to the masculine point of view, at odds with the rest of the text, might suggest that performing fellatio is not in itself pleasurable, so that what is articulated from the women's point of view is the perceived dilemma in its satisfactory execution, rather than the experience as sexual pleasure.

If the text of *Lace* often reads like a sex manual for women, it also contains a critique of male sexuality, which is seen to range from Robert's arrogant incompetence to Abdullah's accomplishments in oral sex (he is described as the 'Nijinksy of cunnilingus'!). Despite the rather stereotypical racist echoes here of ideology's claims for the sexual prowess of black men, it is made clear that Abdullah's 'prowess' is a skill which had to be learned, of which women are the main beneficiaries. These judgments on male sexual competence, from a female perspective, are very different from those of romance fiction, whose heroes are always assumed, and sometimes shown, to be naturally expert, 'virile' lovers.

Thrills and Spills

Sado-masochism has proved a problematic subject for feminism: from the critique of pornography to the debates at the London Lesbian and Gay Centre in 1985, the linking of sex with any suggestion of violence, even in play, is obviously dangerous ground for women. The relationship depicted in *Lace* between Maxine and Charles is one which, while possibly giving rise to masturbatory pleasure for women readers, relates to this problematic. On return from their honeymoon, they are inspecting the wine cellars of his château, when, with the workmen still busy in the vicinity, Charles seduces Maxine. Despite her reluctance, he overpowers her physically until she submits with abandon. The sexual excitement derives partly from the social unacceptability of the situation: owner and wife on a tour of inspection find it impossible to maintain physical control. Charles orders Maxine not to wear 'panties':

> 'I want to know that if I care to feel you at any time, you will be ready for me . . . in just a few matters, I expect to be obeyed by you without question.'[19]

Before long Charles would only have to

> . . . look hard at her, across a room of impeccably dressed, important people, and he would have the immediate satisfaction of seeing Maxine give a little jump and blush.[20]

The more inappropriate the setting, the greater the excitement, and:

> Maxine had never dreamed that married life would be so laced with hazard and surprise or that her lingerie bill would be so large. She loved every dangerous moment of it . . .[21]

The foregoing scenario can be read in two ways. On the one hand, there is a subversive appeal in the notion that sexual passion overcomes social convention. By refusing to 'stay in its place', sex constitutes a disruption of the social order, with its constructed rules and rankings, by that which is 'natural', personal, individual – which is why, perhaps, it is such a standard pornographic/erotic scenario. On the other hand, that Maxine is always available, never initiating sex and entirely passive is objectionable because the notion of ever-present availability comes close to a form of consensual rape. Despite her business acumen, economic superiority and independence, the underlying message is that she still wants to be sexually dominated. As Ann Barr Snitow comments:

> In pornography, the joys of passivity, of helpless abandon, of response without responsibility are all endlessly repeated, savored, minutely described. Again this is a fantasy often dismissed with the pejorative 'masochistic' as if passivity were in no way a pleasant or a natural condition.[22]

The problem for women, of course, is that to be passive is their designated role rather than their choice, which makes it difficult ever to see passivity for women as an uncomplicated pleasure.

In contrast, a second scenario deals with an incident of sado-masochism with the female character taking the active role. Judy has a relationship with Griffin, a powerful, wealthy, married executive. When Griffin inadvertently makes it clear that Judy is only the most recent in a long line of extra-marital affairs, she 'punishes' him by acting out a sado-masochistic game. She ties him up, gags him, cuts off his (expensive) suit with a pair of shears, covers him in olive oil, whisky and meringue, treats him as a '. . . sexual object to bring herself to orgasm' and finally finger fucks him anally to bring him to a climax. She then leaves the apartment with him still tied to the bedposts:

> Griffin was furious . . . But he was also impressed . . . There had been real fury behind what Judy did . . . she had kept him at the point of orgasm for an hour and a half, teasing him almost beyond endurance until his nerves were raw. He had been humbled, if not humiliated . . .[23]

As the text suggests, this is both a game and 'real'. Humiliated by his attitude towards her, Judy does not submit, complain or walk out: she asserts physical control over him and thereby alters the balance of power between them:

> From that moment, the pattern of their relationship shifted, and Griffin treated Judy with a great deal more care and respect, not because he was afraid of her, but because she had done exactly what she said she would do – she had punished him![24]

The cutting up of Griffin's clothes brings to mind both the threat of castration and the links between materialism, power and sexuality. The suit becomes a kind of metonymic signifier for this, which has to be destroyed before equality can be achieved between them.

In contrast to the Maxine/Charles relationship, here we are given the female character taking the dominant role. In her psychoanalytic critique of *The Story of O* Jessica Benjamin defines the dynamic of sado-masochism as the conflict in the individual between 'self-assertion' and 'transcendence' which is developed through the parent/child relationship: 'True differentiation means maintaining the essential tension of the contradictory impulses to assert the self and respect the other.'[25] Thus the desire to dominate/be dominated within sado-masochism is an attempt to re-adjust on a fantasy level unconscious psychic imbalances which are not inherently polarised on gender distinctions. The scenario between Judy and Griffin is a literal rather than an unconscious attempt to achieve mutual recognition. But for the reader it presents a (playfully?) sadistic act, from the female point of view, which has little to do with the desires of the male.

Critique of the Sexual Object

The darker side of the 'permissive society' is depicted in the character of Lili, the daughter of Judy and Abdullah, who is exploited by the male-controlled sex industry, first as a pornographic model and later as a sexualised film star. Forced into an abortion at thirteen, used and abused by men who claim to love her, she is rather like a dark version of Monroe. It may seem ironic to find such a critique of pornography in a work that might itself be deemed pornographic.

But Lili struggles against her role as victim, and while searching for her mother, ironically manages to quarrel with all four of the women who had maintained her until she disappeared from their view during the invasion of Hungary. Meanwhile, she unwittingly searches for her father in a series of relationships with older men, and even more unknowingly finds him and becomes his mistress. The underlying enigmas of the narrative concern Lili: the enigma concerning her mother is resolved when Judy declares herself, although all four women had shared responsibility for her as a child, which makes for an interesting comment upon motherhood as natural or social. The enigma concerning her father is resolved for the reader, but not for Lili, and thus constitutes the narrative's underlying problematic.

As with the treatment of rape, however, these conventionally traumatic plot elements are not sensationalised as irrevocably destructive or tragic: Lili too has the personal resources to surmount her adverse circumstances. In this respect *Lace* dispenses with traditional assumptions about women's sexuality which represent it as vulnerable to permanent damage.

Whatever Turns Us On?

If romance fiction, through its denial of direct sexual expression, is a form of sexual sublimation, what position is offered the reader of blockbusters, where female sexuality is so prominently and explicitly placed? As Rosalind Coward argues, images are defined by their context: images of women, naked or otherwise, are not inherently pornographic, but only become so when contextualised by a 'regime of representations' – i.e. a particular set of codes with conventionally accepted meanings – defining them as such for the viewer.[26] The way images in pornographic magazines are pinned down by captions and text presenting them explicitly for male titillation suggests that visual images alone – even of naked women in obviously provocative poses - cannot be relied upon to be unambiguous.

Whether or not *Lace* was actually written for a female readership, it has a clear appeal to women. It is women who are its central characters, while men feature mainly for their sexual (and sometimes financial) gratification. Its narrative concerns combine the professional and the personal lives of its protagonists in ways quite untypical of masculine genres of fiction, and, albeit from within a conservative discourse, challenge the conventional socio-economic position of women. And all this from a female perspective.

This is not to say that the women in the text are not objectified, but this objectification is for the female reader. It offers both glamorised images of powerful, sexy women, together with, at times, the more mundane reality assumed to lie behind the glamour. These women are not mere passive victims: even when abused and exploited, they fight back and their collective sisterhood provides them with an emotional and economic support network, which would seem to be an appropriation from feminism. The question is whether the context of this objectification alters the relationship female readers can have with it, or whether it merely colludes with conventional, sexist ways of seeing women.

It is open to question whether or not the kind of sexual scenarios to be found in *Lace* do appeal to women's masturbatory fantasies. Rosalind Coward suggests not: 'Most women still prefer the sublimated masochism of romance to explicit pornographic material and feel uneasy rather than envious about men's use of pornography.'[27] This stems, as she sees it, from pornography's function as a sexual aid for men, which is linked to a different understanding between men and women about masturbation. She argues, rightly, that masturbation is not the problem, but that in so far as men use pornography as a kind of 'health aid', the fear is that they might view women's bodies, both in pornography and in the real world, as always 'available to meet men's sexual needs'.[28] But while women may be uneasy about the kind of pornographic material displayed in local newsagents shops and consumed by men, they do not seem to be uneasy (if sales figures are any indication) about consuming the kind of explicit sex to be found in blockbuster novels like *Lace*, aimed presumably at women, which I would argue is quite removed from the 'masochism of romance'.

Pornography for Women?

In her book, *Pornography: Men Possessing Women*, Andrea Dworkin attempts to illustrate the direct relationship between pornography and male violence towards women. She contends that within our contemporary misogynist society men use pornography as a means to inculcate and celebrate male power. Through all pornographic forms, she argues, women are victimised by male violence, sexually object-ified, humiliated and degraded.[29] The message of pornography is therefore that women exist to be used and abused, that they are contradictorily both sexually animalistic and inherently masochistic with a passive desire to be dominated. As long as pornography exists, she concludes, women cannot hope to gain sexual self-determination.[30]

It is certainly true that the commercial sex industry is currently run by and for men: the women who work in it have no control over production. There is also no doubt that much of the sexually explicit material produced by it is degrading to women. But so, to differing degrees, are many other forms of representation (advertisements being the prime example) which not only exploit women as sex objects, but may more insidiously exploit them as inferior beings in all social spheres. Dworkin's pornography-equals-rape argument ignores all the other discourses through which power is mediated – of which pornography is just one, if important, constituent.

Although Dworkin argues that the original definition of 'porno-graphy' – the depiction of whores – still underlies its now current sense of the explicit depiction of sex, she also claims that 'erotica' is merely a high-class, euphemistic way of saying the same thing. This would appear to leave us with no possibility of representing sex, or women's bodies, that is not degrading to women. On the other hand, to distinguish erotica from pornography on the grounds that 'erotic' represents sexual *love* makes the difference that between making love and fucking and returns us to the discourse of romance. Ann Barr Snitow offers an alternative definition of pornography which might point a way out of this impasse:

> Though pornography's critics are right – pornography is exploi-tation – it is exploitation of *everything*. Promiscuity by definition is a breakdown of barriers. Pornography is not only a reflector of

social power imbalances and sexual pathologies; it is also all those imbalances run riot, run to excess, sometimes explored *ad absurdum*, exploded. Misogyny is one content of pornography; another content is the universal infant desire for complete, immediate gratification, to rule the world out of the very core of passive helplessness.[31] (original emphases)

In other words, Snitow argues, pornography is capable of expressing sexuality beyond the typical active/passive or male subject/female object dichotomies. You can have different forms of pornography: an explicit depiction of sex that can be instructive and/or pleasurable; or one that exploits, privileging, and thereby inculcating, heterosexual power relations, whether in heterosexual or homosexual/lesbian contexts.

Snitow's argument runs into problems when we consider the ideological implications of all sexual activity: can't it ever be ideologically free? And by what criteria do we judge its ideological status? In addition, we need to ask how the context of representation affects how it is read. The same representation of lesbian sex, for example, might be acceptable to women in a lesbian context, and unacceptably pornographic in a context for male consumption.

Susanne Kappeler suggests that we should therefore understand pornography not as a specific form of sexuality, but as a form of representation:

The traditional debate has focused on 'porn' at the expense of 'graphy', an emphasis duly reflected in the customary abbreviation to 'porn'. 'Porn', in this slippage, has gradually come to mean 'obscene sex' or 'violent sex' – forms of sexuality we disapprove of. We do not like them (or would not like them) in real life, therefore we do not want them represented . . . Sex or sexual practices do not just exist out there, waiting to be represented; rather there is a dialectical relationship between representational practices which construct sexuality, and actual sexual practices, each informing the other.[32]

I agree with Kappeler's analysis in terms of the relationship between representation and reality, but I don't think it is possible to claim that women do not get pleasure from pornographic images, 'obscene sex' or even 'violent sex' – whether or not they are represented as the object of desire, and despite the fact that this pleasure might be troubling to women.

Recent theories about the representation of women have drawn heavily on Lacan's psychoanalytic theory, which postulates that, given the phallocentricity of psychic/linguistic structures, women can only occupy the object/other position in social discourse. Therefore, it has been argued by feminists such as Laura Mulvey, writing about film, that formal conventions themselves, along with the associated pleasures, must be challenged by alternative representational structures.[33] This is because, within conventional forms, it is impossible for the female spectator not to position herself as the object, rather than the subject, of desire. In other words, it is impossible, especially with regard to sexuality, to argue for a female gaze. E. Ann Kaplan summarises this view:

> ... in locating herself in fantasy in the erotic, the woman places herself as either passive recipient of male desire, or, at one remove, positions herself as watching a woman who is a passive recipient of male desires and sexual actions.[34]

In *Lace* we are presented with a number of scenarios where the female characters are 'passive recipients of male desire'. But this is not *always* the case. Just as often, the female characters *actively* desire sex, usually with men, but sometimes by themselves. They recognise their own sexuality as distinct from men's. Moreover, this occurs within a narrative in which women (almost) always occupy the dominant subject position. While the subject/object division is a pervasive component within the dualism of Western thought, it is certainly not an inherent psychic structure, as Susanne Kappeler suggests when arguing for notions of 'collectivity' and 'intersubjectivity'.[35] While I agree with the need to challenge objectification (certainly with the need to challenge the wholesale objectification heaped on women by men), I do think that representation has to involve objectification to some extent. As Mariana Valverde puts it: 'An eroticism that is both sexy and egalitarian is one in which both partners are simultaneously subject and object, for one another as well as for themselves.'[36]

Part of feminism's problem in dealing with issues of pornography and erotica, is that on the one hand we see ourselves bound by patriarchal discourse, and on the other we are actively desiring within them. This can be a very contradictory experience. Heterosexual feminists have been very much on the defensive in recent years, but, as Ehrenreich, Hess and Jacobs point out, not to confront the issue is tantamount to capitulation to dominant ideologies:

Contemporary feminists who campaign against pornography do not go so far as to say that sex itself is an ordeal or insult to women, but what else can be meant by their frequent insistence that every *representation* of heterosexual sex – however 'soft-core' – is an insult to women and an assault on our rights? For if sex is the ratification of male power, then will it not always be a secret refutation of everything feminism stands for? Does feminism have any real option but to be puritanical or, what almost amounts to the same thing, utterly silent on the subject of sex?[37]

Popular Feminism?

Lace (which outrightly denounces socialist feminism at one point as a waste of time)[38] could not have been written or widely consumed as morally acceptable if the Women's Liberation Movement had not been in the vanguard of the recent challenging of traditional male views of female sexuality. The text is a testimony to the kind of contradictions involved in sexuality and representation. Through the discourse of bourgeois liberalism it offers the possibility of change for women, but only through existing structures: as a sort of mirror image of the *Cosmopolitan* type of magazine produced by characters in the novel itself. Sex is on the agenda, not only because it is an important subject, but because it sells. There is a strong didactic function that tells you how to do it, combined with passages that turn you on so that you want to do it. Sex is still firmly heterosexual (anything else is deviant) and 'real' fulfilment is still defined as penile penetration; but we do not have sublimated masochistic fantasies allied to romance and marriage. And if men and sex and love remain important to women, money – your own money – is more important. Which perhaps puts sex in its place!

Blockbuster fiction offers both the 'excitement of pre-marital romance' and the more realistic ups and downs of adult sex. I think this level of realism is one that has to be acknowledged. These novels have filled a vacuum left by feminist writers, who have moved into other genres, subjects and forms. Capitalism and its ideology have appropriated this space, articulating an active female sexuality to an individualist ethic. Some may see this as worse than a feminist hangover, but I think that feminism has managed some small, but valuable, intervention into the mass market.

7
Joan Collins and the Wilder Side of Women
Exploring Pleasure and Representation

Belinda Budge

The power, impact or 'indecency' of the role of Alexis Carrington in the soap opera *Dynasty* was being discussed at a seminar on feminism and popular culture; but while the power of the image was the stated subject, the debate of the moment was whether it should ever have been raised. Even to suggest that Joan Collins' role as Alexis Carrington was a sufficiently important issue to warrant inclusion on the day's agenda proved extremely contentious. Was it not a ridiculous waste of time? Alexis – in the opinion of the two back rows at least – was a 'floozy' and a 'bitch', too fantastically rich and powerful to be of relevance to feminism. What was the point of looking for subversive elements (if, indeed, that was the point) in a media product like *Dynasty*, which so obviously upholds and reinforces dominant patriarchal ideologies? Examination of the female gaze of Alexis could surely only reveal its construction as a 'con', articulating stereotypical male fantasies about the way women think?

The point at issue is, of course, pleasure. In the case of soap opera, the pleasures for many women spectators are legion. Addiction, anticipation, repetition and interruption are among them. And what about recognising that the fantasy engendered by *Dynasty* is not so much about fulfilling our desires as about being allowed to make fun of them? Or the pleasure of enjoying it as melodrama, or satire (or both!)? Or the pleasure of discussing the form and limits of serial soap as part of the pleasure of consumption?[1]

These were the possibilities dismissed in the seminar room, where the overall feeling was one of hostility towards not only soap opera in general but *Dynasty* in particular, and especially Alexis Carrington.

It would appear we still think that women watch *Dynasty* passively, pathetic and unwitting victims of its deceptive messages. And hence the issue of pleasure, long a problem for feminist cultural politics, remains a problem. In dismissing the role of Alexis as irrelevant to feminism, the women watching are also dismissed. For the pleasures described above are those of an *active* audience.

A Glimpse of the Wildside

Such a reaction is particularly telling in the 1980s – a period when we are bombarded with images that beg a new understanding of representation and pleasure. Selling female sexuality to women is different from selling it to men. Though the two operations have much in common, the body of a woman is coded in differing ways so as to produce particular kinds of pleasure. The pleasure 'on offer' to men differs from the pleasure on offer to women.[2]

Moreover, a flip through any contemporary women's magazine reveals images that seem to defy traditional feminist interpretations of representation and pleasure. Take the summer of 1986 as an example. Issues of *Elle* magazine were 'Blazing into Summer' with 'High Cuts' swimwear: 'Black on the Sand' and 'Zipped up for Action'. *Company* suggested that you 'Dress to Thrill' – 'dare a little more, wear a little less'. *Cosmopolitan*, meanwhile, offered advice on 'What to Wear for An Affair'. For its part, *Vogue* displayed the 'wilder shores of summertime, in and out of breathtaking shapes'.

As female buyers and spectators, we are being offered the vision of a *wilder* side of woman, and she shouldn't be ignored! She is not the 'passive' female with whom John Berger concerned himself in *Ways of Seeing*[3] – a woman on display only for the ideal spectator (who is always assumed to be male) – or the 'to-be-looked-at' woman recipient of the 'male gaze'.[4] She can be seen in the newer advertisements for Russell and Bromley shoes. Gone are the simple black and white line drawings of 1960s shoes and the 'women as legs' images of the 1970s. In the eighties we are confronted with a mysterious and desirable 'whole woman' who seems exclusive, expensive, luxurious, elegant and (naturally) leggy.

Are we merely passive spectators of these readily available, sexualised images of women designed specifically to appeal to us? That has certainly been the dominant feminist view in the past. Many feminist interpretations of such images have argued that what they offer for consumption is an ideal version of self. But is this all? The visual pleasure for women involved in looking at 'attractive' women is certainly inscribed in the image; yet is this just about women being continually seduced into a search for the ideal version of self, simply in order to appeal to 'their man'? Isn't one of the pleasures on sale here that of seeing female sexuality presented in a way that does not adhere to the terms of vulnerability, accessibility or availability of the pornographic image to men?[5]

Our definitions of how images can be read have become too narrow to account for their complexity – our theory has remained peculiarly underdeveloped relative to the practice of the media. The frequently employed concept of 'objectification', for example, has acquired a specific meaning within feminism. It describes a process of representation in which women are reduced to the status of objects, often becoming mere commodities to be visually consumed, from which women's social and psychological selves are alienated. Or it can be used in terms of Freud's concept of sexual fetishism, to describe objects or parts of the anatomy which have become symbols of, and substitutes for, the socially valued phallus.

Indeed, a Freudian reading can be made of the Russell and Bromley advertisements, which clearly depict female sexuality through the representation of a stiletto-shod foot – isolating and fragmenting the sexual by focusing on a part of the anatomy and fetishising the foot by valorising it as a phallic symbol. A psychoanalytic interpretation of this image suggests that the stiletto as phallic symbol serves to 'give' the woman her missing phallus, rendering her safe by circumventing the castration threat she poses to male sexuality.

The stiletto is only one example of a repertoire of conventionalised symbols which have become imbued with fetishistic associations. Yet while psychoanalysis does provide one way to interpret their dominant associations in our culture, is it useful to interpret all forms of sexualised imagery in terms of phallic substitution? As Myers rightly points out, symbolisation is not a closed system of limited or fixed meaning: 'Symbolism is polysemic, there always exists the possibility of powerful symbolism which works to activate forms of sexual expression which are not recognised by phallocentric interpretation.'[6]

If this is so, is it not time to start creating a new vocabulary to describe the pleasurable associations for women of looking at images of other women? The emphasis on demystification and deconstruction, whilst essential, must partially cede to reconstruction and redefinition in an attempt to illuminate the relationship between pleasure and representation. We need to start looking at the pleasures of an *active* audience and to celebrate the visual pleasure of women looking at 'attractive' women. The 'wilder side of women' engenders a fantasy that re-introduces into our vocabulary the notion of the *erotic* for women.

This is the challenge presented to us by the images of the mid 1980s and that includes the much-maligned but thoroughly enjoyed Alexis Carrington Colby Dexter.

Walking on the Wildside with Joan

Who is this woman who occupies such a place of honour in our culture? On the face of it, Alexis Dexter is merely one of a myriad of roles necessary for the never-ending world of soap opera. In terms of popular notoriety, she is much more. *Dynasty* has commanded the attention of the popular daily press, which features leaks and rumours of plots to come, as well as gossip about, and interviews with, the stars. Accompanying all this has been the Joan Collins story, with publicity and press releases, serialised memoirs and confessions, interviews and studio pictures, and coverage of her relaunch as star and sex symbol via the film *The Stud* and its sequel *The Bitch*. The latter is an epithet which has stuck (thus the *Guardian* headline of November 1985: 'The Bitch Gets Hitched Again') and lives on in the character of Alexis. The names are often merged and used interchangeably. Our contact with Joan 'Alexis' Collins is not short-lived, casual or superficial; it is renewed virtually every morning with our daily newspaper.

The boundaries of reality and fiction have become so enmeshed that it is little wonder that when we watch Alexis in *Dynasty* we feel as if we know her well. Yet what we know best about her is her enigmatic unpredictability. Life in Denver, Colorado, is nothing if not surprising, and we can never tell for sure how Alexis will react to the latest dilemma in the inherently problematic world of the Carrington Dynasty. This is the nature of soap opera, where unhappiness is the rule rather than the exception. As Ien Ang says, 'A utopian moment is totally absent in soap opera narratives; circumstances and events continually throw up barriers to prevent the capture of that little scrap of happiness for which all characters are none the less searching.'[7]

Accordingly the women in soaps can never be entirely happy. Is this due to the demands of the form, with its need for endless problematics? Or is it perhaps a result of the positioning of women at the centre of the narrative? Caught between the traditional female destiny imposed on them by patriarchy and its non-viability for the women themselves, their representation in soap opera frequently exposes the contradictions generated by patriarchy. The nature of soap, with its interminable narratives and lack of 'happy endings', means that these contradictions are never truly resolved. What is distinct about Alexis as a character is that she actively highlights these contradictions, in sharp contrast to many of the women characters in this (and other) series. Unlike them, Alexis does not accept unhappiness as her norm. Presented as strong, intelligent, independent and powerful (if destructively so), she continually fights to maintain and improve her position, manipulating and disturbing the patriarchal status quo. In this respect, love her or hate her, Alexis can be seen as a role-breaker in the representation of women in soap opera, and, indeed, as a role model for women in patriarchal society.

It may be argued that Elsie Tanner of *Coronation Street* was Alexis' forerunner as the middle-aged woman transgressive of the female role in the family and in control of her sexuality; and she was, in addition, a more truly 'popular' character, in her representation of a powerful working-class woman. The difference is, however, that while Elsie Tanner was aware of her sexuality in terms of being active in pursuit of her own desires, she was not really in control of it. Unlike Alexis, Elsie was constantly and obviously unhappy in her relations with men. In this respect then, she represented less a role model to empower women than a point of identification for women viewers with their own desire and its perpetual disappointment in relationships with men. Clearly, Alexis' sexual power is closely meshed with her socio-economic power: she does not need men, as Elsie does, for economic survival or status in the community.

In fact, the active challenge to patriarchy epitomised by Alexis echoes that of another genre – that of the 'dark lady', the 'evil seductress', the 'spider woman' of the *film noir* thrillers of the 1940s and 1950s. She follows in the footsteps of Joan Crawford as *Mildred Pierce* and Barbara Stanwyck as Phyllis Dietrichson in *Double Indemnity*: that remarkably potent image of sensual women who are strong, dangerous, erotic and, above all, exciting sexually; women defined by their sexuality, who at the same time have access to it and derive power from that access.

Like the women of *film noir*, Alexis is central to the intrigue of *Dynasty*. Within the social formation of this soap, she takes on many different roles – business tycoon, mother, wife, lover, seductress – and in all of them she initiates intrigue. Her displacement from one fixed familial role represents a threat to the stable worlds of marriage, work and the family, and hence to their underlying dependence on female submissiveness. The threat of her active female sexuality is evoked by her displacement from the traditional family structure, whose bounds cannot contain her character. She may be the Mother of the Carrington Family, around which everything in *Dynasty* resolves, but she is no matriarch to be relied upon to serve the interests of other members in that family.

In *Loving with a Vengeance* Tania Modleski points out that in soap opera 'misery becomes not . . . the consequence and sign of the family's breakdown, but the very means of its functioning and perpetuation.'[8] Nowhere is this more obvious than in the character of Alexis, who, far from attempting to hold the family harmoniously together, is seen constantly adding to the existing misery and upset, if not actually occasioning it. By so doing, however, she challenges ideological assumptions about woman's place in the family, and it is this that makes her unique. For instance, in the episodes of the 'Moldavia Massacre',[9] we see Alexis in a sense 'selling' her daughter Amanda to Prince Michael of Moldavia. The plot provides us with possible motives for this apparently most un-motherly behaviour. At the time, Alexis wanted to remove Amanda as a threat to her own marriage to Dex Dexter; to invest in the Moldavian economy for financial profit; and to cement her reacquaintance (and apparently unrequited love) with Prince Michael's father, King Galen. Or was it out of genuine concern for her daughter's happiness that Alexis wanted to unite Amanda and Michael? In their conversation about love, Alexis sounds sufficiently genuine to convince Amanda; but does she convince us? Alexis' controlled expression reveals nothing of her inner feelings or 'real' motives. In this, she resembles the strong silent hero whose strength lies precisely in his silence. Moreover, because there is no narrative closure in the soap-opera genre, we can never know the 'truth' about her. Any defeats (in favour of, say, Blake) are temporary: there is no permanent judgment on her like imprisonment, exile or death. Unlike the female power of the *film noir* heroine, hers is not finally contained within a narrative framework that controls her and defines her as evil.

Alexis has seized on those aspects of a woman's life which normally render her powerless and turned them into weapons. In her 'mothering' role, for example, there is no question of allowing her children to rule her life, of putting their interests before her own. It is her ex-husband Blake Carrington who suffers the conventional 'female' anxiety about their children's fates. Although it may be noted that, as a man, this never seems to conflict with his self-interest as a business man.

As in *film noir*, Alexis' 'spider woman' image is reinforced by another female character who, in representing an ideologically 'positive' female archetype, defines her transgression. In *Dynasty* this role is occupied by Krystle, Blake's wife – the virgin mother (fair where Alexis is dark), innocent nurturer of husband and children (including Alexis' own – 'All the people you love happen to be *my* children,' Alexis tells her pointedly). She is the blonde, sensual woman-as-redeemer. It is she who dispenses love, understanding and forgiveness. Generally depicted as visually static, it is not unusual for

Krystle to remain silent throughout entire scenes. Thus female viewers of *Dynasty* are confronted with conflicting definitions of femininity: the passive woman who is 'good', and the active woman who is 'evil'. Or is she? And if she isn't, is Krystle really 'good'?

The structure of soap opera organised around a family dictates that the latter's preservation is of primary importance, and, in a notably unprogressive theme, that its persistent unhappiness can only be solved from within it. By presenting us with this family in constant turmoil, an appeal is made to the spectator to understand its conflicts and evils while hoping that harmony and good will somehow triumph - except that then the series would end. Thus the conflict is essential to the existence of the dynasty! One consequence of this is that we, the viewers, are invited to identify with many more characters than the one character of the classic (male) narrative film, 'structured', as Mulvey points out, 'around a main controlling figure with whom the spectator can identify'.[10] In *Dynasty* this means, for example, that in the opposition between Alexis and Krystle we are not clearly positioned to identify consistently with one of the antagonists, but with each alternately, or simultaneously, or with neither. Thus our visual and narrative positioning does not resolve the contradictory definitions of femininity they represent.

Another *film noir* theme present in *Dynasty* is that of a man's struggle for the devotion of a woman who refuses to accord him the centrality he expects in her life, and who instead requires that he devote himself to her. In *Sunset Boulevard* Norma Desmond hires Joe Gills to work on the script for her comeback as a movie star. She insists that this means him participating in her life, rather than her being interested in his:

> He dreams he is her pet chimp, and he actually becomes victim of her Salome. Joe finds an acceptable lover in Betty, the young woman who types while he dictates, smells like soap instead of perfume, dreams of *his* career and is content to be behind the camera instead of in front. Self-interest over devotion to a man is often the original sin of the *film noir* woman and metaphor for the threat her sexuality represents to him.[11]

Like Norma Desmond, Alexis will not be defined in relation to a man, submit her interests to his, or make him central to her life. Her (now ex) husband Dex Dexter is shown constantly trying to control her sexuality in order not to be destroyed by it. He resents being seen as 'the husband of Alexis', ornament and sexual object. He asserts his masculinity by 'taking' Alexis in an almost violent way and is always walking out of their apartment asking her to choose between him and something else – be it work or another man. It is a choice Alexis always refuses to make.

The threat of Alexis' overpowering sexuality is also expressed visually. In many frames her image dominates that of the man, or men, often controlling the camera movement as well as directing the gaze of the viewer – this in spite of being presented as an object of desire, at least for the viewer. Just as our first sight of Phyllis in *Double Indemnity* is of her long, lovely legs, so we constantly see Alexis in skirts split to the waist. But if her dress defines her as a woman of desire, this is true in both senses of that phrase: she is desirable, but she is also desiring. Her multiplicity of outfits (silk business suits, sequinned off-the-shoulder evening dresses and elegant lingerie) seems to be chosen by her to define the multiplicity of her public and private roles. If she dresses to signify desirability, this, we assume, is because she wants to be desired – in order to satisfy her own desire, sexual or otherwise. This informs us that she is in control of her own sexuality.

The *femme fatale* of *film noir* ultimately loses control of the action, as both narrative and camera exert mastery over her. At the end of the film she is symbolically imprisoned by the visual composition of her image, just as, in many of the narratives, she is imprisoned, or killed, for her crime. The destruction of the *film noir* 'spider woman' constitutes a moral lesson: the power of the independent woman is an evil that will destroy her. In this respect, *film noir* can hardly be regarded as progressive, for although it does present us with role models who defy their fate, they are not allowed to triumph over it. As Place argues: 'The ideological operation of the myth, the absolute necessity of controlling the strong, sexual woman, is thus achieved by first demonstrating her dangerous power and its frightening results, then destroying it.'[12]

The beauty of Alexis as 'spider woman' is that she avoids the fate of her film predecessors. Soap opera narrative is endless and so is Alexis' defiance. Place says of the *film noir* 'spider women' that 'it is not their inevitable demise we remember, but rather their strong, dangerous and above all exciting sexuality'.[13] This is also what we remember of Alexis, except that it is not couched in the memory that she was finally judged morally wrong. Unlike the *film noir* heroine, Alexis fights on and on and on and on.

Beyond the Wildside?

The character of Alexis Carrington, far from being something that can, or should, be dismissed, represents a far-reaching challenge to feminism. Lurking within the elaborate plots and the glamorous clothing is a pleasurable image of woman in the eighties which constitutes a challenge to stereotyped feminist analysis of represent-ations of women – a challenge which can be extended, for example, to the analysis of advertising and other visual images. Feminists must be willing to look beyond the celluloid and gloss, as well as the established modes of thinking about them, if they are to tackle the issue of women's pleasure in the eighties. The elusive 'whole' woman, who looks out at us from magazines – composed and sensuous, inviting us to look, yet remaining inaccessible – opens up possibilities of reintroducing the notion of the *erotic* through scrutinising the pleasures of an active audience.

It is a notion Roland Barthes would recognise. In his last book, *Camera Lucida*, Barthes examines just what it is that draws us in to looking at a photographic image. His concern is not only with the way in which some photographs move us intellectually, but also with how a particular element of the image moves or captures us really powerfully. He calls this latter element the 'punctum', and argues that once there is a punctum, a 'blind-field' is created.

> It is what I add to the photograph and what is none the less already there. If we define a photograph as a 'motionless image' it not only means that the figures it represents do not move, it also means that they do not emerge – do not leave. They are anaesthetised like butterflies.[14]

Barthes argues that it is the presence (dynamics) of this blind-field which distinguishes the erotic photograph from the pornographic. Pornography typically represents the sexual organs in such a way that it makes of them a motionless object (a fetish). In other words, in the pornographic image, there is no punctum. The extremes of shape and glamour characteristic of *Vogue*'s women are images which, in Barthes' definition, could be termed erotic. But it is not the details of these images that attract us. Instead, the image lures us into what Barthes calls a 'subtle beyond' – a place where we are taken outside the photograph and the photograph animates us and we it.

It is time for feminist analysis to examine this 'subtle beyond'. For within its elusive boundaries lie the pleasures of watching Alexis

Carrington or of looking at the images in *Company* magazine when it invites us to 'dress to thrill'. Analysing the nature of the relationship between representation and the pleasures of an active audience provides a pathway for feminist analysis to tackle anew the notion of the erotic – and to enjoy and celebrate the 'wilder side of women' in the 1980s.

I wish to thank Ann Treneman for her support, help and encouragement in the writing of this piece.

8
Desperately Seeking Difference

Jackie Stacey

Introduction

Feminist film criticism has become increasingly concerned with questions of gendered spectatorship and the pleasures of popular cinema. In this context, one focus has been a critical analysis of the pleasures of looking constructed by dominant cinematic forms, which, it has been argued, reproduce 'an active/passive heterosexual division of labour'.[1] But if these pleasures have been organised in accordance with the needs, desires and fears of heterosexual masculinity, then what is the place of *women's* desire towards women within this analysis of narrative cinema? Indeed, is it possible to analyse representations of desire between women within the psychoanalytic framework characteristic of so much feminist film criticism, or are there other frameworks we could turn to instead?

The article which follows this introduction was originally written for *Screen*, where many of the psychoanalytic debates about the pleasures of narrative cinema have been published. The finished product was the result of a series of negotiations with the editorial board about the differences in our strategies and approaches to these questions. My approach has been both challenged and influenced by the responses of the members of the *Screen* editorial board to early drafts of this article. The debates concerned theoretical and political contradictions. In an area insufficiently theorised to offer easy answers, a problem of labelling presents itself. I want to highlight some of the complexities and contradictions involved in writing about desire between women in narrative cinema and the pleasures for the female spectator, since these questions do not fit neatly into the psychoanalytic terms and concepts employed in previous debates.

Psychoanalytic theory has offered accounts of female homosexual pleasures, conscious and unconscious, in all women. Working within a psychoanalytic framework and yet finding many of its concepts restricting and inadequate must be a frustrating experience familiar to many feminists. There are two main problems for my purposes here.

Firstly, the term female homosexual, by nature of that very qualifying adjective, demonstrates that the connotations of 'homosexual' are masculine. Secondly, since how we desire (masculine/feminine, active/passive), and whom we desire (homosexual or heterosexual object choice) have been separated within psychoanalytic theory, the notion of an active desire between women as anything other than masculine is inconceivable. In other words, the language of psychoanalysis situates desire between women firmly within masculinity. This is an ironic consequence, since my original aim in analysing desire between women in the cinema was to move beyond Mulvey's theory of the 'masculine' spectator.

An alternative discourse which speaks of desire between women is that of recent lesbian feminist politics. Indeed, the naming of that desire has been a political act in itself, but there are several problems here too. Within feminist politics, the category 'lesbian' generally refers to a conscious social and political identity. Since neither film in my article is explicitly dealing with lesbianism, and since my arguments about spectatorship aim to include all women, the term lesbian seems inadequate (or even misleading) to refer to the fascination I explore between women in the cinema.

Despite the limitations of psychoanalytic language and the problem of the category 'lesbian', it is important that these terminological difficulties do not prevent us from addressing questions of desire between women in debates about the female gaze. It seems to me that there is no straightforward answer to this question. Rather, there are several possible avenues of enquiry; I outline three of them briefly in the rest of this introduction, and then pursue one of them in greater depth in the article which follows. In approaching the question of 'the lesbian look' or 'the lesbian spectator' in popular cinema, three possibilities present themselves. These different possibilities overlap in many ways and yet can be distinguished analytically according to the focus of their study. The first concerns the look in lesbian narrative films; the second analyses lesbian spectators' readings of mainstream films not concerned with lesbianism; and the third examines the pleasures of looking between women in narrative cinema available to all women in the audience.

Firstly, then, the construction of the look in lesbian narrative film needs to be interrogated; are women constructed differently as objects of other women's desire, or do the same conventions of looking and desiring merely get mapped on to such representations of lesbianism? The construction of the spectator in relation to these conventions is obviously central here, since we need to understand how the pleasures of spectatorship might operate differently within lesbian films. This approach is exemplified by Mandy Merck's analysis of *Lianna* within the conventions of art cinema and patriarchal ways of looking.[2]

A second approach involves consideration of lesbian audiences and their readings of popular cinema which is not concerned with representing lesbianism. It is now widely accepted that the cultural production of meaning involves active spectatorship, rather than the passive consumption of textually determined meanings. Sub-cultural groups often produce an alternative set of readings of dominant cultural images, based on a different set of shared codes, conventions and experiences. Initiatives of this kind might take a lead from Richard Dyer's 'Judy Garland and Gay Men' in his book *Heavenly Bodies*, which provides a wonderful example of such an analysis in relation to gay male sub-culture.[3] Female stars such as Marlene Dietrich, Katherine Hepburn and Bette Davis also emerged as signifying particular pleasures for lesbian spectators in Claire Whitiker's 'Hollywood Transformed: Interviews with Lesbian Viewers':

> *Judy*: Which films made an early impression on you?
> *Anna Maria*: I loved *All About Eve*, particularly because I had a crush on Bette Davis, a wonderful model. She's a strong bitchy woman who knows what she wants and how to get it and yet has stayed human and sensitive . . . I first saw it when I was 12 and have seen it at least eight times.[4]

One of the limits of this approach may be that a more detailed analysis of lesbian audiences would reveal a diversity of readings and of pleasures or displeasures in relation to mainstream cinema. This question of *the* lesbian spectator, or *the* lesbian look, may be reified and oversimplistic. Indeed, there is likely to be a whole set of desires and identifications with differing configurations at stake, which cannot necessarily be fixed according to the conscious sexual identities of the cinema spectators.

The final possible path of enquiry involves an analysis of film texts where the look is constructed between two female characters and thus offers different pleasures to the spectator from those criticised by Mulvey [5]. This approach broadens the analysis of desire, which has focused on a rather narrow definition of the erotic, to investigate the phenomenon of fascination between women. In a culture where the circulation of idealised and desirable images of femininity constantly surrounds us, the phenomenon of fascination between women is hardly surprising. There is, for example, a great deal of evidence to suggest that women in cinema audiences prefer female stars.[6] One explanation for this has been that women identify with the stars' position as desirable to men. Certainly that is one of the pleasures at stake. But it is not the only one. Another is fascination between women. The analysis of the film texts which follows assumes that all women in the audience may take a variety of conscious or unconscious pleasures in these representations of fascination between women, in which they are cinematically inscribed. Indeed, the pleasurable processes of female spectatorship in relation to the female star are reproduced thematically and structurally in the films themselves.

All About Eve (directed by Joseph Mankiewicz, 1950) and *Desperately Seeking Susan* (directed by Susan Seidelman, 1984) are two films in which the fascination of one woman with another, across the gap produced by their differences, structures the narrative development.[7] This formation contradicts the dominant convention within Hollywood cinema whereby the spectator is said to be inscribed within the look and desire of the male protagonist. What interests me about these films is the question of the pleasures for the female spectator, who is invited to look or gaze with one female character at another, in an interchange of feminine fascinations. This fascination is neither purely identification with the other woman, nor desire for her in the strictly erotic sense of the word. It is a desire to see, to know and to become more like an idealised feminine other, in a context where the difference between the two women is repeatedly re-established.

My analysis of these two films follows a detailed discussion of feminist theories of visual pleasure which have drawn heavily on psychoanalysis to explain patterns of gendered spectatorship. This discussion is important because the article was written as a response to and a critique of feminist work of this kind and its exclusion of questions of desire between women. Indeed, an exposition of the psychoanalytic arguments is crucial here, since I argue that this exclusion is a result of the basic structures and concepts of the psychoanalytic theory upon which so much feminist work on cinema has been based.

An Investigation of Desire between Women in Narrative Cinema

During the last decade, feminist critics have developed an analysis of the constructions of sexual difference in dominant narrative cinema, drawing on psychoanalytic and post-structuralist theory. One of the main indictments of Hollywood film has been its passive positioning of the woman as sexual spectacle, as there 'to be looked at', and the active positioning of the male protagonist as bearer of the look. This pleasure has been identified as one of the central structures of dominant cinema, constructed in accordance with masculine desire. The question which has then arisen is that of the pleasure of the woman spectator. While this issue has hardly been addressed, the specifically homosexual pleasures of female spectatorship have been ignored completely. This article will attempt to suggest some of the theoretical reasons for this neglect.

Theories of Feminine Spectatorship: Masculinisation, Masochism or Marginality

Laura Mulvey's 'Visual Pleasure and Narrative Cinema'[8] has been the springboard for much feminist film criticism during the last decade. Using psychoanalytic theory, Mulvey argued that the visual pleasures of Hollywood cinema are based on voyeuristic and fetishistic forms of looking. Because of the ways these looks are structured, the spectator necessarily identifies with the male protagonist in the narrative, and thus with his objectification of the female figure via the male gaze. The construction of woman as spectacle is built into the apparatus of dominant cinema, and the spectator position which is produced by the film narrative is necessarily a masculine one.

Mulvey maintained that visual pleasure in narrative film is built around two contradictory processes: the first involves objectification of the image and the second identification with it. The first process depends upon 'direct scopophilic contact with the female form displayed for [the spectator's] enjoyment'[9] and the spectator's look here is active and feels powerful. This form of pleasure requires the separation of the 'erotic identity of the subject from the object on the screen'.[10] This 'distance' between spectator and screen contributes to the voyeuristic pleasure of looking in on a private world. The second form of pleasure depends upon the opposite process, an identification with the image on the screen 'developed through narcissism and the constitution of the ego'.[11] The process of identification in the cinema, Mulvey argued, like the process of objectification, is structured by the narrative. It offers the spectator the pleasurable identification with the main male protagonist, and through him the power indirectly to possess the female character displayed as sexual object for his pleasure. The look of the male character moves the narrative forward and identification with it thus implies a sense of sharing in the power of his active look.

Two lacunae in Mulvey's argument have subsequently been addressed in film criticism. The first raises the question of the male figure as erotic object, [12] the second that of the feminine subject in the narrative and women's active desire and the sexual aims of women in the audience in relationship to the female protagonist on the screen. As David Rodowick points out:

> her discussion of the female figure is restricted only to its function as masculine object-choice. In this manner, the place of the masculine is discussed as both the subject and object of the gaze: and the feminine is discussed only as an object which structures the masculine look according to its active (voyeuristic) and passive (fetishistic) forms. So where is the place of the feminine subject in this scenario? [13]

There are several possible ways of filling this theoretical gap. One would use a detailed textual analysis to demonstrate that different gendered spectator positions are produced by the film text, contradicting the unified masculine model of spectatorship. This would at least provide some space for an account of the feminine subject in the film text and in the cinema audience. The relationship of spectators to these feminine and masculine positions would then need to be explored further: do women necessarily take up a feminine and men a masculine spectator position?

Alternatively, we could accept a theory of the masculinisation of the spectator at a textual level, but argue that spectators bring different subjectivities to the film according to sexual difference, [14] and therefore respond differently to the visual pleasures offered in the text. I want to elaborate these two possibilities briefly, before moving on to discuss a third which offers a more flexible or mobile model of spectatorship and cinematic pleasure.

The first possibility, then, is to argue that the film text can be read and enjoyed from different gendered positions. This problematises the monolithic model of Hollywood cinema as an 'anthropomorphic male machine' [15] producing unified and masculinised spectators. It offers an explanation of women's pleasure in a narrative cinema based on different processes of spectatorship, according to sexual difference. What this 'difference' signifies, however, in terms of cinematic pleasure, is highly contestable.

Raymond Bellour has explored the way the look is organised to create filmic discourse through detailed analyses of the system of enunciation in Hitchcock's work.[16] The mechanisms for eliminating the threat of sexual difference represented by the figure of the woman, he argues, are built into the apparatus of the cinema. Woman's desire only appears on the screen to be punished and controlled by assimilation to the desire of the male character. Bellour insists upon the masochistic nature of the woman spectator's pleasure in Hollywood film:

> I think that a woman can love, accept, and give positive value to these films only from her own masochism, and from a certain sadism that she can exercize in return on the masculine subject, within a system loaded with traps.[17]

Bellour, then, provides an account of the feminine subject and women's spectatorship which offers a different position from the masculine one set up by Mulvey. However, he fixes these positions within a rigid dichotomy which assumes a biologically determined equivalence between male/female and the masculine/feminine, sadistic/masochistic positions he believes to be set up by the cinematic apparatus. The apparatus here is seen as determining, controlling the meaning produced by a film text unproblematically:

> . . . the resulting picture of the classical cinema is even more totalistic and deterministic than Mulvey's. Bellour sees it as a logically consistent, complete and closed system.[18]

The problem is that Bellour's analysis, like those of many structural functionalists, leaves no room for subjectivity. The spectator is presumed to be an already fully constituted subject and is fixed by the text to a predetermined gender identification. There is no space for subjectivity to be seen as a process in which identification and object choice may be shifting, contradictory or precarious.

A second challenge to the model of the masculinised spectator set up by Mulvey's 1975 essay comes from the work of Mary Ann Doane. She draws on Freud's account of asymmetry in the development of masculinity and femininity to argue that women's pleasures are not motivated by fetishistic and voyeuristic drives.

> For the female spectator there is a certain over-presence of the image – she *is* the image. Given the closeness of this relationship, the female spectator's desire can be described only in terms of a

kind of narcissism – the female look demands a becoming. It thus appears to negate the very distance or gap specified . . . as the essential precondition for voyeurism.[19]

Feminist critics have frequently challenged the assumption that fetishism functions for women in the same way that it is supposed to for men. Doane argues that the girl's understanding of the meaning of sexual difference occurs simultaneously with seeing the boy's genitals; the split between seeing and knowing, which enables the boy to disown the difference which is necessary for fetishism, does not occur in girls.

> It is in the distance between the look and the threat that the boy's relation to the knowledge of sexual difference is formulated. The boy, unlike the girl in Freud's description, is capable of a re-vision . . . This gap between the visible and the knowable, the very possibility of disowning what is seen, prepares the ground for fetishism.[20]

This argument is useful in challenging the hegemony of the cinema apparatus and in offering an account of visual pleasure which is neither based on a phallic model, nor on the determinacy of the text. It allows for an account of women's potential resistance to the dominant masculine spectator position. However, it also sets women outside the problematic pleasures of looking in the cinema, as if women do not have to negotiate within patriarchal regimes. As Doane herself has pointed out:

> The feminist theorist is thus confronted with something of a double bind: she can continue to analyse and interpret various instances of the repression of woman, of her radical absence in the discourses of men – a pose which necessitates remaining within that very problematic herself, repeating its terms; or she can attempt to delineate a feminine specificity, always risking a recapitulation of patriarchal constructions and a naturalization of 'woman'.[21]

In fact, this is a very familiar problem in feminist theory: how to argue for a feminine specificity without falling into the trap of biological essentialism. If we do argue that women differ from men in their relation to visual constructions of femininity, then further questions are generated for feminist film theory: do all women have the same relationship to images of themselves? Is there only one feminine spectator position? How do we account for diversity, contradiction or resistance within this category of feminine spectatorship?

This problem arises in relation to all cultural systems in which women have been defined as 'other' within patriarchal discourses: how can we express the extent of women's oppression without denying femininity any room to manoeuvre (Mulvey, 1975), defining women as complete victims of patriarchy (Bellour, 1979), or as totally other to it (Doane, 1982)? Within the theories discussed so far, the female spectator is offered only the three rather frustrating options of masculinisation, masochism or marginality.

Towards a More Contradictory Model of Spectatorship

A different avenue of exploration would require a more complex and contradictory model of the relay of looks on the screen and between the audience and the diegetic characters.

> It might be better, as Barthes suggests, neither to destroy difference nor to valorize it, but to multiply and disperse differences, to move towards a world where differences would not be synonymous with exclusion.[22]

In her 1981 'Afterthoughts' on visual pleasure, Mulvey addresses many of the problems raised so far. In an attempt to develop a more 'mobile' position for the female spectator in the cinema, she turns to Freud's theories of the difficulties of attaining heterosexual femininity.[23] Required, unlike men, to relinquish the phallic activity and female object of infancy, women are argued to oscillate between masculine and feminine identifications. To demonstrate this oscillation between positions, Mulvey cites Pearl Chavez's ambivalence in *Duel in the Sun*, the splitting of her desire (to be Jesse's 'lady' or Lewt's tomboy lover), a splitting which also extends to the female spectator. Mulvey's revision is important for two reasons: it displaces the notions of the fixity of spectator positions produced by the text, and it focuses on the gaps and contradictions within patriarchal signification, thus opening up crucial questions of resistance and diversity. However, Mulvey maintains that fantasies of action 'can only find expression . . . through the metaphor of masculinity'. In order to identify with active desire, the female spectator must assume an (uncomfortably) masculine position: '. . . the female spectator's phantasy of masculinisation is always to some extent at cross purposes with itself, restless in its transvestite clothes.'[24]

Oppressive Dichotomies

Psychoanalytic accounts which theorise identification and object choice within a framework of linked binary oppositions (masculinity/femininity:activity/passivity) necessarily masculinise female homosexuality. Mary Ann Doane's reading of the first scene in the film *Caught* demonstrates the limitations of this psychoanalytic binarism perfectly:

> The woman's sexuality, as spectator, must undergo a constant process of transformation. She must look, as if she were a man with the phallic power of the gaze, at a woman who would attract that gaze, in order to be that woman ... The convolutions involved here are analogous to those described by Julia Kristeva as 'the double or triple twists of what we commonly call female homosexuality': 'I am looking, as a man would, for a woman'; or else, 'I submit myself, as if I were a man who thought he was a woman, to a woman who thinks she is a man.'[25]

Convolutions indeed. This insistence upon a gendered dualism of sexual desire maps homosexuality on to an assumed antithesis of masculinity and femininity. Such an assumption precludes a description of homosexual positionality without resorting to the manoeuvres cited by Doane. In arguing for a more complex model of cinematic spectatorship, I am suggesting that we need to separate gender identification from sexuality, too often conflated in the name of sexual difference.

In films where the woman is represented as sexual spectacle for the masculine gaze of the diegetic and the cinematic spectator, an identification with a masculine heterosexual desire is invited. The spectator's response can vary across a wide spectrum between outright acceptance and refusal. It has proved crucial for feminist film theorists to explore these variations. How might a woman's look at another woman, both within the diegesis and between spectator and character, compare with that of the male spectator?

This article considers the pleasures of two narrative films which develop around one woman's obsession with another woman, *All About Eve* and *Desperately Seeking Susan*. I shall argue that these films offer particular pleasures to the women in the audience which cannot simply be reduced to a masculine heterosexual equivalent. In so doing I am not claiming these films as 'lesbian films'[26] but rather using them to examine certain possibilities of pleasure. I want to explore the representation of forms of desire and identification in ᴛhese films in order to consider their implications for the pleasures of female spectatorship. My focus is on the relations between women on the screen, and between these representations and the women in the audience. Interestingly, the fascinations which structure both narratives are precisely about difference – forms of otherness between women characters which are not merely reducible to sexual difference, so often seen as the sole producer of desire itself.

The Inscription of Active Feminine Desire

In *Alice Doesn't*, Teresa de Lauretis explores the function of the classic masculine Oedipal trajectory in dominant narrative. The subjects which motivate the narrative along the logic of the 'Oedipus', she argues, are necessarily masculine.

> However varied the conditions of the presence of the narrative form in fictional genres, rituals or social discourses, its movement seems to be that of a passage, a transformation predicated on the figure of the hero, a mythical subject . . . the *single* figure of the hero who crosses the boundary and penetrates the other space. In so doing, the hero, the mythical subject, is constructed as a human being and as male; he is the active principle of culture, the establisher of distinction, the creator of differences. Female is what is not susceptible to transformation, to life or death.[27]

De Lauretis then proceeds to outline the significance of this division between masculine and feminine within the textual narrative in terms of spectatorship.

> Therefore, to say that narrative is the production of Oedipus is to say that each reader – male or female – is constrained and defined within the two positions of a sexual difference thus conceived: male-hero-human, on the side of the subject; the female-obstacle-boundary-space, on the other.[28]

As de Lauretis herself acknowledges later in the chapter, this analysis leaves little space for either the question of the feminine subject in the narrative, or the pleasures of desire and identification of the women in the audience. In order to explore these questions more concretely, I want to discuss two texts; both *All About Eve* and *Desperately Seeking Susan* have female protagonists whose desires and identifications move the narratives forward. In de Lauretis's terms, these texts construct not only a feminine object of desire in the narrative, but also a feminine subject of that desire.

All About Eve is particularly well suited to an analysis of these questions, as it is precisely about the pleasures and dangers of spectatorship for women. One of its central themes is the construction and reproduction of feminine identities, and the activity of looking is highlighted as an important part of these processes. The narrative concerns two women, a Broadway star and her most adoring spectator, Eve. In its course, we witness the transformation of Eve Butler (Ann Baxter) from spectator to star herself. The pleasures of spectatorship are emphasised by Eve's loyal attendance at every one of Margot Channing's (Bette Davis) performances. Its dangers are also made explicit as an intense rivalry develops between them. Eve emerges as a greedy and ambitious competitor, and Margot steps down from stardom into marriage, finally enabling her protégée to replace her as 'actress of the year' in a part written originally for Margot.

Eve's journey to stardom could be seen as the feminine equivalent to the masculine Oedipal trajectory described by de Lauretis above. Freud's later descriptions of the feminine Oedipal journey[29] contradict his previous symmetrical model wherein the girl's first love object is her father, as the boy's is his mother. In his later arguments, Freud also posited the mother as the girl's first love object. Her path to heterosexuality is therefore difficult and complex, since it requires her not only to relinquish her first object, like the boy, but to transform both its gender (female to male) and the aim (active to passive) directed at it. Up to this point, active desire towards another woman is an experience of all women, and its re-enactment in *All About Eve* may constitute one of the pleasures of spectatorship for the female viewer.

Eve is constantly referred to as innocent and childlike in the first half of the film and her transformation involves a process of maturation, of becoming a more confident adult. First she is passionately attached to Margot, but then she shifts her affection to Margot's lover Bill, attempting unsuccessfully to seduce him. Twice in the film she is shown interrupting their intimacy: during their farewell at the airport and then during their fierce argument about Margot's jealousy, shortly before Bill's welcome-home party. Eve's third object of desire, whom she actively pursues, is the married playwright Lloyd Richards, husband to Margot's best friend. In both cases the stability of the older heterosexual couples, Margot and Bill, Karen and Lloyd, is threatened by the presence of the younger woman who completes the Oedipal triangle. Eve is finally punished for her desires by the patriarchal power of the aptly named Addison de Wit, who proves to be one step ahead of her manipulations.

The binary opposition between masculinity and femininity offers a limited framework for the discussion of Eve's fascination with Margot, which is articulated actively through an interplay of desire and identification during the film. In many ways, Margot is Eve's idealised object of desire. She follows Margot from city to city, never missing any of her performances. Her devotion to her favourite Broadway star is stressed at the very start of the film.

Karen But there are hundreds of plays on Broadway . . .
Eve Not with Margot Channing in them!

Margot is moved by Eve's representation of her 'tragic' past, and flattered by her adoration, so she decides to 'adopt' her.

Margot (voice-over) We moved Eve's few pitiful possessions into my apartment . . . Eve became my sister, mother, lawyer, friend, psychiatrist and cop. The honeymoon was on!

Eve acts upon her desire to become more like her ideal. She begins to wear Margot's cast-off clothes, appearing in Margot's bedroom one morning in her old black suit. Birdie, Margot's personal assistant, responds suspiciously to Eve's behaviour.

Margot She thinks only of me.
Birdie She thinks only *about* you – like she's studying you – like you was a book, or a play, or a set of blueprints – how you walk, talk, eat, think, sleep.
Margot I'm sure that's very flattering, Birdie, and I'm sure there's nothing wrong with it.

The construction of Bette Davis as the desirable feminine ideal in this narrative has a double significance here. As well as being a 'great star' for Eve, she is clearly the same for the cinema audience. The film offers the fictional fulfilment of the spectator's dreams as well as Eve's, to be a star like Bette Davis, like Margot. Thus the identifications and desires of Eve, to some extent, narrativise a traditional pleasure of female spectatorship.

Margot is not only a star, she is also an extremely powerful woman who intimidates most of the male characters in the film. Her quick wit and disdain for conventional politeness, together with her flair for drama offstage as much as on, make her an attractive figure for Eve, an 'idealistic dreamy-eyed kid', as Bill describes her. It is this *difference* between the two women which motivates Eve, but which Eve also threatens. In trying to 'become as much like her ideal as possible', Eve almost replaces Margot in both her public and her private lives. She places a call to Bill on Margot's behalf, and captures his attention when he is on his way upstairs to see Margot before his coming-home party. Margot begins to feel dispensable.

> *Margot* I could die right now and nobody would be confused. My inventory is all in shape and the merchandise all put away.

Yet even dressed in Margot's costume, having taken her role in the evening's performance, Eve cannot supplant her in the eyes of Bill, who rejects her attempt at seduction. The difference between the two women is repeatedly stressed and complete identification proves impossible.

All About Eve offers some unusual pleasures for a Hollywood film, since the active desire of a female character is articulated through looking at the female star. It is by watching Margot perform on the stage that Eve becomes intoxicated with her idol. The significance of active looking in the articulation of feminine desire is foregrounded at various points in the narrative. In one scene, we see Eve's devoted spectatorship in progress during one of Margot's performances. Eve watches Margot from the wings of the stage, and Margot bows to the applause of her audience. In the next scene the roles are reversed, and Margot discovers Eve on the empty stage bowing to an imaginary audience. Eve is holding up Margot's costume to sample the pleasures of stardom for herself. The process is then echoed in the closing scene of the film with Eve, now a Broadway star herself, and the newly introduced Phoebe, an adoring schoolgirl fan. The final shot shows Phoebe, having covertly donned Eve's bejewelled evening cloak, holding Eve's award and gazing at her reflection in the mirror. The reflected image, infinitely multiplied in the triptych of the glass, creates a spectacle of stardom that is the film's final shot, suggesting a perpetual regeneration of intra-feminine fascinations through the pleasure of looking.

The Desire to be Desperate

Like *All About Eve*, *Desperately Seeking Susan* concerns a woman's obsession with another woman. But instead of being punished for acting upon her desires, like Eve, Roberta (Rosanna Arquette) acts upon them, if in a rather more haphazard way, and eventually her initiatives are rewarded with the realisation of her desires. Despite her classic feminine behaviour, forgetful, clumsy, unpunctual and indecisive, she succeeds in her quest to find Susan (Madonna).

Even at the very beginning of the film, when suburban housewife Roberta is represented at her most dependent and childlike, her actions propel the narrative movement. Having developed her own fantasy narrative about Susan by reading the personal advertisements, Roberta acts upon her desire to be 'desperate' and becomes entangled in Susan's life. She anonymously attends the romantic reunion of Susan and Jim, and then pursues Susan through the streets of Manhattan. When she loses sight of her quarry in a second-hand shop, she purchases the jacket which Susan has just exchanged. The key found in its pocket provides an excuse for direct contact, and Roberta uses the personals to initiate another meeting.

Not only is the narrative propelled structurally by Roberta's desire, but almost all the spectator sees of Susan at the beginning of the film is revealed through Roberta's fantasy. The narrativisation of her desires positions her as the central figure for spectator identification: through her desire we seek, and see, Susan. Thus, in the opening scenes, Susan is introduced by name when Roberta reads the personals aloud from under the dryer in the beauty salon. Immediately following Roberta's declaration 'I wish I was desperate', there is a cut to the first shot of Susan.

The cuts from the Glasses' party to Susan's arrival in New York City work to the same effect. Repelled by her husband's TV commercial for his bathroom wares, Roberta leaves her guests and moves towards the window, as the ad's voice-over promises 'At Gary's Oasis, all your fantasies can come true.' Confronted with her own image in the reflection, she pushes it away by opening the window and looking out longingly on to Manhattan's skyline. The ensuing series of cuts between Roberta and the bridge across the river to the city link her desiring gaze to Susan's arrival there via the same bridge.

At certain points within *Desperately Seeking Susan*, Roberta explicitly becomes the bearer of the look. The best illustration of this transgression of traditional gender positionalities occurs in the scene in which she first catches sight of Susan. The shot sequence begins with Jim seeing Susan and is immediately followed with Roberta seeing her. It is, however, Roberta's point of view which is offered for the spectator's identification. Her look is specified by the use of the pay-slot telescope through which Roberta, and the spectator, see Susan.

In accordance with classic narrative cinema, the object of fascination in *Desperately Seeking Susan* is a woman – typically, a woman coded as a sexual spectacle. As a star Madonna's image is saturated in sexuality. In many ways she represents the 1980s 'assertive style' of heterosexual spectacle, inviting masculine consumption. This is certainly emphasised by shots of Susan which reference classic pornographic poses and camera angles; for example, the shot of Susan lying on Roberta's bed reading her diary, which shows Susan lying on her back, wearing only a vest and a pair of shorts over her suspenders and lacy tights. (Although one could argue that the very next shot, from Susan's point of view, showing Gary upside down, subverts the conventional pornographic codes.) My aim is not to deny these meanings in *Desperately Seeking Susan* in order to claim it as a 'progressive text', but to point to cinematic pleasures which may be available to the spectator *in addition* to those previously analysed by feminist film theory. Indeed, I believe such a project can only attempt to work within the highly contradictory constructions of femininity in mainstream films.

Susan is represented as puzzling and enigmatic to the protagonist, and to the spectator. The desire propelling the narrative is partly a desire to become more like her, but also a desire to know her, and to solve the riddle of her femininity. The protagonist begins to fulfil this desire by following the stranger, gathering clues about her identity and her life, such as her jacket, which, in turn, produces three other clues, a key, a photograph and a telephone number. The construction of her femininity as a riddle is emphasised by the series of intrigues and misunderstandings surrounding Susan's identity. The film partly relies on typical devices drawn from the mystery genre in constructing the protagonist's, and thus the spectator's, knowledge of Susan through a series of clues and coincidences. Thus, in some ways, Susan is positioned as the classic feminine enigma; she is, however, investigated by another woman.

One line of analysis might simply see Roberta as taking up the position of the masculine protagonist in expressing a desire to be 'desperate', which, after all, can be seen as identifying with Jim's position in relation to Susan, that of active desiring masculinity. Further legitimation for this reading could be seen in Jim's response to Roberta's advertisement to Susan in the personals. He automatically assumes it has been placed there by another man, perhaps a rival. How can we understand the construction of the female protagonist as the agent and articulator of desire for another woman in the narrative within existing psychoanalytic theories of sexual difference? The limitations of a dichotomy which offers only two significant categories for understanding the complex interplay of gender, sexual aim and object choice, are clearly demonstrated here.

Difference and Desire between Women

The difference which produces the narrative desire in *Desperately Seeking Susan* is not sexual difference, but the difference between two women in the film. It is the difference between suburban marriage and street credibility. Two sequences contrast the characters, using smoking as a signifier of difference. The first occurs in Battery Park, where Roberta behaves awkwardly in the unfamiliar territory of public space. She is shown sitting on a park bench, knees tightly clenched, looking around nervously for Susan. Jim asks her for a light, to which she timidly replies that she does not smoke. The ensuing cut shows Susan, signalled by Jim's shout of recognition. Susan is sitting on the boat rail, striking a match on the bottom of her raised boot to light a cigarette.

Smoking is again used to emphasise difference in a subsequent sequence. This time, Roberta, having by now lost her memory and believing she may be Susan, lights a cigarette from Susan's box. Predictably, she chokes on the smoke, with the unfamiliarity of an adolescent novice. The next cut shows us Susan, in prison for attempting to skip her cab fare, taking a light from the prison matron and blowing the smoke defiantly straight back into her face. The contrast in their smoking ability is only one signifier of the characters' very different femininities. Roberta is represented as young, inexperienced and asexual, while Susan's behaviour and appearance are coded as sexually confident and provocative. Rhyming sequences are used to emphasise their differences even after Roberta has taken on her new identity as Susan. She ends up in the same prison cell, but her childlike acquiescence to authority contrasts with Susan's defiance of the law.

Susan transgresses conventional forms of feminine behaviour by appropriating public space for herself. She turns the public lavatory into her own private bathroom, drying her armpits with the hand blower, and changing her clothes in front of the mirror above the washbasins as if in her own bedroom. In the streets, Susan challenges the patronising offer of a free newspaper from a passer-by by dropping the whole pile at his feet and taking only the top copy for herself. In contrast to Susan's supreme public confidence, Roberta is only capable in her own middle-class privacy. Arriving home after her day of city adventures, she manages to synchronise with a televised cooking show, catching up on its dinner preparations with confident dexterity in her familiar domestic environment.

As soon as Roberta becomes entangled in Susan's world, her

respectable sexuality is thrown into question. First she is assumed to be having an affair, then she is arrested for suspected prostitution, and finally Gary asks her if she is a lesbian. When the two photographs of Roberta, one as a bride and one as a suspected prostitute, are laid down side by side at the police station, her apparent transformation from virgin to whore shocks her husband. The ironic effect of these largely misplaced accusations about Roberta's sexuality works partly in relation to Susan, who is represented as the epitome of opposition to acceptable bourgeois feminine sexuality. She avoids commitment, dependency or permanence in her relationships with men, and happily takes their money, while maintaining an intimate friendship with the woman who works at the Magic Box.

Roberta's desire is finally rewarded when she meets Susan in an almost farcical chase scene at that club during the chaotic film finale. Gary finds Roberta, Des finds 'Susan' (Roberta), Jim finds Susan, the villain finds the jewels (the earrings which Susan innocently pocketed earlier in the film), Susan and Roberta catch the villain, and Susan and Roberta find each other . . . The last shot of the film is a front-page photograph of the two women hand in hand, triumphantly waving their reward cheque in return for the recovery of the priceless Nefertiti earrings. In the end, both women find what they were searching for throughout the narrative: Roberta has found Susan, and Susan has found enough money to finance many future escapades.

Roberta's desire to become more like her ideal – a more pleasingly co-ordinated, complete and attractive feminine image[30] – is offered temporary narrative fulfilment. However, the pleasures of this feminine desire cannot be collapsed into simple identification, since difference and otherness are continuously played upon, even when Roberta 'becomes' her idealised object. Both *Desperately Seeking Susan* and *All About Eve* tempt the woman spectator with the fictional fulfilment of becoming an ideal feminine other, while denying complete transformation by insisting upon differences between women. The rigid distinction between *either* desire *or* identification, so characteristic of psychoanalytic film theory, fails to address the construction of desires which involve a specific interplay of both processes.

I would like to thank Sarah Franklin, Richard Dyer, Alison Light, Chris Healy, Maureen McNeill and the Women Thesis Writers Group in Birmingham for their inspiration, support and helpful comments during the writing of this article.

9

Black Looks

Jacqui Roach and Petal Felix

All the women are white,
All the blacks are men,
But some of us are brave.[1]

A Black Female Gaze?

Is there a black female gaze? This collection explores the possibilities of finding, in contemporary popular culture, a perspective which is specifically female, which can counter and subvert the dominant masculine perspective in popular representations. Our concern in this chapter is to ask how black women can relate to the gender politics of representation. How many of the debates surrounding these issues are relevant to us? Are we automatically included as women? Or does our colour exclude us in a culture where 'black' signifies the opposite of 'white' and has negative connotations within the dominant linguistic system?

We live in a culture in which the dominant gaze is not only male, but white. It is not just that there are more representations of white people and of white people's perspectives – this might not seem surprising as they constitute over 90 per cent of the population. The point is that all too often this perspective excludes us, stereotypes us, ghettoises us; denying our subjectivity by treating us as 'other' to *their* problems, calling us a 'blot' on *their* landscape, controlling us as objects of *their* gaze.

There have been alternative representations to those described above. Yet when black culture has been recognised, when a black perspective has been expressed, it has been overwhelmingly a male one. From Richard Wright to Linton Kwesi Johnson, from Paul Robeson to Michael Jackson, from Joe Louis to Daley Thompson, black has meant black men. In the past only as singers – and a handful at that – have black women managed to make their mark on an international scale.

Things have changed in the last decade, of course. Black women writers, especially Americans like Alice Walker and Toni Morrison, have gained international recognition, and even that ultimate accolade, a Hollywood 'film of the book' in the case of *The Color Purple*. Black women athletes like Tessa Sanderson have become media stars. Black women appear in television soap operas, from *Dynasty* to *EastEnders*. Women's magazines feature black women fashion models, albeit predominantly light skinned; Iman, the top international fashion model from Somalia is perhaps one of the few exceptions. What is the impact of this increased presence in the mainstream? Is it just more of the same objectification, with black women stereotyped as victims or signifiers of the exotic?[2] Is it merely a token presence to appease the liberal conscience? Or might it represent a real intervention by black women in the culture as a whole? One which enables our voice to be heard, our view of the world to be represented?

While objectification and tokenism cannot by any means be dismissed as things of the past, we believe nevertheless that there is a black female presence in British popular culture today. This presence is one that projects a black female gaze upon a world otherwise dominated by whites and males. It is no more a single point of view than is that of, say, white women or black men: inevitably it is as multifaceted as the experience of black women in this society. In order to explore this multifacetedness, we interviewed three black women working in popular cultural forms. The diversity of their experiences and their approaches will, we hope, demonstrate the richness and the contradictions of black female creativity, and identify and reappropriate the positive meaning of the phrase 'black looks', which currently has negative significance in terms of dominant circulation.

In so far as their prominence has made the women we discuss role models for other black women, they carry the burden of all those from subordinated groups who become visible as a minority: they come to *represent* black women in the society, both to black women themselves and to others. Their choices become more than individual ones, because – unfairly – black women as a whole are judged through them, and black women judge them knowing this, and because of this the vulnerability as well as the clarity of their gaze is all the more important.

Joan Riley

One woman who is acutely aware of this is the novelist Joan Riley, author of *The Unbelonging, Waiting in the Twilight* and *Romance*. She considers the perspective of her work to be a primarily realistic one. But as she discovered when *The Unbelonging* was published in 1985, definitions of reality differ. Of course, there are always debates about what does or does not constitute 'realism'. In the past, orthodox Marxist critics, like the Hungarian Georg Lukács, have expressed dissatisfaction with any movement (modernism, for example) that did not carefully reflect unequal class relations, 'the reality of capitalism'.[3] Joan Riley's work, which considers variables such as 'gender' and 'race' as well as 'class', has been heavily criticised, not for 'escapism' from capitalism, but for not being 'positive' enough! The reality Joan Riley saw, and sought to represent in her novel, was one whose existence and significance her critics denied, or felt should not have been represented in the current political conjuncture. For this novel, narrated from the point of view of Hyacinth, a young black woman imbued with a sense of self-hatred, deals with incest and violence within the black family.

So here was the first novel written by and about a black woman based in Britain, and what was it saying? That black men rape their children, that the black family is torn apart by cruelty; that black people desperately want to be white? Was this not playing directly into the hands of white racists, with their stereotypes of black men as beasts? Did it not reproduce the 'liberal' stereotype of black families as broken apart by oppression, of black people as 'their own worst enemies'? Did *The Unbelonging* represent a black female gaze at all? Or was it not rather an example of the imposition of the white (male) gaze upon a black consciousness informing its view of itself and the world?

This problem is not a new one for black writers. Early black American writers, for example, tended to idealise black people and black life, rather in the way that Hollywood films of the fifties, in trying to break away from racist stereotypes, felt able to represent black men only if they were perfect in every way.[4] When a black male writer like Richard Wright began to write more 'realistically', he was criticised by black critics for presenting, in his character Bigger Thomas, a view of the black American man as a murderer and rapist of white women. James Baldwin was criticised for representing the black man as a homosexual. Ralph Ellison was surely conscious of this when, in *Invisible Man*, he has his protagonist embarrassed by a white person being introduced to a sharecropper whose wife and daughter are both pregnant by him. More recently, Alice Walker has shown awareness of the risk she takes in writing a story about the rape of a white woman by a black man.[5] In a racist society does the black writer have an obligation to present black people only in positive terms? Is her work otherwise complicit with inverted racism?

Joan Riley thinks not. She was initially surprised at the fury of some black people in responding to her novel, which she feels *was* written as an expression of a black female point of view. She says:

> I got a lot of criticism from people I didn't expect to get it from. A lot of criticism from blacks and radicals. People's attitude was that it [incest] only happens in white families and you certainly shouldn't discuss it, or attack black people even if it does happen in their families. I feel very strongly that we should be allowed to be vulnerable and establish our right to humanity, which we are not doing if we deny some aspects of being black and accept some. We must deal honestly with all different aspects of ourselves, whether they be good or bad, and not always try to present this one-dimensional force. We must try to challenge the white-tailored stereotype of ourselves, and not create one of our own.[6]

But *whose* reality does Joan Riley's writing represent? How many black men are harbingers of sexual violence and general misery? How many black women suffer as miserable victims? Naturally, the proportion is smaller than suggested by the media generally, but where these contradictions exist are they ones we want to identify for ourselves? Judging by the response from 'ordinary' black people, Joan Riley has no doubt her vision touched on reality for some:

> The ordinary person on the street was coming up to me and saying, 'Oh yes, great. I can see myself. I know somebody who . . .' etc. They welcomed the fact that for once they had somebody who was a real person, somebody they could identify with. They got frustrated with Hyacinth, they got annoyed with her, they felt her triumphs with her, but for God's sake she was a human being, she wasn't one of these cardboard blacks who at the end either becomes a lesbian or suddenly gets blackness. It doesn't work like that, people aren't like that. So the ordinary people welcomed the book. I got lots of support. It was really tremendous. But the radicals, they felt they couldn't say what I wrote was wrong, but they were saying I had no right to write it, I had no right to expose the black community. I believe their criticism goes back to white people again. It was not only what I was saying, but that white people were looking at me.[7]

This is the crux of the matter. Should the black woman writer temper her vision according to what she thinks white people will think when they read her book? If she wants to write about black women's experience for other black women, must she nevertheless keep one eye on how white readers will interpret it? Would this not allow her vision to be skewed, and ultimately corrupted, by white racism? On the other hand, can she afford to ignore how a racist society might appropriate her work and use it against black women?

Joan Riley is unrepentant. Her second novel, *Waiting in the Twilight*, traces the life of Adella, a black woman who came to Britain in the fifties to join her husband, and subsequently struggled to keep her family and home life together while maintaining some sort of dignity in a society which made very clear that dignity was definitely not something to which she had a right. When a black male colleague was asked his opinion of the work, his reply was: 'Oh, that depressing book about a woman who's a cleaner, whose husband leaves her, who suffers a stroke – too depressing, man. I hated it.' Joan Riley's second novel was unambiguous in its depiction of the oppression of the black immigrant woman in British society. Her radical critics shifted their ground: now her writing was too gloomy; black people's lives weren't really that dreadful – were they?

People say I write depressing books because I write about reality, basically. You know, one of the reasons I wrote *Waiting in the Twilight* was because again it comes back to the black intelligentsia, and me being horrified at the way they treated their parents; so many people are ashamed. If their parents are cleaners, they won't talk about it, or they talk about their parents as if they were all some sort of sub-species, and for me if you don't respect your elders that is the beginning of the end for your community.[8]

Once again we are confronted with the question of whether the novel reinforces white prejudices about black people in British society. Adella's husband is lazy, faithless and violent. Adella herself is a cleaner – a role whites conventionally associate with black women. Why reinforce that association rather than undermine it? Joan Riley responds with a question of her own:

Shouldn't we look beyond the mop and look at why she's a cleaner, look at who she really is? I see the woman behind the mop, because I don't agree with this thing that if you have a degree you're better, and the less status society gives to a job the more the person doing it is regarded as inferior. I feel the wisdom of older people has been lost because we have taken on a set of values which says that black is inferior, and the more black you are the more inferior you are, and if you are in what society terms a 'low status' occupation, the less brains you have.[9]

Joan Riley feels that her works celebrate a people often forgotten in the annals of history: people who may be as vulnerable and weak as Hyacinth or Adella, but who are not *only* victims; on the contrary they are 'survivors'. She feels that their presence in this country is itself evidence of their courage. Adella, for example, despite her many failings, is also a heroine by virtue of having made a voyage into the unknown, and, with no thought of travelling so far to be 'just' a cleaner, struggled to survive. As Joan Riley says of her protagonist:

When you talk about women like Adella, you are talking about women who left their countries, women who didn't even know where they were going. They didn't have accommodation, but they wanted to make a better life for their children, they wanted to give them an education. How many people now would get on a ship and go anywhere for their children? You talk about pioneers of the twentieth century: the greatest pioneers were the West Indians.[10]

She is therefore critical of those who accuse black women writers of presenting a depressing picture of black female life:

Some white people have said it [*Waiting in the Twilight*] was depressing, and one black person said it was all right to talk about Adella's life, but it didn't have any humour in it: what about all that black humour, we're always running around singing and jumping and laughing, what about all that? Yet white reality makes good books . . . We can sit down and read all this white reality and say, what a good book. If I'd put a white cleaner in *Waiting in the Twilight* as the central character, I don't think I would have got so much criticism. The fact is the lowest of the low in everyone's mind is a black cleaner, and the fact that I choose to say this person is not low, this person is a human being and I'm going to take you forcibly behind the mop is what I get a lot of criticism for. That's what all this talk about it being depressing is really all about.[11]

However, the question is, when does a representation cease being a long-awaited record of the lives of women who have been ignored or dismissed as worthless and become instead a culpable reinforcement of stereotypical images? Which is the more effective strategy? Do we want black women writers to encourage positive images of black women by creating heroines who are lawyers, teachers or doctors rather than cleaners and rape victims? Won't we then be accused of being 'unrealistic', or at least 'untypical'? After all, professional black women are still rather thin on the ground in Britain. Or do we prefer them to try to remain true to their own vision of reality, however grim that may be, in order that we may confront the painful complexities of our history? For that, perhaps, is the only way we can transcend it.

Part of the problem may lie less in the specific vision of one writer (i.e. this is *not* an issue about 'author's intention') than in the burden it obliges us to carry as representing 'black women's lives'. If there were simply more writing by black women (and black men for that matter!) representing a variety of visions of black women in the 'popular', collectively it might amount to a fuller, more complex and contradictory picture. Joan Riley herself feels that there is not yet enough of such writing available in Britain to supply a context which could sustain the force and grimness of her own work. In other genres, however, black women are visible via representations which are more obviously positive, and which counterbalance Joan Riley's particular 'realistic' vision.

Judith Jacobs

Judith Jacobs' face has become a familiar one in most households in Britain. For she plays Carmel, the black health worker in the popular television soap opera *EastEnders*. A twice weekly show, with an average audience of some 16 million, is potentially a powerful medium. *EastEnders*, like other popular soaps, gets wide coverage in the tabloid press and popular women's magazines; the actors who appear in it have become media stars. For many viewers, who are not themselves Eastenders, this *is* the East End, full of predominantly white 'cockneys', who may have problems but who know how to be 'jolly' in the pub! Similarly, for many people who are not themselves black, the black characters in it *are* black people. Issues about the National Front, unemployment, heavy policing and economic deprivation, which led to the events at Broadwater Farm, are of course repressed by this romantic fantasy of a small, caring and sharing community, in which everyone has a place and where social melodrama over Arthur's unemployment, for example, often makes Charles Dickens look understated.

In this scenario Carmel can certainly be seen as a positive representation: she is a professional woman, a responsible adult, who is in a position of some authority in relation to the predominantly white population of Albert Square. True, her introduction to the programme was focused on her affair with a (black) man some ten years her junior. But the 'scandal' of this was finally denied when the conflict between the man and his parents over the age difference was resolved by their acceptance of her. Moreover, she subsequently terminated the affair in an admirably 'mature' way.

Carmel's 'positive' representation in *EastEnders* hasn't invited much comment from the black community, although the depiction of the black family where the husband, Tony, is shown as lazy, the wife Hannah is shown as a nagging shrew, and their daughter is shown as a thief, has been very heavily criticised. Worse, there has been at least one exposé of racism among script writers and cast. Yet Judith Jacobs is quite defensive about this and the programme itself: '*EastEnders* is the only programme on television with a black family, yet it gets criticism.'[12] Well, it isn't any more, because the black family has been written out – some say as a direct result of racism! Judith Jacobs believes differently: 'People are generally scared, or wary, about putting black people on television.'[13]

How does Judith Jacobs feel about her role as an actress generally? Does she think of herself as 'just an actress', as so many of our more famous black stars are fond of referring to themselves? Or does she think of herself as a specifically *black* actress?

I feel I could never call myself just an actress, as opposed to a black actress, until I get offered a part where I can look at the script without thinking, 'My God, how can I do this without offending anybody?' I look forward to the day when I make something of a character without vetting the script first.[14]

Judith Jacobs has been an actress from the age of fourteen. She had her first real 'break' when she got a part in *Angels*, a soap opera set in a hospital, where she played – yes, you've guessed it – a nurse. She maintains:

I wouldn't do anything that would degrade or insult black women. If a black woman plays a prostitute, people think, that's typical. To offset that we need positive representation. I have played strong women, caring women, but why have I never been asked to play a psychiatrist or an accountant? Why are there not any black people in advertisements doing ordinary things like eating cereal or buying cars? Before we can get this positive representation, there have to be more black people behind the scenes, and in the decision-making positions. At the moment there are only two black technicians at Elstree: one is in costumes, the other in make-up. There is not one black producer.[15]

So does she think that positive representation on television, even if it does not accurately reflect the real position of black people in society, can change the way black people are perceived and perceive themselves?

Of course. The main reason why black people play so many negative roles is because they are the only ones they are offered. That's why I think *EastEnders*, with all its faults, was a good thing for black actors and actresses in this country. I would never play the archetypal maid, who had no sense, but there will be black people who will take those roles.[16]

How might this change come about? How can black actresses, who are so often called upon to play characters who are subservient, stupid or morally dubious, intervene in the dramatic media to present a specifically black and female perspective? Judith Jacobs feels that black actresses have something important to offer, both because there are so few of them visible in a mass medium like television, and because of their strength. Unlike Joan Riley, she does not consider the 'strong black woman' to be just a stereotype. Before we get on to the small screen, she believes the presence of black actresses will be felt in the theatre. Indeed, most of the cast of *No Problem*, the black Channel 4 sitcom in which Judith Jacobs was one of the stars, started out in the Black Theatre Co-operative, and are still part of it. It is through theatre, she suggests, that a black perspective is really given a chance to express itself, and it is here that her loyalties lie. 'I do not rely on the white system. My main commitment is to the Black Theatre Co-operative, where we can generate our own work, and do things that we all have a commitment to.'[17]

However, transferring positive representation from the arena of black culture to the mainstream may have its dangers. Might it not lead to white complacency – producers and viewers saying, 'Look, how wonderful, a black woman playing a doctor! Twenty years ago she would have been cleaning the wards or a prostitute brought in because her pimp had beaten her up. See what progress has been made!' There is also the problem of credibility. Given inner-city deprivation, abysmal educational provision, institutionalised racism, and sexism, these factors obviously reduce the chances of a black woman getting to be a doctor. Won't the positive representations be dismissed as fantasy? Does the black woman in *Dynasty* or the black female police officer in *Cagney & Lacey* empower us by supplying role models of wealth and success? Or do they insult us by ignoring the reality of most black women's lives? It is easy for us in Britain to imagine that the situation for black women in America is far preferable. But on what evidence do we base such assumptions? We are back to the question of realism.

One way out of this *political* dilemma may be to focus on a dimension which, for the purposes of this piece, we may call the *spiritual*.

Judy Boucher

Judy Boucher, a 35-year-old singer originally from St Vincent, rocketed to fame with her number one hit single, 'Can't be with you Tonight'. This song tells of a woman who can't see her lover because of her involvement with someone else. Now this may seem like a strong female perspective, a gaze in control of relationships and of self. Moreover these lyrics, sung by a black woman, constitute a welcome counter to all those sad songs about black women betrayed, deserted or standing by their men. But Judy Boucher sees it primarily as a love song which provides people with an opportunity to grope each other on the dance floor.

> I wasn't at all surprised that it was successful, just at the speed with which it become popular. I always felt it was a good song. In fact, someone said to me that this song is dangerous, because a woman told him that whenever it plays the men are all over her and he said, well, whenever it's played the women are all over me.[18]

Not the desired effect – or is it?

> 'Can't be with you Tonight' has a lot of feeling. I think a lot of people identify with the lyrics, that's why it touches so many people.[19]

Judy Boucher is one of our 'stars', who definitely believes that she is 'just a person', and therefore has no particular gaze – black or white, male or female. If you don't write about love, what do you write about? War? Well, we would like to think there are a few subjects in between, but let's not be too hasty in concluding that this indicates a total abdication of a point of view:

> I really don't want to write about war or nuclear disarmament, so I write about the nicer things. Everybody wants to be loved, and everybody wants a bit of romance. I basically just want to be a successful singer. I don't want any barriers which say because she's black she shouldn't be up top. Let's just accept me as a person.[20]

Some people might be led to conclude from this statement that Judy Boucher doesn't regard black singers whose black perspective does inform their music as 'people'. Or is she referring to the white music industry, which promotes non-contentious songs about love, and shies away from songs about South Africa or starvation in Ethiopia – unless, of course, the main movers and shakers are white. Rather than consider such questions in relation to her music, Judy Boucher prefers to compare her career to her role in rearing her children, which she considers more important than her singing, as can be observed from her following comments:

> I'm a lot more open with my daughter than my mother was with me. She has more freedom than I did, because in the West Indies they believe that if a girl doesn't go out to clubs or parties she won't get pregnant. Life doesn't work that way. I have a close relationship with both my children, and don't differentiate between my son and daughter. Whatever happens in singing, my children come first.[21]

So her children get the benefit of her strength and her point of view on the world: they perhaps get a non-sexist upbringing. But what of her audiences? All they get is a lot of lyrics about love and infidelity to turn them on. For what Judy Boucher wants is a fair chance for herself and for her family, in this world. And she appears to feel that this is synonymous with feminism:

> Sometimes I wonder what feminism is really. I would fight for equality, so if that means I am a feminist then I probably am one, because I would want a fair chance in this world same as anyone else.[22]

This kind of 'spiritual' and romantic gaze, focused on the family and the 'nicer' things in life, appears to transcend the merely political whilst actually ignoring it. We cannot pretend that popular music can change the world, 'Live Aid' notwithstanding; but neither can we dismiss it as meaningless and without important effects on how we see ourselves and our concerns. A lot of popular music is about 'love', and this in itself makes a statement about the significance of romantic heterosexual relationships in our lives. When songwriters and singers produce songs about other subjects they claim an importance for these. Are we content for black women singers to continue to imply, in their choice of music, that a 'good man' is all we need? The singer Janet Jackson has, in our opinion, a more pragmatic idea of how to inscribe a black female gaze in popular culture; it's 'a story about control, control of what I say and control of what I do'.[23]

We are not saying, then, that Janet Jackson's work is straightforwardly *positive*. Rather, we are arguing that black women need more control over where and how black female 'looks' develop in the future. This situation is clearly of wider political significance. Here, we have simply tried to show the strengths and weaknesses underlying individual strategies.

Where do we stand?

It will be clear from the above that black women are becoming visible in a wide range of popular cultural forms, making their presence felt, their views known. But the mere fact of being black and female is no guarantee of a homogeneous black female perspective. These three women view their respective roles very differently in terms of how they relate as prominent, creative individuals to black women in general. We may regard each as adopting a different strategy in order to achieve our goal: making a black female gaze felt in mainstream cultural life. Each strategy may be seen to have its own advantages and disadvantages, its own way of intervening, its own risks. Joan Riley is convinced that only by telling the grim truth as she sees it can she transcend that grimness and begin to change it, whatever the risks of white appropriation for stereotyping. Judith Jacobs feels that it is important for black women to secure positive representations of themselves in mainstream popular culture in order to alter the image of black women held by themselves, by black men, and by white people – even if such representations may not always be entirely 'realistic'. Judy Boucher, by contrast, is not concerned with wider issues of racism and sexism in our society; she is concerned with her right as an individual to participate in the culture 'like anyone else', and therefore challenges any assumption that her blackness and femaleness either disqualify or obligate her.

Perhaps all three strategies have a part to play in establishing black women's presence and perspectives in British culture. Each can tackle problems to which the others are blind, each avoid risks the others cannot. Clearly, for any strategy to work there needs to be a genuine plurality of approach. This particularly applies, we think, to Judy Boucher's 'just like anyone else' individualist stance: should this become the dominant mode of intervention for black women? Personally, and politically, we could not regard this as a progressive development. Yes, in one sense we know that we are 'like anyone else'. But then again we aren't: we are black and we are women; we have our own reality, our own history, our own gaze – one which sees the world rather differently from 'anyone else'. As black women we need to assert this difference, whilst keeping one eye on our collective strength!

10
The Status of Women Working in Film and Television

Anne Ross Muir

Recent feminist debates have used psychoanalytic theory to explore why the 'male gaze' is dominant in mainstream cinema. But there may be a more concrete (if related) explanation: that the masculine point of view is prevalent simply because men control the industry.

One has only to watch the credits roll by at the end of a film or television programme to realise that women are sadly under-represented in the worlds of cinema and broadcasting. One major reason for this state of affairs is that women have been discriminated against, and have been barred from many jobs in the film and television industry. It is a depressing picture. Over the years a large number of very talented women have tried to break down those barriers – and failed. Pessimists point out that such discrimination is so entrenched and longstanding that it could take generations to wipe out. It is not surprising, therefore, that many women don't even try to enter the industry. They are defeated before they begin.

Yet it is because of this attitude that women are in danger of losing an unprecedented opportunity to sweep aside the barriers which have kept them out of key jobs in film and television. The conditions for change are right. For example, many of the major broadcasting organisations have now agreed, in principle, that women should have an equal opportunity for careers alongside men.

It is, however, a fragile opportunity. If past experience is anything to go by, such policies may make little difference unless women take them at their word and make things happen. It's up to us.

There is no doubt that the present situation is desperately in need of improvement. In 1975 the results of an enquiry into the status of women in the film and television industry conducted for the ACTT (Association of Cinematograph, Television and Allied Technicians) showed that the position of women had not improved since the Second World War and had, in fact, deteriorated.[1] In the 1950s women worked in a wide variety of grades and represented 18 per cent of the labour force within the industry. By 1975 they constituted only 15 per cent and had been buried in ghetto jobs, that is, in jobs held almost exclusively by women, which are often lower paid and which are given little status.

By 1986 the situation was hardly better. The figures for employment provided by the ITCA (Independent Television Companies Association) showed that of 306 camera operators, only 12 were women; there were only 8 female sound technicians compared to 269 male ones; while of 1,395 engineers, 19 were women. On the other hand, none of the production assistants or secretaries were male.

A survey of the situation of women within the BBC conducted by Monica Simms and released in 1985 reached similar conclusions.[2] In the BBC's top grade of personnel, there were 159 men and only 6 women, while only 8 per cent of staff in the category which includes heads of department, senior producers and correspondents were female. When I interviewed Michael Grade, then Controller of BBC1, he admitted that, at his level of decision-making, there were no women involved.

The film industry is, if anything, worse. It's true that the National Film School has now increased its intake of female students from 1 out of 25 when it opened in 1971 to around 30 per cent in the last few years. Yet although qualifications from the NFS have been a passport to success for a number of male graduates, it has not helped many women to break into mainstream film-making. Sir Richard Attenborough can be moved to tears at the racial discrimination suffered by Gandhi yet women (black and white) are more likely to be scrubbing studio floors than directing movies and that doesn't seem to worry anyone.

In fact, it is easy to get the impression that women have simply *never* figured in the film and television industry – except as performers, production assistants and secretaries. Yet all recent research by film critics and historians has shown that women helped to lay the foundations of the modern cinema.

The movie business started up around the beginning of the century and Hollywood was soon established as one of the main centres for film-making. In most histories of those early days women are allocated a place on screen, portraying girlish innocence or vampish sexuality. However, this had little to do with the reality of their careers. Mary Pickford might embody the masculine ideal of demure femininity in her films, but in real life she was a hard-headed business woman, setting up United Artists (which was still a major film company until very recently) with Douglas Fairbanks and Charlie Chaplin. Women worked in every part of the industry. The critic Molly Haskell has counted at least 26 female directors in the period

1913–23.[3] Another film historian, Antony Slide, refers to Dorothy Dunn, Grace Davison and Margery Ordway as just three of the successful camerawomen in those early days.[4] John C. Mahoney points out that the majority of important screen writers between 1914 and 1930 were female, including Frances Marion, June Mathis and Anita Loos, who won Oscars for *The Big House* and *The Champ*.[5]

Many of these women were outstandingly successful. Lois Weber was one of the best-paid directors in Hollywood during the period 1916–34. Dorothy Arzner's 1932 movie, *Merrily We Go To Hell*, was one of the highest grossing films in a period of forty years, according to *Motion Picture Daily*. Leontine Sagan directed *Mädchen in Uniform*, which was voted one of the ten best pictures of 1933 by *Film Daily*. Women were particularly distinguished as editors. Barbara Rose Maclean was Darryl Zanuck's editor and received several Academy nominations, before finally winning an Oscar for *Wilson* in 1944. Margaret Booth worked for Louis B. Mayer at MGM and has been described by the noted film historian, Kevin Brownlow, as 'one of the great motion picture editors'.[6]

Even in those early days, however, there were signs of unease about allowing women a creative identity and power. Molly Haskell argues that one reason why women were allowed to direct films at all during these formative years was because it was not yet considered a glamorous job. Nevertheless, the critic Nancy Ellen Dowd has discovered that some of the work of Alice Gay Blaché (who directed almost every kind of movie in Hollywood during the early years of this century) was wrongly attributed to Emile Cohl and Victorin Jasset.[7] The same researcher also states that in 1922 the work of Alla Nazimova was released under the name of her husband, Charles Bryant.

It is clear from such examples that the process of discrimination had begun even in those early days of the cinema. As the film industry became less of a maverick operation and more a part of the economic establishment, that process gained momentum. When cinema's potential for profit and power was realised, the social conventions and prejudice against women began to have a greater impact. During the twenties and thirties women were gradually elbowed out and discouraged or actively barred from creative and decision-making jobs in the industry.

The process was reversed during the Second World War, however, when women had to take on jobs previously done only by men. By that time there was a thriving British film industry and women like Dorothy Thomson, Roseanne Hunter and Yvonne Fletcher were given the opportunity to direct. At the BBC women were offered the chance to move up the career ladder, provided they gave up their jobs when the menfolk returned from fighting. Some did lose their promotions when that happened but others were able to hang on. Only a few years later the television network began to expand, attracting many of the bright young men and leaving the way clear for women to establish themselves quite successfully in radio, where some rose to the rank of Controller.

Generally, however, once the war was over the pattern of discrimination was re-established. A study conducted by the Policy Studies Institute in 1968 concluded that most of the really senior women in the BBC had taken advantage of unprecedented opportunities during the war and had no obvious successors. The results of a follow-up study by the same group begun in 1979 confirmed those findings and even suggested that the position of women at the top in the BBC had deteriorated.[8]

Within the film industry, the experience of Kay Mander was typical. She started out as a 'continuity girl'. When the war broke out, she was given the opportunity to direct and write scripts 'because there weren't any men around so it was much easier to get work'. When peace returned she went to Java, where she continued directing films with her husband. A few years later, following her return to Britain, she co-scripted and directed *The Kid From Canada*, which won a special award at the Venice Film Festival. In spite of this success, she says that 'from 1957 onwards, I failed to get any satisfactory work as a director, so I went back to feature continuity'. Michael Balcon, one of the most influential figures in British cinema at the time, told her 'quite flatly, that women couldn't handle film crews and anyway there weren't any suitable films for women to direct'.[9]

Given such attitudes, it is not surprising that the role of women in the film industry declined. Some were able to find work in the less lucrative and less prestigious areas of documentaries or educational and training films. As in the pre-war days, any creative power which women did have in feature film-making was often either simply not recognised, or else it was disguised. Thus, Nancy Ellen Dowd's research revealed that Ida Lupino's first film, *Not Wanted* (1949), was credited to Elmer Clifton. Two years later, in 1951, Muriel Box had a similar experience in Britain, when, having already won an Oscar for co-scripting *The Seventh Veil*, she decided to try her hand at directing. She records in her autobiography *Odd Woman Out* that 'the hardest part initially was to persuade artists to accept an unknown director and a woman into the bargain. To avoid difficulties . . . agents were told it would be a joint directorial effort between my husband and myself.'[10] Even though she then went on to direct over a dozen international features, Muriel Box is listed in Roy Armes' *A Critical History of British Cinema*, published in 1978, as the 'script-writer wife' of Sidney Box.[11] Since she retired from the cinema there have been almost no female directors in feature film-making and many of the prejudices against women have changed little since the 1950s.

A few women continued to be successful as editors in the post-war period, among them Adrienne Fazan, who won an Oscar for *Gigi* and who also cut classics like *Singin' in the Rain* and *An American in Paris*. Margaret Booth went on to become one of MGM's top executives as Editor-in-Chief. Yet her promotion was exceptional. As John C. Mahoney points out, very few female editors made the step up to directing, unlike many of their male colleagues.

The impact of such historical research is to demonstrate beyond any doubt that women have not been excluded from key positions in the film and television industry because they couldn't do the work. Whenever women have been given the opportunity, they have proved themselves as competent as their male counterparts and, in many cases, far outshone them. Their exclusion is not only unfair to women, but represents a great loss of talent to the film and television industry.

The lack of female representation in the media also has wider implications. It affects us all – not just those women who would like careers in film and television. The EEC has targeted the media as being instrumental in any campaign against sex discrimination, recognising that television, which is heavily viewed by children and is the main source of news for adults, can shape social attitudes. If a film or television company is a mini sexist society, with women congregated in the lower-paid service and support jobs, how can we expect the image of women produced by it to be anything but sexist?

For example, most sportscasters are male, as are the majority of those who produce, film and record our news programmes. Accordingly, it is not surprising that women's sports are rarely treated seriously or at length and that women and the issues affecting them are often ignored in the news. Betty Heathfield, the wife of Peter Heathfield, general secretary of the NUM, told an audience at the Edinburgh Television Festival in 1984 how a rally of 10,000 miners' wives to support their husbands' strike action was ignored by the media. Even the language used on news bulletins can render women invisible – for example, by referring to '500 men' who have been laid off, when there are often a number of female workers amongst them.

If there are no true records of women and their lives, the way is clear for a false picture to prevail which can then be misused. Researchers exploring the US National Archives found that news film of women in the pre-war era referred to them as 'girls' and portrayed them at events that supported this image, such as beauty contests or Easter parades. Yet during the war women were no longer shown in such a frivolous light; they were shown working for the war effort. Thus the images of women presented were not a documentary record, but tailored to suit social and political expediency.

In more modern times, we are presented with situation comedies, dramas and commercials portraying women in roles which bear no relationship to the reality of most of our lives. Some entrepreneurs still make large sums of money from broadcasting beauty contests which treat women's bodies as objects to be rated. We are bombarded by commercials which use images of women to sell everything from cars and washing machines to alcoholic drinks and record albums.

To sum up, the exclusion of women from many of the key jobs in film and television means that we are denied opportunities for work which is not only challenging, creative and well paid, but which can influence the ways in which women are perceived and view themselves in our society. We are also being shut out from an important means of self-expression and a form of communication which could link women across this and other countries. As it is, children are being shown a one-sided (basically male) view of the part that women play in our society. Women themselves are presented with role models which are very far from reality, which make individuals feel isolated and aberrant when they do not conform to the stereotypes, and which tend to inhibit, rather than stimulate, women's belief in their own strength and capabilities.

But I did say at the beginning that conditions are right for change. For example, we are now at a stage where almost every ITV company advertises itself as an equal opportunities employer. This may not be the case in practice, but it does mean that they are recognising their responsibility in this respect, and are receptive to the idea of women working in television. They can now be challenged to live up to their claims in a way that they couldn't before.

The same is true of the BBC. In 1987 their Board of Governors included three women. According to Monica Simms, it was at their suggestion that her survey on the status of women within the BBC was commissioned. As a result, she has come up with 19 recommendations, including the two-year appointment of a Women's Employment Officer, job sharing and flexible hours – all heady stuff for the BBC. Moreover, in 1985 Michael Grade reached a landmark decision –

made purely on principle, he insists – not to broadcast the Miss Great Britain Contest, because it was out of step with the modern role of women in our society. According to Grade: 'The important thing was to have made the public statement as to why we were dropping it.' Nothing is more likely to end the degrading spectacle of beauty contests than the withdrawal of the funding and publicity generated by television coverage.

More than any other company, however, Channel Four has forged a path through prejudice to give women a chance. They have shown a willingness to hire women in key positions and to broadcast programmes giving serious consideration to issues affecting women. In addition, their policy of commissioning material from outside producers has created sufficient work to allow many women to leave dead-end jobs with the BBC and ITV and set up their own production companies. Channel Four has also provided the backing for a number of workshops which, in turn, have given many women access to training and facilities.

Women also have potentially far more political clout in broadcasting than we seem to realise. Television companies differ from ordinary businesses in that they are answerable to government-appointed bodies. Yet Nigel Willmot has discovered that only 7 out of 34 BBC governors and only 8 out of 27 IBA members over the past ten years have been female.[12] As voters, tax-payers and television licence holders, women have the right to demand fairer representation. Individual complaints may have little impact, but if women's groups around the country, from the most conservative to the most radical, could make common cause on this issue then they would undoubtedly be heard and effect a change for the better.

Within the film industry there has been less dramatic progress, largely because it has a freelance, constantly moving workforce, which makes it more difficult to organise campaigns for reform from within the ranks. On the consumer side of the industry, however, there has been a growing interest in films made by women about women's lives. A number of movies – mostly from the United States or Europe – which have been written and directed by women, and in which the central character is female, have been highly acclaimed in this country. Money talks – and the box office success of a film like *Desperately Seeking Susan* established that movies made by women about women are worth backing, thus paving the way for other female directors, writers and technicians.

The argument in favour of more productions of this kind has been given weight in recent years by a new wave of academic scholarship.

When E. Ann Kaplan began lecturing about women and film in 1972, she found that she was working in a vacuum and that there was very little serious research done on the topic.[13] Now there is a body of feminist film criticism which has been able to identify some of the ways in which the cinema discriminates against women and perpetuates images which are harmful to all of us.

There has also been a remarkable groundswell of support for equal opportunities from the trade unions associated with the entertainment industries – largely because of the tireless campaigning of some very brave and committed women within their midst. Many unions have now appointed a member of staff who has specific responsibility for women's issues and have set up committees on equality to lobby for improved working conditions and opportunities for women. One outstanding example of how successful women can be when they organise is evident within ACTT. Since the appointment of a full-time Equality Officer in 1981, women (who represent only 20 per cent of the membership) now participate at every level of union management. As a result of their efforts to change attitudes amongst their male colleagues, they have gathered support to pass motions condemning pornography and endorsing equal opportunities, maternity and paternity benefits, workplace nurseries and the appointment of a full-time Training Officer.

It all adds up to one thing: equal job opportunities for women in the television and film industries have been given support, in principle, by employers, trade unions and critics alike; but unless women make it happen, it may well never progress from principle to practice.

The BBC is under financial and political pressure. It may find it easier to make some token concessions to Monica Simms' recommendations and quietly drop the rest. Certainly, the BBC has ignored some damning evidence of discrimination against women in the past, following reports made by the Policy Studies Institute. Michael Grade admitted, 'I personally point out whenever I see the worst examples of sexism and will pull the producer or head of department aside and make them think a bit harder. That's about the best I can do. You can't make edicts about a subject matter like this.' From this statement we can deduce that the BBC feels no active commitment to the fair representation of women in its programmes. Within the ITV companies the recent economic recession has cut advertising revenue and could lead to a period of retrenchment and unwillingness to promote change. There are also many men who see the advancement of women as a threat to their jobs. Others resist change because it would disrupt the pattern of their lives. Some men base their identity on an image of themselves as superior to women and are unwilling to give that up.

In addition, the direction the film and television industries seem to be taking could make it far more difficult for women to press for equal opportunities in the future. One emergent trend is the move towards cutting permanent staff jobs in television and film production companies and casualising the workforce. This may not bode well for women. Freelancers are notoriously hard to keep track of. Contracts can be very short, and hiring and firing done on the spur of the moment, making it very difficult to implement or monitor equal opportunities policies. Short-term staff are less likely to join forces and campaign for their rights for fear they won't be re-hired. There is also the danger, already prevalent, that permanent jobs will be given to men, while women are employed on short-term contracts and become an expendable workforce, so that whenever there are cutbacks, female workers are the first to go.

Another development with serious repercussions for women is the transition to ever more sophisticated technology. Many jobs which previously demanded little or no knowledge of electronics now require considerable technical expertise. For example, editing has traditionally been thought of as a creative, artistic job in which women have been very successful. But with the advent of video, many companies are now recruiting their editors from amongst the engineering staff, which means that, since there are so few women working in technical areas, there may be almost no female editors in the future. If women do not get a toehold in, and grow with, the new technology, then we may be left hopelessly behind.

In other words, women must act *now*, if we are to take advantage of opportunities for equality in film and television. What is needed is a greater number of female workers in the industry, preferably in key positions. All the evidence suggests that the more female candidates there are for jobs in film and television, the more women are successful. According to Christina Driver of BETA (British Entertainment Trades Alliance), the same percentage of female applicants as male ones are successful in getting jobs in the BBC. It's just that fewer women apply in the first place, so fewer end up being employed. It is important also that those who do apply are well qualified for the work. Otherwise, if employers do hire a woman, they may do so for the wrong reasons, because she has nice legs or seems biddable. It is only too easy for employers to sabotage equal opportunities policies by appointing a woman who is not qualified and who can't do the job. That's the best excuse they could have for not hiring more women.

So the situation is in the balance. The potential for overcoming discrimination against women in film and television is there. And only when we have complete access to these important media for self-expression and mass communication, when we really share control of the means of production, can we fully establish a 'female gaze' within popular culture and present women's point of view in all its fascinating multiplicity.

11

Cashing in on the Curse
Advertising and the Menstrual Taboo

Ann Treneman

The year is 1958. The month is May. The magazine, *Good House-keeping*. A woman sits with her back to us – a stranger without face or front. Medium-length brown hair curls over her neck; bare shoulders contrast sharply with the back of a dark, one-piece bathing suit. Her upright posture is as controlled as the perfect wave in her hair. She is without life – a static image sitting in the left-hand corner of page 16, as wooden as the original pulp material of what she is meant to be selling. She is an ad for tampons.[1]

But how images can change. Jump ahead 28 years and check out *Company* in the mid-1980s. Oops! You've just caught sight of her before she roller-skated off the page – a vision of activity in emerald satin shorts and tank top, long blonde hair streaming, arms pumping. She's just rounding the corner, wheeling past a department store window as she heads into a night-time world of neon and excitement. Left behind are the store window mannequins – specimens of a world without motion, a frozen place populated by statues wearing bathing suits and staring vacantly. A ball and chain lies discarded on the pavement, unlocked by the Lil-lets 'key of freedom'. Freedom herself is on the move . . .[2]

Eclipsed in her wake is that lifeless form of 1958. How dated that primness now seems. And how absurd the slogan 'Don't be home-bound when you should be beach bound!' when there's not a grain of sand in sight. 'Feel confident in a bathing suit', we are told. But it's hard to feel confidence in this woman – who can't even meet our gaze, a female gaze, much less the probing eyes of a beachful of people. We are told that no one will guess her 'secret'. But we already have. For this woman – mocked by the vacant eyes of the store window mannequins of the 1986 ad – still seems shackled by *that* secret. In contrast, the 'street-wise' emerald-clad whiz on wheels seems to have thrown off such shackles for good. She's not looking at us either, but that's because she's too busy living her life! She's unlocked herself from *that* kind of thinking – and the ball and chain stand abandoned as proof.

But which way is the Lil-lets 'key of freedom' really turning? The 'liberated' roller-skater may be able to 'travel light' because of her choice in tampons, yet that image harbours a meaning which can only increase the burden for menstruating women in our society. Far from being a step forward, the advertising image of the eighties is in many ways a step back from the uptight non-swimmer of the fifties. For such ads sell more than products to women; they sell shame as well – and it is the contemporary image which carries the heavier load. The 'key of freedom' is a con, and one that can only succeed by co-opting the female gaze. Its power to do this derives from the way it marries the slick advertising techniques of modern times with the strictures of an ancient taboo against menstruating women. Hedged in by such a dynamic duo, is it any wonder our eyes play tricks on us, and that we are seduced by a pairing which confirms our imprisonment in the modern menstrual taboo?

Such a statement must seem slightly fantastic on first reading. We live in an age in which the meaning of the word taboo has somehow been transformed. This is perhaps best revealed by turning again to the world of advertising. This time the female gaze falls upon two figures, their lips meeting above a piano keyboard. It seems a kiss of passion, a stolen moment, a realised desire. Perhaps it is the music that aroused such feelings – even as they embrace he flourishes a violin, she caresses the ivory keys. Such a romantic time bubble seems far removed from menstruation. But the two lovers do have a message for us. For theirs is a story of taboo – or Tabu, to be precise. It is, the ad tells us, a forbidden fragrance. For the ad viewer, it is a concoction which is a brew of mystery, romance, excitement.[3]

Such exotic notions of taboo make it difficult to associate the concept with the monthly mini-dramas of menstruation. Worries about smells and stains, and how to dispose of bloodied towels and tampons that won't flush, seem mundane – hardly the stuff of which taboos are made. The concept seems far more applicable to those cultures which still retain a visible form of taboo. The 'menstrual hut' can be observed by anthropologists and the surrounding rituals duly recorded. The evidence of our menstruation taboo is not so easily identified.

And when it is found, how drab it seems by comparison! 'The concentration with which today's pre-pubescent girl ponders the menstrual manuals supplied by the napkin manufacturers and probes the mysteries of the tampon box is only a pale vestige of the rituals observed throughout history and earlier to mark the onset of menstruation,' note the authors of *The Curse*.[4] Yet all is not necessarily as it seems, as is evident from these thoughts recorded in the chapter 'Barbarous Rituals' in *Sisterhood is Powerful*:

> Woman is . . . being told nothing whatsoever about menstruation, so that you think you are bleeding to death with your first period; or, being told all about it in advance by kids at school who titter and make it clear the whole thing is dirty; or, being prepared for it by your mother, who carefully reiterates that it isn't dirty, all the while talking just above a whisper and referring to it as 'the curse'. . .[5]

Paula Weideger describes a girl's introduction to the menstrual taboo in her book *Female Cycles*:

> The sense of shame about menstruation is instilled as soon as menstruation begins. From the time of menarche, a girl learns to be ashamed of her body; she is told it limits her freedom, just because of the way it naturally functions . . . Where there is a vacuum [of education] there is plenty of folklore to fill it: 'Hide menstruation, don't go swimming or wash your hair or take a bath or touch plants . . .' These are some of the rumours whispered to young girls. How are they going to learn to be proud of being a woman?[6]

Such whispers pass along our invisible taboo as surely as menstrual huts define it in other cultures. And it is this voice that is relied on in ads for menstrual products. For it is crucial to the success of any ad that those reading it will be able to grasp its message. To ensure this, ad-makers exploit systems of knowledge that are woven into a society. A good example of this process is described by Judith Williamson in her book *Decoding Advertisements*, when discussing the Catherine Deneuve ad for Chanel No 5. The success of this ad – which is composed of nothing but Deneuve's face and the name of the product – hinges on our prior knowledge of Deneuve as glamorous, French, and beautiful. Possessed of this knowledge, we can transfer it to the product and translate what this means to us: Deneuve and Chanel No 5 are French, beautiful and glamorous and, if we use this perfume, we can be too.[7] This is a lie of course. Short of radical plastic surgery, few of us can ever hope to become like Catherine Deneuve no matter what perfume we use. We know this, but, because in our culture beauty is so prized, the ad can still succeed: we might buy the product because a dab of scent might make us *feel* more glamorous. The makers of this ad are thus relying on two systems of knowledge for the ad to work: readers must be able to grasp what Deneuve is, and they must want the

ies that she embodies for themselves. Williamson calls the bits of
kground information we bring to the ad 'referent systems' and
ys: 'To fill in the gaps (in ads) we must know what to fill in, to
decipher and solve problems we must know the rules of the game.'[8]

Of course the biggest rule of the advertising game is simple: 'Thou
must sell' is tattooed upon the consciousnesses of the Saatchi and
Saatchis of this world. And while a referent system provides a basic
ingredient for this maxim, it is the powerful tool of mythical image
which ensures that this commandment will be realised. Such images –
surveyed by Roland Barthes in *Mythologies* – are premeditated
conjurings dedicated to the production of hidden meanings. Barthes
describes how this process works, using the example of a picture in
which a young black soldier in a French uniform is shown saluting
with eyes uplifted: 'I see very well what it signifies to me: that France is
a great Empire, that all her sons, without any colour discrimination,
faithfully serve under her flag, and that there is no better answer to the
detractors of an alleged colonialism than the zeal this young black
shows in serving his so-called oppressors.'[9] Thus a simple 'natural'
picture, evoked in such a way as to rationalise a nation's global
colonialism, infects the reader with its meaning.

A key aspect of mythical imagery is that, while appearing perfectly
'natural', its meaning has been constructed for us. This is particularly
obvious in advertising where the success of an image is gauged by its
ability to convey the right sales message. Thus ads prey upon our
stock of previous knowledge, using familiar objects and concepts in
order to allow their constructed meanings to flow effortlessly into our
thoughts. It is a conjuring-trick and a very sophisticated one at that.
For the magician pulls a rabbit out of a hat and we are not impressed –
we know this is unnatural, a trick of some kind, and treat it
accordingly. But the mythical image – masquerading in its 'natural-
ness' – tends to evoke a different reaction. Barthes says that if we read
such images innocently, we will accept them as fact.[10] Even if we read
such images suspiciously – deciphering and analysing – the concealed
meanings are hard to shake. The most cynical of us, if honest,
probably do see Chanel No 5 as imbued with some kind of intrinsic
glamour. Even when we resist the myths, they often connect with or
feed into other female mythologies.

Such is the process at work in modern menstrual product
advertising. For the ad industry listened to our mothers' whispers
(menstruation is a burden that must be hidden) and transformed them
into fact (the embarrassingly visible ball and chain) and then used its
imagery (a 'liberated' roller-skater) to create a palliative message

designed to sell (tampons can free you too). How different such a process is from the voices of our mothers or friends. For the production of manipulative meanings has acted upon those whispers like a voice synthesiser: amplifying and distorting a folklore into an ideology of institutionalised shame.

This process has a history. For the taboo existed long before the ad industry pounced upon it. Our dirty, bloody menstrual 'problem' cannot be blamed solely upon the fertile imagination of ad creators. Its roots lie within our society – in an attitude to women and their monthly cycle of fertility that is intent on obscuring a process that the average woman undergoes around 400 times during her lifetime. 'The emphasis is on behaving normally during the menstrual period, and be she housewife or career woman, or both, today's woman is determined to prove that she can do her job "like a man" even when she is feeling most like a woman.'[11] These words, although alluding to modern times, also seem to have been true of 1921, when the first Kotex towel appeared on the market. It could be argued that such a product was created to make life easier on women who were fed up with washing and wearing menstrual diapers. But the first menstrual product advertisement did not carry such a straightforward message. Instead, American readers of *Good Housekeeping* opened the magazine in 1933 to find a woman in a shadow for the 'new phantom Kotex'. A key selling point of the product was that it was thick and 'protective' but had tapered ends to help 'eliminate those tell-tale outlines'.[12] And so the seeds of advertising shame were sown, ironically in the very ad which broke the taboo of silence on the subject.

And through the decades those seeds have thrown up a continuing array of guilt-ridden menstruators. The shadowy woman of the thirties in turn became the dainty demure creature of the fifties. In the sixties menstrual ads reflected the rise of youth, becoming a curious shrine to the young and sporting woman who, by the seventies, also had an obsession with being 'natural'. Only the forties model, who was depicted as using menstrual products to get on with war work, represented a real change; and she lasted only as long as society needed her.[13] Now, in the eighties, we face sophisticated and 'liberated' images of women who, conversely, suffer terribly at the mere thought of a leaking towel, an inactive moment, watery weight gain or 'unfeminine' smells. The woman of the eighties may be portrayed as roller-skating into freedom, but in reality she's probably heading to the nearest store to buy some more protection.

The trick of the modern menstrual ad campaign is to masquerade shame as liberation – by co-opting the ideas behind the modern

Women's Liberation Movement, while undercutting them with a meaning that is constrictive. It is specifically directed toward the female gaze; men can only grasp ads for menstrual products by their second-hand knowledge of the taboo and of menstruating women. (To test this, try imagining what an ad for sanitary products aimed at the male gaze would look like.) Only a woman knows first-hand the effects of the taboo, and whenever the subject of menstruation comes up within an all-female group, the anecdotes flow. A woman not only immediately recognises the ball and chain of the Lil-lets ads – she knows what it feels like to wear a bulky sanitary towel wedged between her legs and she knows the feeling she has when, suddenly, a red stain starts to spread over her clothes. The ads prey upon this first-hand knowledge and exploit such concepts as 'liberation' and 'freedom' to seduce us into thinking that there is a ready-made individual cure to what is, in fact, a societal curse.

This is how the female gaze is co-opted and it is a sleight of mind achieved by the cleverest of means. Take for example the recent Dr White's ad featuring a man dressed only in lacy bra and French knickers. Holding his head in his hand, he appears to be in some pain and the headline asks us: 'Have you ever wondered how men would carry on if they had periods?' Several friends came to me while I was researching this piece, waving the ad, saying: 'This is great! Can you believe it! What do you think?' Well, I must confess that, at first, I *was* delighted. The ad, its depiction of cross-dressing itself breaking another taboo, carried a direct allusion to something women have long suspected: 'At the risk of sounding sexist, we must observe that men can be terrible babies when they're ill . . . If men had periods, the cry would go up for a three-week month, never mind the five-day week.' The ad goes on: 'The fact is, it's women who have the periods. . . . And far from carrying on, women are busy, for the most part, soldiering on.'[14]

The message is 'Women are superior to men' – and what a seductive pitch it is! Of course, helping us carry the torch in our silent struggle is the good doctor: 'After 104 years in the business, we aren't naïve enough to imagine we could make your period a lot of laughs, exactly. But we're certain we can make it less of a (dare we say it?) bl**dy nuisance.' Such coyness masks an interesting twist on the idea that shame sells. We emerge from reading this ad – our egos nicely massaged and our sense of humour tickled – feeling pretty good. It has gone beyond the area of many menstrual product ads. It only occasionally alludes to our burden, and presents Dr White as our bosom buddy who helps 'make your life more bearable, whatever kind of periods you have to put up with'. But with friends like this, we don't need enemies. For in addition to reinforcing the idea that our periods are a burden that we must hide, the doctor has just sold us the idea that the reason for our superiority is that we have been so successful in hiding our shameful secret!

The moral behind such an effort is that you don't need the ball-and-chain imagery of Lil-lets to make sure the customer feels liberated. And, in the case of menstrual ads, you can always be sure there's a sting in the tail. Take for instance another Dr White's effort: the ad features a cartoon couple with the man thinking, 'I just hope my darling that this will last forever . . .' while the woman's bubble says, 'I just hope this towel lasts till I get home. . .' Another delightful image that poses the problem of menstrual anxiety in a non-threatening way. The man is shown as a romantic fool, and this makes us laugh a little. The accompanying copy would also be laughable except that its message is no joke: 'In actual fact, the ultimate in embarrassing events happens to very few women. But that doesn't stop the awful possibility from haunting pretty well every one of us, does it? (When did you last wear a white skirt on your heaviest day . . .?)'[15]

Such words illustrate the customer image that must prevail at Dr White's – the consumer as neurotic. Another example is found in an ad in which one page is completely taken up by a pinkish-coloured square headed 'Deep blush'. The opposite page reads: 'To stop you going this colour, our new slim towel is individually wrapped . . .' and goes on: 'To find out if you're a 100 per cent liberated lady, answer this question: "What would you do if you spilt the contents of your handbag and your spare towel landed at your feet (or, worse still, at his feet)?" Drawing on our 105 years' experience, we'd say that, even if you have decidedly 1986 attitudes to life and love, chances are you'd blush to the roots.'[16] By first identifying its readers as liberated the ad takes the sting out of its pathetic message: that we live in such fear of anyone finding out our 'secret' that we must buy a product just to guard against something falling out of handbags.

Who is talking to us in menstrual ads? On the face of it, the 'voice' of the Dr White's ads is that of the oh-so-understanding expert. In our society, that usually means a male. But while I have assumed that Dr White is, in fact, male, he does not speak to us directly. Instead, there is an intermediary – someone who is at pains to be understanding and someone who knows our worries and our fears. Such a voice, when addressing menstruation, has to be female. (Imagine it read out loud, on television or radio: a male voice would seem incongruous.) The 'voice' is that of a wise woman, a woman who knows best, a knowledgeable version of our mothers. She soothes us, assuring us that it is normal for liberated women to be embarrassed by menstruation, and then offers us a solution. She addresses our consciences, and we can't help but listen.

The voice in the Lil-lets 'ball-and-chain' magazine series also appears to be that of a woman. She has less to say than Dr White's intermediary, but then her message is slightly different. She is, literally, a commentator, and her job is to tell us what the world of the 'liberated' Lil-lets woman is like and then advise us on how to achieve it. Thus she says of the roller-skater: 'Street-wise. Personal Hi-Fi. Personal wheels. Personal hygiene. More than ever, small is beautiful. Neat, discreet, Lil-lets tampons slip into any pocket. Let you travel light.'[17] This is also the voice of a wise woman – but a distinctly hip one. The message of liberation here is not the wordy understanding of a Dr White's ad. Rather it is that of an admirer of the roller-skater and her message: 'If you buy this tampon, you can be free too.'

Using a female 'voice' to sell shame to women is ironic, but the world of menstrual advertising is overladen with ironies. Another is that by their very existence, the ads appear to break the taboo upon which they rely to sell their products. But while the ads do break the silence surrounding menstruation, they are promoted and constructed in such a way that the very thing they are breaking ultimately remains intact. The ads are placed so that they are likely to be seen only by women: they are regularly found in women's magazines, but I have yet to see one on a hoarding or in a general circulation publication – and that goes for newspapers like the *Daily Mail* which have traditionally pitched themselves at women. By restricting the ads as much as possible to the female gaze, they keep within the limits of the societal belief that menstruation is for a woman's eyes only. (TV ads, of course, vary from this as they cannot be pitched at such a sex-selective audience. Research has yet to be done on how the male gaze reacts to the sanitary product ads being beamed into their front rooms, and a study on this would make for fascinating reading.) The taboo is also evident in how the ads are constructed. Menstrual products usually reside in bathrooms yet, as is the case with toilet paper, in the ad world they never seem to get near the porcelain. It is also unthinkable to show them being used. Thus advertisers find themselves plunging tampons into clear water to prove their points on absorbency. And the colour red itself seems to be forbidden: witness the lengths Dr White's went to in its Deep Blush ad to replace the red blush of embarrassment with the colour pink. Blood must not even be suggested, let alone actually mentioned. The language of the ads is often coy and euphemistic to the point of being adolescent. Why copywriters believe that we have to be talked down to in this way can only be speculated upon. Whatever the reasons, the result is that these ads – which purport to break the taboo – use language that only serves to reinforce it.

If ads are limited in where they appear and what they contain, they show no such reticence when it comes to discovering new guilty secrets – for the modern woman has much more to worry about than 'tell-tale outlines' (as if that weren't enough). In the 1980s, we are under an advertising mandate to act 'normal' at all times – a state that evidently has nothing to do with our monthly cycles. We are to remain active; we must not show any pre-period bloat; we must guard against 'unfeminine' smells; and generally organise our lives so that no one even suspects that periods exist. Fifty-five years after the first towels came on the market, our periods have become a complex series of monthly problems requiring a massive undercover effort. And in adhering to the requirement to be 'normal', we 'liberated' women support a 500 million dollar industry manufacturing approximately 50 products.[18]

It seems a high price to pay to hide a few fluid ounces of blood each month. But the idea that menstrual shame can be eradicated in the time it takes to buy a packet of tampons has been so inculcated that it is hard to see our compulsive buying of menstrual products as anything out of the ordinary. Indeed, the menstrual product industry has been so successful in selling this idea to women in Britain that a 1983 World Health Organisation survey found that only one per cent of UK women surveyed used home-made protection, a phenomenal finding given the cost of the mass-manufactured products. (A price boosted in the UK by VAT – evidently the Government still sees menstrual products as luxury items even if no one else does.) This compares with somewhere like Egypt where 27 per cent of the women used no protection at all and 57 per cent used home-made towels.[19] Such a comparison begs a number of economic and cultural explanations, but it is revealing that such behaviour is almost beyond imagination in Britain where our costly crusade to hide menstruation is viewed as 'normal'.

Part of the reason that we are such avid consumers of menstrual products is that the purchase of a box of tampons and/or package of sanitary towels provides peace of mind. But we also get something else. For the survey also showed that only seven per cent of the UK women thought that menstruation was 'dirty'.[20] Yet one needs only to look at the referent systems of ads (Lil-lets ball and chain or Dr

White's dramatic copy) to realise that we do see menstrual blood as dirty – so much so, indeed, that not only must it be hidden from view, its presence must not even be suggested. Thus we are told to buy towels that look like 'freshen up squares or sachets of shampoo' to avoid embarrassment.[21] As Weideger says: 'The taboo tells us that menstruation must be hidden, we feel ashamed of menstruation and menopause as a result, and by acting upon shame, we reinforce the taboo.'[22] But such a cycle of shame is invisible. For our thoughts on menstruation, like those of the 93 per cent surveyed, rely on the belief – incessantly pushed by the myths of menstrual product advertising – that menstruation is only 'dirty' if it is not concealed through use of the correct products.

So, in one neat purchase, we solve our monthly 'problem' and, in the process, buy the idea that we really don't see menstruation as anything 'dirty' at all. Thus the taboo – so cleverly concealed as a 'normal' fear in advertisements – itself becomes cloaked. And we, its 'liberated' victims, become ever more deeply mired in a pattern of thought that denies our sex. For the taboo affects more than our buying habits; it influences how we think of ourselves.

In her book *Implicit Meanings*, Mary Douglas identifies several social uses for the taboo among 'primitive' societies. The most applicable to our 'advanced' society would appear to be that the taboo acts to assert male superiority and to reinforce separate male and female spheres.[23] The first can be seen in the now hackneyed, but oft-repeated, jokes about emotional females who, during *the time of the month*, can't be trusted to be logical. The second is summed up in these interconnected thoughts from Weideger:

> While Western women do not walk about in the drapery of Purdah, the veils of secrecy, shame and disrespect similarly constrict the female personality.

and:

> Modern-day women are not required to live in menstrual huts . . . because women have so conscientiously and completely internalised the assumptions underlying the taboo. It is as though we have constructed menstrual huts around our hearts and minds and the building blocks of these huts are shame and guilt.[24]

In *Female Cycles*, Weideger examined her own self-made hut and discovered that she immediately discounted such of her feelings as were associated with her period – irritability or sexual desire, for example – as 'unreal', as somehow not a part of the real 'her'. This habit of denying our own feelings during menstruation is reinforced in advertisements which prescribe 'normal' behaviour for the menstruating woman (bicycling is normal but taking a nap is strictly out). She also recounts the views of the husband who refuses to take his wife seriously if she's near her period and the tale of the girl who began her first six months of fertility by sticking toilet paper into her underwear rather than pluck up the courage to ask her mother to buy sanitary towels for her.[25]

This is the direct, and indirect, burden that women carry as a result of their periods and it is a weight made ever heavier by modern advertising. In 1958 the embarrassed menstruator couldn't face the camera. She was embarrassed despite her 'liberating' tampon, and she certainly wasn't overly keen on this going to the beach business. The referent system works; we all recognise her problem as being 'natural'. But the myth that tampons can cure it fails because the image itself isn't convincing. At least this is the impression of hindsight. This ad reflects a time when women weren't quite sure how they were supposed to act if they had a period. Now we know, and if the ad were to be redrawn today you can bet that woman would be running towards us – splashing in the waves, laughing and lissom. She wouldn't admit to any problems – and that is a problem for those of us trying to live up to her image.

However, it would be wrong to hold up the 1958 image as an ideal. For she is only a generation removed from the happy-go-lucky eighties. And rooted to some degree in both images is that shadowy 'phantom' of half a century ago. For advertising is an insidious medium – given a sound idea, it knows no limits. Its unchecked growth is characterised by Williamson as: 'The constant reproduction of ideas . . . which are used or referred to "because" they "already" exist in society and continue to exist in society "because" they are used and referred to . . .'[26] In 1933, an ad creator looked at a societal taboo and packaged it to sell Kotex. Over the years, ads have continued to build upon the maxim that 'shame sells' until, gradually, the selling point became so well known that the women populating such ads need show no shame at all. Like periods themselves, it became a hidden reality.

Perhaps the ultimate irony of menstrual advertising is that it seeks to instil a desire to erase the very thing the product is designed to service. Ad-makers harp continually – if increasingly subliminally – on the problems of menstruation, with the goal of implanting the idea that a product can erase a problem. Given the power of advertising, and its ability to co-opt not only our liberation movements but our periods as well, it is perhaps 'natural' that many women, given the choice, would prefer to forgo periods altogether. This is precisely the finding of Weideger's survey, which found that 69 per cent of women would rather not menstruate – an answer she views as a result of taboo pressure and one that acknowledges, however negatively, the belief that men's biological make-up is the superior model.[27] It can only be speculated how much ads themselves – by reinforcing and, I would argue, to a certain degree transforming, the taboo – have contributed to such a climate.

In this article, I have argued that the female gaze is co-opted in an especially underhand way by menstrual product advertising which purports to minimise the very problem that it feeds. The co-option of the female gaze is not new, of course; it is constantly being sought out by ad-makers pushing everything from margarine to fashion, cars to baby-strollers. But such ads do not usually rely so exclusively on the female gaze; they may be pitched towards women readers, but their appeal is not necessarily limited to them. Nor are they dependent upon a referent system like the menstrual taboo, which is so ingrained in our culture and has such a grip on women's everyday lives. The power of this taboo is the real force behind sanpro ads, and its ad-assisted pull is what blinkers the female gaze so successfully. Shame will continue to sell only too well until the taboo is significantly altered or enough people openly defy it, taking away some of its power.

There are attempts being made to do this. The campaign seeking to remove VAT from menstrual products brings the subject out in the open, as does the discussion of how the taboo has contributed to the lack of truly hygienic sanitary product disposal units in public lavatories.[28] Others have sought to confront the taboo more directly; one idea being that women having periods could wear something red to work and 'work quietly and peacefully, and expect fewer demands'.[29] Another suggestion was to give parties for girls who have just started their periods. Such suggestions may seem laughable in our society, but they would not seem so far-fetched if our attitude towards menstruation were to change to one that prized and welcomed it.

Or imagine that women suddenly, magically, had a choice about whether to menstruate. What panic that could cause in advertising circles! Shame would be out as a selling point, for menstruation could hardly be presented as a burden then. Instead, it would have to be sold as something to be desired, something to be proud of, something to choose. We would be urged to have periods and, of course, to buy towels and tampons – perhaps bulky ones which (like female codpiece equivalents) advertised our fertility and were carried around in brightly coloured cases clearly marked SANITARY PAD HOLDER. The possibilities are intriguing – for capitalism would want to keep on cashing in on the curse, even if it became a blessing. But without the blinding nature of the taboo, perhaps the female gaze would be more in control of how it viewed, and reacted to, such ads.

Gloria Steinem, in 'If Men Could Menstruate', examines how society might change if it were men who shed blood once a month. 'Clearly menstruation would become an enviable, boast-worthy, masculine event,' she says, and imagines this exchange on the street corner:

'Man, you lookin' good.'
'Yeah man I'm on the rag!'[30]

But men don't menstruate. As a recent Librofem ad proclaims, 'Periods are part of being a woman',[31] and until they're not, advertisers seem hell bent on doing everything to make us pay their price for this biological fact. In the 1980s, that means that being 'on the rag' seems destined to remain something to bemoan, not to shout about. And that really does seem a shame.

I would like to acknowledge Sue Brattle for her help and advice in preparing this chapter.

12
Care to Join me in an Upwardly Mobile Tango?
Postmodernism and the 'New Woman'

Janet Lee

As we move into the late eighties, it becomes clear that the only certainty in the emotional arena is confusion. So much has happened to sweep away all the ground rules that a consensus seems almost impossible. All those ideals that were once held as absolute truths – sexual liberation, the women's movement, true equality – have been debunked or debased.[1]

The above quotation, taken from an article in *Elle* magazine, entitled 'The Age of Confusion', in many ways reflects the current postmodern predicament. For some, postmodernism is the catch-phrase for a contemporary malaise, a term used to define a society characterised by fragmentation, eclecticism and nihilism, whose cultural forms include pastiche and parody; one in which life is played out on a surface without depth or meaning, in an eternal present where images are no longer merely representations, but are themselves reality. In Western society, postmodernists argue, meaning has collapsed, and with it political certainties. We can no longer believe in what Jean-François Lyotard calls the 'grand narratives' of progress, truth, technology and utopia.[2] In short, the meta-narratives which were once characteristic of bourgeois society are no longer viable. Instead, we are left with a multiplicity of shorter narratives, which, arguably, allow space for intervention and rupture.

As a prime site for the representation of ideas about 'life on the surface', popular culture attracts considerable attention in post-modernist politics. As Lyotard has argued:

I believe that the only line to follow is to produce programmes for TV, or whatever, which produce in the viewer or the client in general an effect of uncertainty and trouble. It seems to me that the thing to aim at is a certain sort of feeling or sentiment. You can't introduce concepts, you can't produce argumentation. This type of media isn't the place for that, but you can produce a feeling of disturbance, in the hope that this disturbance will be followed by reflection. I think that's the only thing one can say, and obviously it's up to every artist to decide by what means s/he thinks s/he can produce this disturbance.[3]

This is a strategy with important political implications, which have been utilised by feminists in an attempt to 'disturb' representations and definitions of the 'feminine' and the 'masculine', exploring the power relations that authorise some representations and invalidate others.

However, there are problems with Lyotard's thesis. Above all, it can be argued that, in dismissing one set of grand narratives, Lyotard is, in turn, simply creating another – one which advocates fragmentation. Hence, as the earlier *Elle* quotation says, it is not surprising that 'a consensus seems impossible'.

I am primarily concerned with the place of feminism in these postmodernist debates. Does postmodernism also signify postfeminism? According to Craig Owens, in his essay 'The Discourse of Others: Feminists and Postmodernism',[4] postmodernism evolved from feminist ideas and practices. Taking feminism as his paradigm, he therewith highlights a paradoxical feature of postmodernist debates – their neglect of feminism as an important issue. Yet, as Rosa Lee argues:

Owens, in pointing out this 'remarkable oversight', reappropriates and subsumes feminist insights and interventions under the rubric of 'postmodern thought'. Owens negotiates the 'treacherous course' between postmodernism and feminism by a fairly simplistic means of incorporating that which has been excluded (that is, the work of feminist artists and writers on the issue of sexual difference) into the mainstream 'corpus' of ideas and theories of postmodernism. As marriages go, this one appears to be decidedly unequal: the insistent feminist voice speaks in a vacuum.[5]

Essentially, what Owens has done is transform a multiplicity of differing, even dissenting, feminist positions and strategies into one homogeneous, universal movement, implying that their sole aim was to attack patriarchal meta-narratives. This is a distortion: a single unified subject position was never constitutive of the feminist gaze. It might sound simplistic, but, in a nutshell, Owens doesn't appear to realise that not all feminists are alike!

Feminism(s), along with many other 'isms', have developed within
an increasingly fragmented political scene. Feminists have challenged
the frontiers (created by history, by modernity, by men) of what can
be represented and what cannot; and although their impact has been
enormous, there are clearly many areas where feminism has only
scratched the surface – and not only in relation to postmodernist
theories. So how can we begin to talk about *post*-feminism? Who are
the post-feminists? Who are these 'new women'?

The 'New Woman'

The term 'new woman' seems to reappear with nearly every
generation – from the 'new woman' of the late nineteenth century,
who so shocked society with her 'independence', to that of the present
day, who so preoccupies the theorists of 'post-feminism'. Through the
decades it has served as a recurrent sales technique. At different
periods Dior and Chanel both pioneered clothes for the 'new woman';
it was marketing magic that made them rich and 'infamous'. During
the Second World War the propaganda machine got women to work
by celebrating the 'new woman' as one who could labour and love in
perfect unison. And when the war was over, that very same 'new
woman' was the one who preferred housework to paid work.
Similarly in the sixties, the enjoyment of sex was presented as yet
another role for women. The advent of 'the Pill' meant that women
were suddenly being encouraged from almost every direction to have
more sex.

It seems that whenever someone has something to sell to women –
be it clothes, careers or contraception – we are urged to change
ourselves into the 'new woman' of the moment, by adopting whatever
definition of liberation or modernity is current and buying whatever
signifies that we have not been left behind as the 'old woman'.
Representations of the 'new woman' are ultimately bound up with the
politics of identity. The techniques change, but essentially what's
happening is that women are being sold a variety of subject positions
along with their new clothes and contraceptives. The self is being sold
to 'you' – who, naturally, do not want to be left behind.

In the late eighties, bored by feminism and its unglamorous
connotations (after all glamour is big business), the media in general,
and particularly advertising agencies, have decided that we've *done*
feminism and it's time to move on. We can call ourselves 'girls', wear
sexy underwear and short skirts; because feminism taught us that
we're equal to men, we don't need to prove it any more. Which seems

to mean something not so very different from earlier, sexist, encodings of women's sexual availability. Take, for example, the 1987 'Desert Boots' campaign from Clarks. The 'new man' is displaying his naked foot sexily for the woman's gaze. But what of the woman? High heels, sheer stockings, with a flash of bare thigh visible above her stocking top. Is this post-feminism or anti-feminism?

Women's magazines like *Cosmopolitan* and the newer, slicker *Elle* have actively engaged with the concepts of post-feminism and the 'new woman'. *Cosmopolitan* opened up the options for her in the seventies, with articles brashly celebrating the female orgasm. But in representing women's independence as synonymous with heterosexual sex and love, it could be argued that it constructed the liberation of women in the interests of men's sexual desire. *Cosmo* exhorts the female reader to construct herself through self-discipline, and the reward for this is physical pleasure – or, more specifically, sexual pleasure. It does this by constantly offering advice on how to be fit, fun and generally fabulous. It posits questions that you can't say no to – 'Do you want to be sexy/stylish/successful?' It insists that you can and you will. *Cosmo* always assumes its readers are part of a heterosexual couple, or aspiring to be; whatever the text says, there's no mistaking the images. The 'new woman' *Cosmo*-version is the sexy woman. Sex equals not only fun, but independence and success. And *Cosmo* claims to have the knowledge that will tell you how to have it all – sex, success and liberation.

While it would be inaccurate to define *Cosmopolitan* as a post-modernist magazine, some of its feature articles have recently shown evidence of responding to, or perhaps initiating, certain changes which might be termed postmodernist. Of late there has been extensive media coverage of those classified as 'Yuppies' – young, upwardly mobile people on high salaries which enable them to live in a consumers' paradise. They can transform advertising and magazine images into reality for themselves, because they can afford to buy the products behind those images. The important thing about 'Yuppies', however, is not just that they have a lot of money. It is not a matter of crudely displaying wealth, but of aesthetics and taste, and how individual items contribute to an overall image and lifestyle – with the emphasis on 'style' rather than 'life'. A stereotypical 'Yuppie' would drive a black Golf GTI, use a black leather Filofax, own a flat furnished with matt-black furniture and wear designer clothes probably by the fashion designer Katharine Hamnett. The concept of the 'Yuppie' can be linked to postmodernism in so far as both evince the importance of images, are concerned with style rather than content, and have dispensed with history.

The Capitalist Feminist

A recent article in *Cosmopolitan*, entitled 'Cheers for the Capitalist Feminist', by Leah Hertz, engages with this new materialism:

> What has gone wrong is the hijacking of the women's movement by the left, whose interpretation of feminism is in terms of the rejection of capitalism and with it women's traditional roles, the family structure and the economic rat race. The rationale behind their rejection of capitalism was that, as women were under-privileged, and as capitalism was the oppressor of the under-privileged, women who wanted equality had to reject capitalism. What utter nonsense! The route to women's equality is through economic and political power.[6]

Leaving aside the implication that feminism is a thing of the past ('their rejection of capitalism was that . . .'), what Leah Hertz's argument neglects is the power of the patriarchal structures informing economic and political power. It blithely ignores the statistics about women's relatively lower incomes than men's and the link between this and the perennial problems arising from 'women's traditional roles' in the family structure. Even the capitalist feminist has to take ultimate responsibility for childcare arrangements.

However, we cannot just dismiss the implications of this article or, more generally, of cultural phenomena like *Cosmopolitan*. Leah Hertz is clearly appropriating feminist ideas, but from a different political perspective than that of the women's movement, in Britain at least. And *Cosmopolitan* is not itself monolithic. There are levels of co-option, but also of genuine consonance with feminism. For example, it does not concern itself predominantly with domestic issues in the way that the older women's magazines do; and its articles often deal seriously with practical feminist issues concerned with health, employment, the law, and so on. In this way, for many readers, it may map out a route, however unsophisticated and stereotypical, towards feminine independence.

Elle magazine, being newer (at least in this country, where it was first introduced in 1985) is more in tune with 'style' magazines like *The Face* and *I-D* which appeal to both women and men. Concerned with life on the surface, it exudes glamour and wealth, and a good deal of effort is required to distinguish between the editorial material and the advertisements. In true postmodernist fashion, *Elle* documents consumption as a metaphor for life: the only choice is to consume – everything from clothes and cooking to personalities and politics – and all are accorded equal importance. This articulates with a whole series of other media developments – which elevate the importance of the image over the written text. But *Elle* develops a postmodern aesthetic in a more clear-cut, self-conscious manner than many other media forms, in its flattening out of the world by elevating trivia and then trivialising everything else.

Essentially, *Elle* is *the* magazine for the 'new woman' of the eighties – cool, confident, stylish and rich. In this magazine independence is no longer sex but money: there are no problem pages and no articles on orgasms. *Elle* is for women who have been there and done that – for middle-class, educated, professional women, who are perfectly in tune with the new materialism, and exploit it with style.

Yet I really enjoy *Elle* magazine. I can't resist at least glancing through it on display stands. It *is* stylish, and that stylishness is appealing. Its standard of production is very high, with beautifully shot photographs. I rarely read the written text, but when I do I find that it doesn't tell me what to do and it doesn't keep offering me advice. It takes it for granted that women are articulate, confident and independent; that they have a sense of humour. That, in short, they are grown up enough to work out for themselves what they should do. It assumes, too, that they have been informed by feminism – as 'The Age of Confusion' article illustrates. This was a long article in which journalists Robert Elms and Brenda Polan delivered their views on the 'battle of the sexes'. Brenda Polan, long-time editor of the *Guardian* Women's Page, in arguing for a 'new' kind of feminism, points to differences between contemporary feminism and that of twenty years ago. She points out that if feminist voices are not so audible in the late eighties:

> it is simply because the latest generation of women to reach maturity does not need consciousness-raising in any formal or structured way. It has sucked in feminism with its mother's milk and takes its essential equality for granted. Its confidence is not so easily undermined as ours was and it no longer needs to examine the whys and hows of sexism; the research has been done, the analysis made.[7]

To a certain extent I agree with Polan. Representations of feminism have changed. The feminist is no longer always assumed to be a brown-rice-eating, dungarees-clad dyke.[8] There is certainly no longer (though I doubt there ever was) just one feminism, but rather feminisms marked by a multiplicity of difference, of class, race and age; but also of varying theoretical positions – essentialist, culturalist, structuralist, separatist, Freudian, anti-Freudian, etc.

Where I differ from Polan is in her assumption that we can now stop analysing, stop researching. This implies not only that we now know everything we need to know about the world from a feminist perspective, but also that culture is static. Far from being at the end of the story, as *post*-feminism implies, I think we are still only at the beginning. Walk down any street, into any dole office, into any classroom, any factory or office; take a look around and listen and I doubt one could still seriously argue that we are in a post-feminist era. Post-feminism is a luxury the majority of women can't afford. Along with the 'new woman' it is a media concept, with its eye on the profits. The 'new woman', if there is one, is rich, she can afford to consume clichés. But working-class women, struggling with unemployment, the double shift, cuts in welfare services, etc. need more practical feminist ideas. They can't afford to buy post-feminism any more than they can afford the magazines which advocate it.

But young women are not currently buying feminist magazines either. So we can't just wash our hands of the 'new woman'. On the contrary, we should try to look through the cracks which are so obviously being plugged by the fashion for this new style 'liberation'. There are clearly lessons to be learned from the marketplace about women's needs, which neither feminism nor post-feminism is adequately meeting.

13
Feminism and the Politics of Power
Whose Gaze is it Anyway?

Shelagh Young

It's exactly twenty years since the first bra was burnt and the Women's Lib movement was born. Those were the days when a woman's place was in the home, unequal pay was taken for granted and men always offered you their seat in a crowded bus.

Today we have the Pill, an Equal Opportunities Commission, a Sex Discrimination Act, and even the office groper can be sacked for sexual harassment . . . But a lot of women would argue that being liberated is a mixed blessing.

Daily Mirror, 8 December 1986

It has long been a complaint of many women that introspection has gradually displaced insurrection as the defining factor of feminist politics. In 1986 the supposed achievements and failures of members and ex-members of the women's movement were paraded before us in an astonishing number of books and articles devoted to reviewing those difficult 'feminist years'. But for some, when the tabloid newspapers began to reflect on 'twenty years of feminism', this 'celebration' of feminism began to look suspiciously like a wake . . .

To those who feel threatened by feminist politics and ideas, defining and categorising them is probably a way of making them safe. After all, summing up twenty years of 'women's lib' in terms of its effect on the 'office groper' doesn't exactly exaggerate the impact of feminism on contemporary society. But why have feminist theorists also been so concerned to map out both a feminist past and a feminist future? I would argue that there are two major motivating factors behind this latest bout of intense introspection: the development of various intra-feminist struggles and the emergence of the mysterious realm of generational politics. To put it bluntly, having grown old while fighting many a bitter battle in the name of feminist politics, veteran campaigners now have to come to terms with the fact that to most young women their vision of a feminist future is a big yawn. However, I do not believe for a moment that such a response indicates the failure of feminism; paradoxically, this apparent resistance is a measure of the force of feminism's impact upon contemporary cultural forms and practices.

That Was Then and This Is Now

The second wave women's movement in Britain emerged over twenty years ago in the context of an exciting 'internationally oriented left radicalism'.[1] Yet there is no denying that it soon appeared to be dominated by women who were white, middle class and formally educated. Some of these feminists, whether airing their views in the relative privacy of their consciousness-raising group or writing some enormous theoretical tome, clearly assumed that they spoke for all women. Black women, older women, working-class women and lesbians are just a few of the marginalised groups whose dissenting voices have since felt the need to fight for a place within British and American feminist discourse. As a result of such struggles feminism itself has become a nebulous concept, subject to endless discussion and redefinition. For example the 'outrageous' proposals of 'equal rights' feminism are now not only encoded in the law but are seen to be largely a matter of common sense. This absorption of feminist ideas and principles suggests a widening of the terrain of feminist thought, which now enjoys an unprecedented degree of popularity.[2]

Feminism in the eighties is more than just an 'interesting area of study', for although its influence upon mainstream media is by no means stable, the ebb and flow of feminist intervention in these areas is relevant to everyone. However, while academics struggle to extricate some coherent threads from a tangled web of feminist theory, the media seem happy to repeatedly wheel out Germaine Greer in order to represent feminism to the masses. The 'personal' may well be 'political', yet as feminists begin to contemplate their relationship to the mainstream and the place of feminism within popular culture, we find ourselves wondering whether the popular 'personality' can really be 'political'. It seems that at the heart of the current debate there is a disconcerting confusion over the role of the political activist and the exact nature of political struggle. After all these years it isn't really clear what being 'in' the women's movement means when for many – especially younger women – the term no longer has the power to impart a sense of belonging to, or involvement in, a common struggle.

For me, the burning question is not whether a feminist activist can enter the mainstream media without 'selling out', but rather in what ways feminism, as a theoretical and political practice, has made any significant impact upon the dominant media and their audience. The painful debates around the question of differences between women are a reminder that, when arguing the case for a feminist gaze and an effective feminist intervention in mainstream culture, it is prudent to consider just who is looking at whom!

Post-feminism, Postmodernism and the Problem of the Popular

Sometimes it seems that the dominant intellectual project of the last few years has been to prove that the *popular* is also the *political*. Women have led the way in challenging the high/low dichotomy that has traditionally dominated our notion of what constitutes culture or art. In seeking to undermine the conventions of artistic production and exhibition, feminist artists have often incorporated so-called 'domestic' crafts such as weaving, knitting and embroidery in their work. This aspect of feminist art practice has evolved as a challenge to 'the hierarchy of art forms which led to the domination of painting and sculpture in the first place', as well as working to validate women's traditional work in the crafts.[3] Judy Chicago's controversial work 'The Dinner Party' probably remains the most widely publicised example of this practice. Impressive by virtue of its sheer size and its exclusive dedication to women's achievements, 'The Dinner Party' is described here by Michèle Barrett:

> The central conception is a triangular dining-table, along the sides of which are placed symbolic representations of thirty-nine women: pre-Christian goddesses; historical figures such as Sappho and Boadicea; women like the suffragist Susan B. Anthony and the artist Georgia O'Keefe. (This dining-table echoes the 'last supper' so significant to our male-dominated Christian culture.) Each of the figures at the table has a place setting of a runner, cutlery, goblet and plate, whose different designs evoke her particular character. From these thirty-nine women the names of 999 less resoundingly famous, but still reasonably well-known, women radiate in inscriptions on the 'heritage floor' . . . The dining-table itself totals nearly 150 feet in length, each woman's place setting using about three and a half feet of space. The combination of this impressive scale and

the lavish, beautiful, solid, ceramics and embroidery made the experience of being there an obviously moving one for many women.[4]

Women have certainly felt 'moved' by the experience of viewing 'The Dinner Party', but many were moved to express discomfort rather than admiration. Chicago's use of vaginal imagery in each sculptured place setting and her uncritical ranking and selection of the 'great women' whose names feature in her work has attracted charges of essentialism and élitism. Another problem raised by 'The Dinner Party' concerns its equivocal status as a work of art: should its exclusive occupation of a whole floor of the San Francisco Museum of Modern Art in 1979 be seen as a subversive triumph for feminist art practice or as its co-option by the art establishment? If the latter, what does the relegation of 'The Dinner Party' to a warehouse in Islington on its GLC-funded exhibition in 1985 signify?

Both events certainly attracted a large number of women but in Britain, feminism's enthusiastic reclamation of quiltmaking, knitting and weaving as hitherto underrated women's 'arts' probably reached its popular creative climax with the construction of a four-and-a-half-mile long patchwork dragon at Greenham Common. Weaving its way around the perimeter fence, this stitched-up serpent evoked comforting images of fireside sewing circles presided over by Granny Greenham with her bag of scraps. As a symbol of domestic creativity the dragon has a place, but why are so few feminists equally willing to applaud the less cosy examples of women's cultural production? Dressmaking is also a traditionally female pastime but where can we find a confident celebratory reclamation of women's work in the high fashion industry? Lonely is the woman who turns up at a dragon festival wearing a designer frock; we should ask whether *designer dykes* or *designer feminists* exist anywhere other than in the imagination of Julie Burchill?[5]

Clearly what constitutes feminist 'art' or political practice is very much dependent on how the commentator defines feminism. The roots of feminism's homespun philosophy that values the amateur over the professional, the shabby over the chic, can be found in socialist politics. In Britain feminist discourse has tended to be dominated by the Left and more specifically by socialist feminists. Thus it is hardly surprising that women who seize power, and who are seen to be actively and unashamedly contributing to and participating in the capitalist system of production, are generally frowned upon within feminist circles. Feminists, and the Left in general, are caught on the horns of a dilemma: should they crave or scorn popularity and profitability? Play the system or fuck the system?

A simplistic equation of financial success with the loss of political credibility has led some women to imply that 'success' and 'feminism' are totally incompatible. For Marilyn French 'success' is a wholly undesirable goal and is antithetical to 'women's values'. In her analysis success 'demands the sacrifice of almost everything in life that does not advance power'.[6] Author of the bestselling book *The Women's Room* (the novel which purports to 'change women's lives'), French is no stranger to the phenomena of success and power herself. Does this make her less of a feminist, or, following the logic of her own argument, *less of a woman*? Of course it doesn't; but 'success' for feminists remains a troublesome issue. Many women have been justifiably critical of the recent growth of feminist publishing into an increasingly lucrative and competitive industry. As Grace Evans explains:

> The marketing of political ideas creates contradictions. If feminist books become more easy to get hold of, so much the better. If the books become prestigious, then so does feminism. Or does it? Perhaps only feminism as defined by the books in the mainstream. How do ideas fare in the vagaries of the market place? If feminist publications come to be sold primarily through mainstream outlets, then it is the larger, richer publishers whose titles will be favoured and we have already seen how their choices tend to omit certain categories of women's writing; the writing of Black women, particularly Black British women and Third World women.[7]

Michèle Barrett has shown that cultural politics are crucially important to feminism precisely because they involve struggles over meaning,[8] yet coming out as a *Dynasty* addict can still be a problem for feminists. Although various studies have examined the ways in which the subject 'woman' has been constructed in the discursive formations of the popular media, until recently there have been very few investigations of the ways in which feminists relate to, or influence the popular. Of course there have been many valuable studies of women's magazines (by Angela McRobbie and Janice Winship, for example) and an enormous amount of feminist research into contemporary cinema (by Claire Johnston, Laura Mulvey, and Annette Kuhn among many others). But we still need to look more closely at the internal contradictions and tensions that affect feminism's relation to popular culture. If feminism is to remain a radical or subversive political force women cannot afford to simply emulate either the old Left's dismissive disdain for mass culture or the new Left's apparently indiscriminate endorsement of anything that appears to be popular. As Judith Williamson stresses:

> . . . often potentially radical drives and desires take the forms offered within the status quo (e.g. charities are fuelled by altruism, wearing 'way-out' clothes may symbolise the wish to disrupt, etc.). But that doesn't make the forms themselves radical. Politically, we are prepared to distinguish between the way things are and the way they might be. Why can this not be applied to popular culture as well?[9]

For me the title of an article about *the* female pop idol of 1985 spelt out the difficulties that haunt this area of political analysis. 'How I learned to stop worrying and love Madonna . . .' was essentially a celebration of one woman's rise to stardom, of her manipulative manoeuvres on the way to the top and of a playful irreverence which clearly had an appeal for millions of teenage girls.[10] The rapacious relation to men that formed part of Madonna's public image undermined the label of 'Boy Toy' on her painted jacket, yet she was still an unlikely feminist idol. After all, Madonna's image encapsulated a wanton celebration of consumer capitalism and her self-designation as the ultimate 'Material Girl' was hardly an advertisement for socialist feminism. When Madonna broke the rules the media applauded her wild sexuality, which contrasts sharply with their treatment of feminist nonconformism. Many feminists justifiably resent the media for constructing a derisory image of the drab dungareed dyke whose most playful pastime consists of peering into her friends' vaginas with a home-made speculum.

While it is true that the media in general have not been overly sympathetic in their portrayal of feminist women, and especially of lesbians (who need not identify themselves as feminists in order to get a raw deal), many feminist women do perpetuate a sort of alternative puritanism which can be very boring indeed. Consciousness-raising groups have proved tremendously empowering for many women, but they have also worked to suppress what is now seen as the 'problem' of pluralism. Far too many women have been alienated by the constraining influence of feminism's puritanical politics. Who needs to feel patronised by a sussed-out sister who has 'moved on' from wearing cosmetics and skirts, when for thousands of girls, clothes and make-up are the tools of their teenage rebellion? Long before Madonna bounced into the charts, adolescent girls were irreverently and immodestly strutting their stuff to the chagrin of parents and teachers. Arguments over the length of my skirt, the height of my heels and the thickness of my eyeshadow were once crisis points in my struggle for autonomy. For me, feminism promised a merciful interruption to the apparently normal feminine progression from adolescent style wars of independence to post-menopausal battles of the bulge. No feminist wants women to confine their rebellion to the limited realm of personal appearance, but the strand within feminist discourse that stresses the 'authenticity' and political potential of a 'natural' look doesn't do justice to the women who dare to dress up.[11] Ironically, in an era that some would argue is marked by a dangerously apolitical celebration of artifice, many feminists, while appearing to believe in the social construction of the gendered subject, are failing to delve beneath its surface. Mirroring the pathetic patriarchal tactic of assessing women not by what they say or do, but by their appearance, the 'authentic' feminists are forgetting that the natural 'look' is as carefully constructed and laden with meaning as any other style. Today, two features of the 'natural' female body – the absence of make-up and the presence of body hair – have become the over-simplifying signifiers of the feminist subject.

The problem posed by Madonna was that she neither looked nor spoke like a really 'right-on' woman. In fact, in order to justify her love for Madonna, Sheryl Garratt had to turn to the fictional narrative of the film *Desperately Seeking Susan*, which, towards the end, has Madonna and her co-star Rosanna Arquette holding hands together 'in triumph'. This was the image, says Garratt 'that meant we could relax and admit all along, we'd loved Madonna'. But isn't it interesting that Garratt should think that 'we' were ever not relaxed about Madonna? Clearly the 'we' of Garratt's text addresses a particular group of women. Garratt is really speaking to the semi-professional feminists, to women who have served their time as timid neophytes in a respectable number of consciousness-raising, therapy and women's studies groups and emerged ready to point the way forward for womankind. Hitting such dedicated politicos with a new concept is, as Garratt assumes, bound to throw them into crisis. What 'we' have all forgotten in the headlong rush to pontificate about popular culture is that some women were always relaxed about Madonna simply because they were never familiar with those strands of feminist thought which have contributed to feminism's own form of puritanism.

For those who *know* about feminism and particularly for those who believe that feminist politics must necessarily be linked with the socialist tradition, Madonna was a problem. After all, while her style may have been a little anarchic and her blunt candour on the subject of sexuality refreshing, her overall strategy was hardly revolutionary:

> I like being with men. I like working with men. I like pulling out all the stops and trying to figure out how to get my own way, how to get what I am after. And if that means being slightly underhand and teasing them, or flattering them or whatever, I don't give a damn. I'll just do it. It's often a very calculating and manipulative way of going about things, but I've always done that.[12]

Madonna speaks? Well no, actually that was Edwina Currie, the Tory MP whose carefully constructed, and just slightly risqué, image has made her a political star. Madonna and Edwina are in many respects two of a kind – they enjoy a rare degree of financial independence and control that only exists at the level of fantasy for most women. Their success embodies a partial fulfilment of many a feminist's dream of emancipation. For women on the Left, however, those achievements are marred by their enthusiastic participation in the machinations of the capitalist economy. Being energetic, independent and sexually assertive are just not enough to effect the transition from right-wing woman to right-on woman and many feminists are eager to expose the ideological wolves lurking in the far from sheepish New Woman's clothing. Judith Williamson pinpoints the hidden wolf when she mentions the way in which Madonna, in spite of her fame, retains an appealing 'ordinariness', for in reality Madonna is far from ordinary.[13]

Margaret Thatcher, as we have pointedly been reminded hundreds of times, is a grocer's daughter; the grammar-school girl from Grantham; the mother of two who swapped her kitchen cabinets for the Cabinet. She too has relied heavily upon this apparently irresistible combination of the special and the mundane to prolong her popular appeal. If Madonna is the 'bedroom dancer come out of the closet', then Thatcher is the housewife with a country to run, while Edwina (who shares the same birthday as Margaret) is playing the flirtatious hostess whose dining room has been turned into a government ministry. Part of their appeal rests not only on ideas about sexuality, luck or fortuitous planet alignments, but also upon the premise that anyone who really tries can do what they have done. Arguably, these 'successful' popular figures are speaking to all women. However, what the rhetoric of libertarian discourse obscures is that clearly not all women are free to become similarly 'successful'. It was never just the self-presentation or representation of Madonna as a woman that worried feminists, it was also what she connoted in politics: the Thatcherite spirit of free enterprise.

Madonna and certain Tory 'ladies' do pose a problem for feminism. It is not that feminist ideas have made no impact on them. Rather, the way in which some aspects of feminist politics have been taken up refuses to conform to any recognisable 'mistress' plan.[14] Feminists have always been keen on planning the future for women; in fact, looking back over the last twenty years, it sometimes seems as though they thought of little else. But the brighter, better, more equal feminist future being planned and publicised was not the product of every woman's imagination. Throughout the seventies and early eighties white, middle-class, Western feminists have decided who should set what agenda for the liberation of women. With the concept of patriarchy at the head of their list, packs of feminist theorists, like extraordinarily persistent bloodhounds, have spent their time tracking down the culprits of the patriarchal system of power. Unfortunately, while they became experts in sniffing out the problems of patriarchy, it has taken much longer for them to identify feminism's major faults.

In clinging on to the idea that a relatively privileged minority of women could concoct a plan for liberation that would be satisfactory for *all* women, Western feminism deludes itself. Founded upon a startling ignorance of questions of age, race, sexuality and class, the shared assumptions of a relatively small number of politically active women on the Left came to form the basis of a feminist discourse that defined the parameters of feminist politics, practices and subjectivity. The realisation that there is life outside the feminist bookshops is long overdue, and the rush to put matters right has only just begun. Meanwhile, the prize for intellectualised understatement should probably go to Michèle Barrett and Mary McIntosh, who recently admitted that their 'work has spoken from an unacknowledged but ethnically specific position . . . its apparently universal applicability has been specious'.[15] You bet it has. But what about those who have been saying as much all along? Marginalised by the predominantly white, middle-class women who originally named and shaped the demands of the women's movement, an increasing number of dissenting groups have voiced their objections and exposed the way in which feminism has evolved as a system of power which can compound their oppression. As Roisin Boyd wrote in 1983:

We talk a lot about power, usually male power, in the women's liberation movement. But seldom is the power some groups of women have in relation to other groups of women acknowledged. Those women outside the 'norm', i.e. white English or American, are not allowed to set the terms of reference in which debates and issues are taken up. Black, Third World, Irish and other groups of women are always struggling to have our voices listened to against the prevailing wind of what's perceived to be 'real' feminism.[16]

This challenge to 'real' feminism from women outside the 'norm' is also revealed in the unanticipated appropriation of elements of feminist discourse by right-wing women. The myth of the 'real' feminist, the notion that there could possibly be a single feminist subjectivity, a single feminist gaze or project equally valid for all women, has been exploded. The surfacing of feminist 'others' within feminist discourse has inevitably resulted in our having to acknowledge more than one feminist subject position. In theory, at least, we are experiencing post-feminist qualms in a postmodern storm.

Relations of power are clearly an under-investigated area of feminist politics and practice, but what exactly is this 'power' that is apparently exercised by some groups of women and resisted by others? According to Michel Foucault, 'Power is everywhere; not because it embraces everything but because it comes from everywhere.'[17] This all-encompassing and rather cryptic pronouncement implies that *all* groups, both dominant and dominated, are constantly engaged in the deployment of power. In support of his argument Foucault posits a relationship between discourse, subjectivity and the operation of power. As Belsey describes it, a discourse 'is a domain of language-use, a particular way of talking (and writing and thinking). A discourse involves certain shared assumptions which appear in the formulations that characterise it.'[18] Feminism is but one of many discursive practices which, according to Foucault, offer a number of subject positions from which it is possible for a specific individual to speak, to write, to think, or to direct their gaze.[19] Of course, no subject is ever the original construction of one specific discourse; we are all always already subjects in discourse and this obviously has a bearing upon any discussion concerning feminist intervention in mainstream culture. In other words, one woman's definition of female 'success' may be another woman's example of the dire failure of the feminist project.

For Foucault, power and knowledge are joined together in discourse. He argues that:

> . . . we must conceive discourse as a series of discontinuous segments whose tactical function is neither uniform nor stable. To be more precise, we must not imagine a world of discourse divided between accepted discourse and excluded discourse, or between the dominant discourse and the dominated one; but as a multiplicity of discursive elements that can come into play in various strategies.[20]

Whilst Foucault never specifically makes the following argument, it seems likely that the resistance of women to male domination can be described as a struggle against a form of power that makes individuals subjects, that causes individuals to conceive of themselves in a limited and limiting way. The form of power in question has been named 'patriarchal' by feminists and the resistance which operates through feminist discourse is explicitly directed against patriarchal power. Foucault claims that there are two meanings of the word subject: one can be physically or mentally subject to someone else by control and dependence, and one can be tied to one's own identity by a consciousness or self-knowledge.[21] For women, consciousness-raising groups and the development of a body of feminist theory and knowledge constitute the more obvious sites of resistance against these patriarchal modes of subjection. In resisting and exposing the workings of patriarchal power feminists have self-consciously opposed the dominant ideologies of femininity and set out to provide an alternative framework for the organisation of female subjectivity.

The irony of this *feminist resistance* is that in opposing the privileges of knowledge and the construction of women as 'feminine' subjects, a form of feminist knowledge, a feminist discourse which actually excludes and oppresses some women has evolved with its own regime for governing the individual. Used in this way 'governing' refers to the exercise of power over the actions of others; the structuring of the possible field of action for others. This process can be identified both in the way in which patriarchy has defined the feminine, and in the way in which a particular range of actions and statements have become defined as appropriate for the feminist subject. All too frequently, the voices of those women who do not conform have been dismissed as irrelevant or defined as non- or anti-feminist.

So how does this apply to Madonna? Does she qualify as a feminist icon? Is she 'right-on' or, after singing 'True Blue', revealed as a woman positioned firmly on the Right? I think the problem of Madonna for feminists was that she transgressed both the category of the feminine and of the feminist. Madonna's self-determinedly aggressive sexual presentation certainly undermined the conventional understanding of feminine sexuality as essentially passive, but in what way does this engage with feminist politics? Janice Winship argues that the popular cultural products of the eighties reveal the 'merest glimmerings' of shifts around gender. The emergence of the 'New Young Woman' and her brother (a late developer) has largely been organised around the notion of 'street-wise':

> To be street-wise isn't to be a feminist (though it could be) but to be alert to those contradictions. To be street-wise isn't to disapprove of Page 3 pin-ups or slushy romantic pulp writers but, if need be, to steer a deliberate path through the thick of those contradictions with street-wise outrageousness . . . If there hadn't been fifteen years of the women's movement and organised feminism there wouldn't be this cultural space to play with gender and hetero-sexuality.[22]

Madonna occupied this 'cultural space' and played around in it, making naughty videos that at first sight may have seemed to confirm a feminist's worst fears about sexualised images of women. When, for example, Madonna confidently returns the fetishist's gaze while wearing his favourite sexual accessories, she reveals herself to be in the possession of knowledge; she *knows* because she has looked and is now *looking back*. This parody of a classic pornographic peepshow[23] reveals the sophistication of a new young female audience that knows the difference between feeling powerful and feeling powerless. As Janice Winship concludes, overtly sexual images of women do not carry the same meanings for the New Young Women of today that they did for the 'older' feminists ten or fifteen years ago:

> That is partly because feminism *has* revealed pornography's abuse of women to women. And it is partly because, however indirectly, feminism has given these young women a knowledge and a strength to act in the world which also allows them to laugh at and enjoy those images in a way many of us could not, and cannot.[24]

These same young women resist the feminist 'power' that seeks to structure their lives and, ironically, in so doing, simultaneously reveal the partial political success of the feminist project. Feminism is at last a force to be reckoned with, a system of power being actively resisted.

But I Still Don't Like Madonna . . .

Clearly not all women approve of these developments and a sense of loss pervades many of the more recent analyses of contemporary feminism. Members of this mournful sisterhood fall into the category of the 'authentic' described by Elizabeth Wilson in her analysis of the relationship between feminists and fashion. In distinguishing between a 'modernist' and an 'authentic' tendency within feminist politics, Wilson may have oversimplified matters, but she has highlighted a possible source of some awkward tensions within contemporary feminist debate, particularly an ideological disjunction between feminist mothers and their apparently reactionary daughters. The yearning for 'authenticity' that Wilson attributes to certain feminists rests upon a resolute belief in 'nature' and the 'true' self. Meanwhile the 'modernist' feminist's belief in the unstable, socially constructed 'subject in process' allows for a more playful, less lugubrious outlook on the very evident conflicts between different 'feminist' positions.[25]

Disagreement is a primary characteristic of political discourse yet the demand that internal differences be quashed for the greater good of an oppositional movement is a familiar one. Feminists were widely criticised by their male 'comrades' on the Left when they refused to accept their subordination in the present for the sake of the long-awaited revolution. Today many members of the Labour Party face similar condemnation when they refuse to abandon their campaign for 'Black sections' within the party. The idea that strength can only be found in unity, and that diversity implies weakness, has proved to be a powerful motivating factor in the organisation of all political movements. If struggles between women have caused the women's movement to fragment, has feminism necessarily lost its ability to challenge patriarchal power effectively and to force social change?

Some theorists have suggested that a general tendency towards social fragmentation and political eclecticism is now evident throughout a range of cultural practices, and that the sort of dissatisfaction with rigid and organised political movements that is voiced by many feminists is symptomatic of a 'postmodern condition'. This general resistance to the suppression of differences in the name of progress cannot be said to have emerged in any one specific area of social life, yet it is a particularly interesting phenomenon when examined in the context of feminist practice. Angela McRobbie has commented on the way in which one of the conditions of contemporary reality is marked by '. . . the coming into being of those whose voices were historically drowned out by the (modernist) meta-narratives of mastery, which were in truth both patriarchal and imperialist.'[26]

Of course for many Western women this 'coming into being' began with their involvement in the women's movement. However, as I have already suggested, the movement was founded upon an illusory unity based on the exclusion and suppression of dissenting voices. Feminism's critique of patriarchy is nevertheless still held to be an important and vital element of the 'postmodern' discovery of the plurality of culture. In the words of Craig Owens, 'women's insistence on difference and incommensurability may not only be compatible with, but also an instance of postmodern thought'.[27] This claim is based upon a particular interpretation of the *symptoms* of a post-modern 'condition':

> Decentred, allegorical, schizophrenic . . . however we choose to diagnose its symptoms, postmodernism is usually treated by its protagonists and antagonists alike, as a crisis of cultural authority, specifically of the authority vested in Western European culture and its institutions. That the hegemony of European civilisations is drawing to a close is hardly a new perception; since the mid-1950s, at least, we have recognised the necessity of encountering different cultures by means other than the shock of domination and conquest.[28]

But have feminists really developed any adequate new means of encountering their 'others'? The depressing news on the feminist front is that, until recently, few of us had attempted to engage with the idea of difference within the category of woman.[29] Plurality and difference, far from being celebrated, have been defined as reactionary develop-ments or as the manifestly dissolute remnants of a sort of wishy-washy liberalism. Unfortunately, the same intellectual arrogance that led white, Western feminists to imagine that they could speak for *all* women, has infected the feminist debate around postmodernism. For example, in the midst of an otherwise perceptive critique of Craig Owens' work, Rosa Lee drops a critical clanger:

> Whether the pluralism of postmodernism is seen as a positive factor, offering even greater scope for 'freedom', or whether it is judged merely as evidencing what Gablik refers to as 'a false complexity that merely covers up a lack of meaning', the feminist 'contribution' to this 'condition' as Owens calls it, is plainly *the root cause* of the postmodern crisis of cultural authority, and *not merely a facet* of it.[30] (original emphasis)

What this blatant example of self-congratulatory feminist back-slapping completely obscures is the fact that if there are any 'root causes' then feminism is only one of many. Lee fails to acknowledge that the postmodern crisis concerns the cultural authority of the West and that it stems as much from political initiatives originating in the Third World as it does from feminist interventions in Europe and the USA. However, if there really can be no single theoretical discourse or political practice that will fulfil every woman's demands and desires, does this force us to accept the demise of feminism as an effective oppositional force?

In the light of Foucault's analysis of the relation between power and knowledge it is interesting to note that postmodernism has been described as the collapse of modernism's legitimating 'Grand Narratives' and, in particular, a loss of confidence in the idea of progress.[31] In this context the term modernism is used to describe a cultural movement that has affected all areas of social life and which is intimately linked to the philosophical project of Enlightenment. At the heart of this project was a drive towards knowledge, to knowing the 'self', and towards the evolution of principles of justice and morality supposedly appropriate for all human subjects. The concepts of individuality, of the individual's rights and freedoms, of the uniqueness of self and the unity of the 'natural' subject are all hallmarks of classical modernism and popular themes in many feminist texts.

There are now some theorists who regard the explosion of the myth of the unitary subject to be a key contributory element in the demise of modernism. The 'self' in the discourse of postmodernity is only an unstable amalgam of identities existing in 'a fabric of social relations that is now more complex and mobile than ever before'.[32] So, if we examine just one of feminism's longstanding interests – the deconstruction of feminine subjectivity – we can begin to understand how feminism can be described as an instance of postmodern thought.

However, in seeking to acclaim certain aspects of feminist discourse as examples of postmodernity, Owens, like Foucault, tends to gloss over the problems of inequitable power relations between women. What I am interested in is not necessarily a full-scale interrogation of the origins and operations of power, but the mere acknowledgment of its widespread effects. Whether we fall into a recognisable 'brand-name' category of feminism, whether we call ourselves post-feminist, anti-feminist or non-feminist, at least part of our sense of identity is derived from our positioning within, and relationship to, the discourses of both popular and theoretical feminism. Acknowledging that forms of difference exist within the category of the subject 'woman' suggests that we should take a fresh look at the operation of conventional feminist discourse, in particular its reluctance to deal with the question of female power. What I am saying here is that we cannot divide women into two neat categories, for there are no solid boundaries between the feminist and the feminine subject, the female and the feminist gaze.

Of course, this notion of confusing, contradictory and unstable subjects feeds into debates around the possibilities of active female or feminist looking. Experiencing one's own subjectivity as a mass of contradictions is a process that must be familiar to all women, particularly feminists. Yet more often than not it is resented rather than investigated. For Stuart Hall the popular success of Thatcherism highlights the complex nature of subjectivity. He describes the material effects of a fragmented subject beautifully when he suggests that:

> . . . a tiny bit of all of us is also somewhere inside the Thatcherite project. Of course, we're all one hundred per cent committed. But every now and then – Saturday mornings perhaps, just before the demonstration – we go to Sainsbury's and we're just a tiny bit of a Thatcherite subject . . .[33]

It is too easy to argue that divergence equals dilution, and anyway who claims the authority to say what is and what is not a feminist representation, or who is and who is not a feminist? To despise and ignore the products of popular culture until they match up to some rigorous and unchanging feminist code of practice is hardly a productive strategy nor a very enjoyable one; and one would have thought the declining sales figures for *Spare Rib*, for example, would have brought home the lessons of such a strategy. It seems to me that contemporary feminists should be searching not for icons but for inroads to the cultural terrain that constitutes the 'popular' and to the systems of power that shape and define the female subject. We could start by listening to the views of those wayward daughters who seem to be so actively resisting, rather than conforming to, any simple feminist model of the New Woman. After all, there must be that little bit of a feminist subject lurking in there somewhere, mustn't there? And if there is, I suspect she's looking back at me.

Notes

Introduction

1. Lewis Carroll, *Alice In Wonderland*, new children's edition, Macmillan, 1980, p. 116.
2. Friedrich Engels, Letter to J. Block, 21 September 1890, in Karl Marx and Friedrich Engels, *Selected Works*, vol. 3, p. 487. See also Louis Althusser, 'Contradiction and Overdetermination' in *For Marx*, pp. 117–18.
3. Michèle Barrett, 'Feminism and the Definition of Cultural Politics', in Rosalind Brunt and Caroline Rowans (eds.), *Feminism, Culture and Politics*, p. 37.
4. For a fuller discussion, see Anne Ross Muir, *A Woman's Guide to Jobs in Film and Television*.
5. Angela Carter, *The Sadeian Woman*, p. 27.
6. Laura Mulvey, 'Visual Pleasure and Narrative Cinema', *Screen*, vol. 16, no. 3, Autumn 1975, pp. 6–18.
7. See, for example, Edward Buscombe, et al., 'Statement: Psycho-analysis and Film', *Screen*, vol. 16, no. 4, Winter 1975/6, pp. 119–30; and Jacqueline Rose, 'The Cinematic Apparatus – Problems in Current Theory' in *Sexuality in the Field of Vision*, where Rose criticises the use of Lacanian concepts – particularly 'the imaginary' – by film critics like C. Metz. In brief, Rose suggests that this usage transforms the Freudian stress on 'disavowal' as the moment of unveiling of lack into 'explanation of the action of perception itself'. She argues this transformation is inappropriate because it shifts the emphasis from unconscious processes that can't be known to perception of the conscious experience in the cinema of 'I know it's not real but I'll pretend it is whilst I'm here'.
8. Mary Ann Doane, 'Film and the Masquerade: Theorising the Female Spectator', *Screen*, vol. 23, nos. 3/4, September/October 1982, p. 77.

1. Watching the Detectives: The Enigma of the Female Gaze

1. Mary Gordon, *Ms*, January 1987.
2. The term 'genre' often appears cloaked under the pejorative term 'formula', but for full discussion of meaning, see S. Neale's *Genre*.
3. I think that Frank Mort, for example, exaggerates the radical implication of male self-consciousness in 'Image Change: High Street Style and the New Man', *New Socialist*, November 1986.
4. Elvis Costello, *Watching The Detectives*, copyright © Demon Label, Street Music Limited, 1984.
5. See discussion of James Bond by T. Bennett in the Open University *Popular Culture Handbook*, Unit 21, 1982.
6. See discussion of fetishism in Annette Kuhn's *Women's Pictures: Feminism and Cinema*, p. 61.
7. See Elizabeth Cowie on the narrative conspiracy of *Coma*, *m/f*, nos. 3/4, 1979/80.
8. I am using the concept of 'overdetermination' in the Althusserian sense; see 'Ideology and the Ideological State Apparatus', in L. Althusser, *Essays On Ideology*.
9. David Byrne, Talking Heads, *More Songs About Buildings and Food*, copyright © Bleu Disque Music Co. Inc./Index Music, 1977.
10. Molly Haskell, *From Reverence to Rape: The Treatment of Women in the Movies*.
11. Nancy Mills, 'The Women's Vroom', *Guardian*, 17 October 1987.
12. Laura Mulvey, 'Visual Pleasure and Narrative Cinema', *Screen*, vol. 16, no. 3, Autumn 1975, pp. 6–18.
13. Julia Kristeva, *About Chinese Women*, p. 37.
14. Ibid., p. 115.
15. Ibid., p. 38.
16. Carlo Ginzburg, 'Morelli, Freud and Sherlock Holmes: Clues and Scientific Method', *History Workshop Journal*, vol. 9, Spring 1980, pp. 5–36.
17. Elizabeth Wilson, 'Psychoanalysis: Psychic Law and Order', *Hidden Agendas*, p. 168.
18. Kristeva, op. cit.
19. Mary Daly, *Gyn/Ecology*.
20. Bridget Smith, *Spare Rib*, December 1985.
21. As discussed on BBC2's *Did You See*, 16 May 1986, with Ludovic Kennedy, Linda Agran and Alistair Cooke.
22. I obtained this information from the extensive 'filenotes' of press releases from Orion Productions circulated with other information by the British *Cagney & Lacey* Appreciation of the Series Society

(CLASS), registered address, 23 Mitcham Road, West Croydon, Surrey, CRO 3RW, England.

23. Christian Metz, 'The Grand Syntagmatique', from *Film Language: A Semiotics of the Cinema*, pp. 217–18.

24. Mulvey, op. cit.

25. John Ellis, *Visible Fictions*, p. 137.

26. Mary Wings, *She Came Too Late*.

27. Tzvetan Todorov, 'The Typology of Detective Fiction', in *The Poetics of Prose*.

28. Ellis, op. cit., p. 137.

29. Craig Owens, 'The Discourse of Others: Feminists and Post-modernism', in *Postmodern Culture*.

30. See discussion in Annette Kuhn's *Women's Pictures: Feminism and Cinema*, p. 17.

31. Mulvey, op. cit.

32. For a discussion of changing definitions of 'avant-garde' see Peter Burger, *Theory of the Avant-Garde*.

33. Her slight revision appears in 'Afterthoughts on "Visual Pleasure and Narrative Cinema"' inspired by *Duel in the Sun*', Framework, nos. 15/16/17, 1981, p. 15.

34. Ibid., p. 15.

35. The most recent statement of Laura Mulvey's position on the 'male gaze' appears in 'Changes: Thoughts of Myth, Narrative and Historical Experience', *History Workshop Journal*, vol. 23, Spring 1987, pp. 1–19, although she seems to be continuing to work/write on this subject.

36. Janet Winship, 'A Girl Needs to Get Street Wise: Magazines for the 1980s', *Feminist Review*, no. 21, Winter 1985.

37. McQuail, Blumler and Brown, 'The Television Audience: A Revised Perspective', in *Sociology of Mass Communications*.

38. Concerning the methods by which a class can become hegemonic, Antonio Gramsci distinguished two principal routes: the first is that of transformism (passive consensus), 'the gradual but continuous absorption, achieved by methods which varied in their effectiveness, of the active elements produced by allied groups – even those which came from antagonist groups', see *Selections from the Prison Notebooks*, p. 59. Gramsci contrasted this 'absorption' with successful, 'expansive' hegemony, which had to consist of the creation of an active, direct consensus resulting from the adoption of the interests of the popular classes by the hegemonic class, which would give rise to the creation of a genuine 'national popular will'.

39. Owens, op. cit.

2. Substantial Women

1. Quoted in Tricia Murray, *Margaret Thatcher*, W.H. Allen, London, 1978, p. 107.
2. For Gramsci's concept of the ideological nature of 'commonsense', see Antonio Gramsci, *Selections from the Prison Notebooks*, pp. 322–51.
3. Laura Mulvey, 'Visual Pleasure and Narrative Cinema', *Screen*, vol. 16, no. 3, Autumn 1975, p. 18.
4. Advertising and pop videos are just two areas in which 'postmodernist' techniques, more usually associated with the avant-garde, are to be found in the mainstream – without necessarily having progressive implications. See, for example, the analysis of MTV by E. Ann Kaplan in *Rocking Around the Clock*.
5. See, for example, Michèle Barrett, 'Feminism and the Definition of Cultural Politics' in Rosalind Brunt and Caroline Rowan (eds.), *Feminism, Culture and Politics*, pp. 37–56.
6. 'Hence the split between spectacle and narrative supports the man's role as the active one of forwarding the story, making things happen.' Mulvey, op. cit., p. 12.
7. Barbara Cartland's romance fiction, for instance, frequently uses 'real' historical figures and events which are narrated from a female point of view as a context for what is relevant to romance, thus inverting the importance attributed to the political and the personal by historians.
8. Leah Hertz, *The Business Amazons*, p. 92.
9. Mulvey, op. cit., p. 12.
10. I am indebted to Sue LeTouze for pointing this out.
11. Hertz, op. cit.; Robert Goffee and Richard Scase, *Women in Charge*.
12. Susan Butler, 'Revising femininity? Review of *Lady: Photographs of Lisa Lyon* by Robert Mapplethorpe', in Rosemary Betterton (ed.), *Looking On*, p. 122.
13. Ibid.
14. See John Berger's discussion of glamour as essentially purchasable in *Ways of Seeing*, 1972.
15. Butler, op. cit., p. 122.
16. Henry S. Galus, *The Impact of Women*, pp. 59–60.
17. On stars, see Robyn Archer and Diana Simmonds, *A Star is Torn*. On schoolgirls, see Michelle Stanworth, *Gender and Schooling*, p. 18.

18. Robyn Rowland (ed.), *Women Who Do and Women Who Don't Join the Women's Movement*.
19. *Guardian*, 14 November 1987.
20. See especially Bertholt Brecht, *Mother Courage and Her Children*.
21. Frantz Fanon, *The Wretched of the Earth*, pp. 73–4.
22. Beatrix Campbell, *The Iron Ladies*, p. 246.

3 Here's Looking at You, Kid!

1. Antony Easthope, *What a Man's Gotta Do: The Masculine Myth in Popular Culture*, p. 54.
2. This point seems to be somewhat overgeneralised and Eurocentric – while it may be true that some men feel alienated from their own bodies, those men brought up in different cultures and classes may experience other kinds of feelings towards their bodies.
3. Rosalind Coward, *Female Desire: Women's Sexuality Today*, p. 230.
4. Martin Raymond in an article 'Boys on Film' in the magazine *Girl about Town*, 16 February 1987.
5. Sam Cooke, lyrics from 'A Wonderful World'.
6. Laura Mulvey, 'Visual Pleasure and Narrative Cinema', *Screen*, vol. 16, no. 3, Autumn 1975.
7. Louisa Saunders in *Girl about Town*, 16 February 1987.
8. Paul Rodriguez, art director of the Athena chain, interviewed in 'Wolf in Chic Clothing' by Brian Kennedy and John Lyttle in *City Limits*, 4 December 1986.
9. Brian Kennedy in *City Limits*, 3 September 1987.
10. Mary Ann Doane, 'Film and the Masquerade: Theorising the Female Sepectator', in *Screen*, vol. 23, nos. 3/4, September/October 1982.
11. Susan Sontag, 'Notes on Camp', in *Against Interpretation*, p. 280.
12. See for instance the work of Robin Lakoff on women and language. She describes women as being in command of a 'vocabulary of trivia'.
13. Nancy Henley, *Body Politics*.
14. John Ellis, *Visible Fictions*, p. 128.
15. Laura Mulvey, 'Afterthoughts on "Visual Pleasure and Narrative Cinema" inspired by *Duel in the Sun*', in *Framework*, nos. 15/16/17, 1981.
16. D. N. Rodowick, 'The Difficulty of Difference', in *Wide Angle*, vol. 5, no. 1, 1982.
17. Footnote to 'The Transformations of Puberty – The Differentiation between Men and Women', in Sigmund Freud, *On Sexuality*, p. 141.

18. Stephen Heath, *The Sexual Fix*.
19. Elizabeth Cowie, 'Fantasia', *m/f*, no. 9, 1984.
20. Ellis, op. cit.
21. Stephen Neale, 'Masculinity as Spectacle: Reflections on Men and Mainstream Cinema', *Screen*, vol. 24, no. 6, November/December 1983, pp. 24–6.
22. Mark Finch, 'Sex and Address in *Dynasty*', *Screen*, vol. 27, no. 6, November/December 1986.
23. Richard Dyer, 'Don't look now', *Screen*, vol. 23, nos. 3/4. September/October 1982.
24. Frank Mort, 'Images Change: High Street Style and the New Man', *New Socialist*, November 1986.
25. Finch, op. cit.
26. Jacqueline Rose, *Sexuality in the Field of Vision*, p. 210.
27. Luce Irigaray, 'When the Goods Get Together', in *New French Feminisms*, p. 108.
28. Margaret Walters, *The Male Nude: A New Perspective*, p. 18.
29. Quoted in ibid., p. 295.
30. Ibid., p. 295.
31. Tony Hodges interviewed on *The Media Show*, Channel Four, May 1987.
32. Roland Barthes, *The Pleasure of the Text*, p. 31.

4 *The Color Purple*: In Defence of Happy Endings

1. Alice Walker, *The Color Purple*, p. 176.
2. Alice Walker, 'Advancing Luna – and Ida B. Wells' in *You Can't Keep a Good Woman Down*. See also Alice Walker, *In Search of Our Mothers' Gardens*.
3. Richard Wright, *Black Boy*, p. 33.
4. *The Color Purple*, p. 211.
5. Adrienne Rich, 'Compulsory Heterosexuality and Lesbian Existence', in *The Signs Reader: Women, Gender and Scholarship*.
6. Ralph Ellison, *Invisible Man*, pp. 42–61.
7. Zora Neale Hurston, 'How it Feels to be Colored Me' in *I Love Myself When I'm Laughing*.
8. Zora Neale Hurston, 'Cock Robin of Beale Street' in *Spunk*.
9. Hilary Bailey, 'Subtext and Artful Dodges', *Guardian*, 19 May 1983.
10. Alice Walker, *The Third Life of Grange Copeland*.
11. Alice Walker, *In Love and Trouble*.
12. *The Color Purple*, pp. 166–7.

13. Ibid., p. 168.
14. Ibid., p. 167.
15. Ibid., p. 92.
16. Ibid., p. 49.

5 Lolita Meets the Werewolf: *The Company of Wolves*

1. *Guardian*, film review, August 1987.
2. *Screen International*, film review, August 1987.
3. Elaine Showalter, 'Towards a Feminist Poetics' in *Women Writing and Writing about Women*, p. 33.
4. Ian McEwan interviewing Angela Carter, *Sunday Times*, November 1984.
5. Sandra Gilbert and Susan Gubar, *The Madwoman in the Attic*, p. 45.
6. Angela Carter, *Heroes and Villains*, back cover.
7. J. M. S. Tompkins, *The Popular Novel in England*, p. 174.
8. Roland Barthes, quoted in *Women Writing and Writing about Women*, p. 11.
9. Tompkins, op. cit., p. 174.
10. Roald Dahl, *Revolting Rhymes*, Penguin, Harmondsworth, 1984.
11. Angela Carter, 'The Company of Wolves' in *The Bloody Chamber*, p. 113.
12, Ibid., p. 113.
13. Ibid., p. 114.
14. Ibid., p. 114.
15. Ibid., p. 115.
16. Ibid., p. 116.
17. Ibid., p. 117.
18. Ibid., p. 117.
19. Ibid., p. 117.
20. Ibid., p. 118.
21. See Angela Carter's discussion of Sade's depiction of female sexuality in *The Sadeian Woman*.
22. 'The Company of Wolves', p. 118.
23. Pre-publicity synopsis, Palace Pictures.
24. David Castell, *Daily Telegraph*, November 1984.
25. Rosemary Jackson, *Fantasy: The Literature of Subversion*, p. 51.
26. John Ellis, *Visible Fictions*, p. 45.
27. 'The Company of Wolves', p. 118.
28. Michael Open, *Irish Film Council Review*, December 1984.
29. Stephen Woolley, quoted in *Screen International*, November 1984.

30. Richard Coombs, *International Film Review*, November 1984.
31. Angela Carter, interview in *Marxism Today*, November 1984.
32. 'The Company of Wolves', p. 118.
33. Herbert Marcuse, 'Art in the One-Dimensional Society', in *Radical Perspectives in the Arts*, p. 58.

6 *Lace*: Pornography for Women?

1. Jane McLoughlin, *Guardian*, 5 June 1984.
2. 'Bodice Rippers seem to have appeared on the marketplace in the mid seventies and often portray the heroine's sexuality as "inadvertent". The bodice ripper formula transforms the hero's desire for the heroine, usually expressed through rape, into a masochistic fantasy whereby female desire is released as a product of pain and as an *effect* of active male desire.' Lorraine Gamman, unpublished paper, 'Dirty Looks in the Bodice Ripper', presented at Middlesex Conference Centre, 5 September 1987.
3. Ann Barr Snitow, 'Mass Market Romance: Pornography for Women is Different', in *Desire: The Politics of Sexuality*, pp. 266–74.
4. Angela Carter, *The Sadeian Woman*, p. 27.
5. For an overall discussion of the impact of feminism on sexual ideology and the marketplace see B. Ehrenreich, E. Hess and G. Jacobs, *Re-Making Love: The Feminization of Sex*. Chapter 6, 'The Politics of Promiscuity – The Rise of the Sexual Counterrevolution', discusses contemporary reversals in the sexual revolution, including feminist reactions to promiscuity.
6. See, for example, Kathy Acker, *Blood and Guts in High School Plus Two*.
7. See, for example, Marge Piercy, *Woman on the Edge of Time*; Joanna Russ, *The Female Man*.
8. Angela Carter, 'The Sweet Sell of Romance' in *Nothing Sacred*, p. 152.
9. Shirley Conran, *Lace*, p. 55.
10. Ibid., p. 68.
11. Ibid., p. 104.
12. Ibid., p. 86.
13. Ibid., p. 56.
14. Ibid., p. 67.
15. Ibid., p. 286.
16. Ibid., p. 513.
17. Ibid., p. 506.

18. Ibid., p. 506.
19. Ibid., p. 237.
20. Ibid., p. 239.
21. Ibid., p. 239.
22. Snitow, op cit., p. 269.
23. Conran, op cit., p. 452.
24. Ibid., p. 452.
25. Jessica Benjamin, 'Master and Slave: The Fantasy of Erotic Domination', in *Desire: The Politics of Sexuality*, p. 295.
26. Rosalind Coward, 'Porn: What's in it for Women?', *New Statesman*, 13 June 1986.
27. Ibid.
28. Rosalind Coward, 'Sexual Violence and Sexuality', *Feminist Review*, no. 11, Summer 1982.
29. Andrea Dworkin, *Pornography: Men Possessing Women*. See opening chapter, 'Power'.
30. Ibid., pp. 199–202.
31. Snitow, op. cit., p. 269.
32. Susanne Kappeler, *The Pornography of Representation*, p. 2.
33. Laura Mulvey, 'Visual Pleasure and Narrative Cinema', *Screen*, vol. 16, no. 3, Autumn 1975.
34. E. Ann Kaplan, 'Is the Gaze Male?', in *Desire: The Politics of Sexuality*.
35. Kappeler, op. cit., p. 212.
36. Mariana Valverde, *Sex, Power and Pleasure*, p. 46.
37. Ehrenreich, Hess and Jacobs, op. cit., p. 203.
38. Conran, op. cit., p. 495: 'Kate attended four meetings of the Women's Liberation group, but found them all disappointing. Every woman's experience was considered of utmost importance, however boring . . . The sisters never seemed to talk about practical considerations; discussion was either directed to experience-sharing or else utopian theorizing. Kate was depressed by the muddled Marxist political thinking.'

7 Joan Collins and the Wilder Side of Women: Exploring Pleasure and Representation

1. The 'pleasures of the popular' are provocatively debated by Judith Williamson in her article 'The Problems of being Popular', *New Socialist*, no. 41, September 1986, and in response by Cora Kaplan's 'The culture crossover', *New Socialist*, no. 43, November 1986.
2. For a discussion of the way in which women's bodies are coded so as

to produce particular kinds of pleasure, see Annette Kuhn, 'Lawless Seeing', in *The Power of the Image: Essays on Representation and Sexuality*, pp. 19–47.

3. John Berger, *Ways of Seeing*, p. 46.

4. Laura Mulvey, 'Visual Pleasure and Narrative Cinema', *Screen*, vol. 16, no. 3, Autumn 1975.

5. Kathy Myers argues this point in 'Towards a Feminist Erotica', *Camerawork*, no. 24, March 1982. Through an examination of a porn image and a fashion image (which at first sight look remarkably similar) Myers argues that debates on representation cannot be confined to the image alone, without looking at its contextualisation, the condition of its production and consumption.

6. Ibid., p. 16.

7. Ien Ang, *Watching Dallas*, p. 122.

8. Tania Modleski, *Loving with a Vengeance: Mass Produced Fantasies for Women*, pp. 11–34.

9. The plot of the 'Moldavia Massacre' revolves around the intended marriage of Amanda (daughter of Blake and Alexis) to Prince Michael of Moldavia. The wedding day in Moldavia sees the (supposed) bloody massacre of the entire Carrington dynasty – another 'cliff-hanger' ending to one series of *Dynasty*!

10. Mulvey, op. cit., p. 12.

11. Janey Place, 'Women in Film Noir', in E. Ann Kaplan (ed.), *Women in Film Noir*, p. 47.

12. Ibid ., p. 45.

13. Ibid., p. 36.

14. Roland Barthes, *Camera Lucida*, p. 57.

8 Desperately Seeking Difference

1. Laura Mulvey, 'Visual Pleasure and Narrative Cinema', *Screen*, vol. 16, no. 3, Autumn 1975, pp. 11–12.

2. Mandy Merck, '*Lianna* and the Lesbians of Art Cinema', in *Films for Women*.

3. Richard Dyer, *Heavenly Bodies*.

4. Claire Whitiker, 'Hollywood Transformed: Interviews with Lesbian Viewers', in *Jump Cut: Hollywood, Politics and Counter Cinema*, p. 107.

5. Mulvey, op. cit., pp. 6–18.

6. See, for example, Leo Handel, 'La bourse des vedettes', *Communications*, no. 2, 1963, pp. 86–104.

7. This pattern is reproduced in the recent detective film *Black Widow*,

directed by Bob Rafaelson, 1987, where the homo-erotic connotations are much more explicit.

8. Mulvey, op. cit.

9. Ibid., p. 13.

10. Ibid., p. 10.

11. Ibid.

12. There have been several attempts to fill this theoretical gap and provide analyses of masculinity as sexual spectacle: see Richard Dyer, 'Don't Look Now – The Male Pin-Up', *Screen*, vol. 23, nos. 3/4, 1982; Steve Neale, 'Masculinity as Spectacle', *Screen*, vol. 24, no. 6, 1983; and Andy Medhurst, 'Can Chaps Be Pin-Ups?', *Ten. 8*, no. 17, 1985.

13. David Rodowick, 'The Difficulty of Difference', *Wide Angle*, vol. 5, no. 1, 1982, p. 8.

14. Mary Ann Doane, 'Film and the Masquerade: Theorising the Female Spectator', *Screen*, vol. 23, nos. 3/4, September/October 1982.

15. Constance Penley, 'Feminism, Film Theory and the Bachelor Machines', *m/f*, no. 10, 1985.

16. According to Raymond Bellour, the term *enunciator* 'marks both the person who possesses the right to speak within the film, and the source [instance] towards which the series of representations is logically chanelled back'. Raymond Bellour, 'Hitchcock the Enunciator', *Camera Obscura*, no. 2, 1977, p. 2.

17. Raymond Bellour, 'Psychosis, Neurosis, Perversion', *Camera Obscura*, nos. 3/4, 1979, p. 97.

18. Janet Bergstrom, 'Enunciation and Sexual Difference', *Camera Obscura*, nos. 3/4, 1979, p. 57. See also Janet Bergstrom, 'Alternation, Segmentation, Hypnosis: An Interview with Raymond Bellour', *Camera Obscura*, nos. 3/4, 1979.

19. Doane, op. cit., p. 78.

20. Doane, op. cit., p. 80.

21. Mary Ann Doane, Patricia Mellencamp and Linda Williams, 'Feminist Film Criticism: an Introduction' in *Re-Vision*, p. 9.

22. Ibid., p. 14.

23. Laura Mulvey, 'Afterthoughts on "Visual Pleasure and Narrative Cinema" inspired by *Duel in the Sun*', *Framework*, nos. 15/16/17, 1981, pp. 12–15.

24. Ibid., p. 15.

25. Mary Ann Doane citing Julia Kristeva, *About Chinese Women*, in 'Caught and Rebecca: The Inscription of Femininity as Absence', *Enclitic*, vol. 5, no. 2/vol. 6, no. 1, 1981/1982, p. 77.

26. For a discussion of films which might be included under this category see Caroline Sheldon, 'Lesbians and Film: Some Thoughts', in *Gays and Film*.

27. Teresa de Lauretis, *Alice Doesn't: Feminism, Semiotics and Cinema*, pp. 113, 119.

28. Ibid., p. 121.

29. See, for example, Sigmund Freud, 'Some Psychical Consequences of the Anatomical Distinction Between the Sexes' (1925), in *On Sexuality*.

30. See Jacques Lacan, 'The Mirror Stage as Formative of the Function of the I as Revealed in the Psychoanalytic Experience', in *Ecrits*, pp. 1–7

9 Black Looks

1. The title of a book by Gloria T. Hall, Patricia Bell Scott and Barbara Smith (eds.), Feminist Press, New York, 1986.

2. When, in Autumn 1987, the *Guardian* featured a black woman modelling 'ethnic' jewellery it received complaints from readers. Of course, we would not, as one reader's response to the complaints 'suggested', prefer a white male model; it is the isolation of the image that is at issue, and the uncritical appropriation of 'ethnic' jewellery for fashion.

3. Georg Lukács, 'The Ideology of Modernism' in *The Meaning of Contemporary Realism*, 1963.

4. See, for example, works by Charles Chessnutt and James Weldon Johnson. Even as late as the Harlem Renaissance black literature tended to idealise black Americans, as well as their African heritage.

5. Alice Walker, 'Advancing Luna – and Ida B. Wells' in *You Can't Keep a Good Woman Down*.

6. Quoted from an interview with Joan Riley held by Petal Felix and Jacqui Roach, 1987.

7. Ibid.

8. Ibid.

9. Ibid.

10. Ibid.

11. Ibid.

12. Quoted from an interview with Judith Jacobs held by Petal Felix and Jacqui Roach, 1987.

13. Ibid.

14. Ibid.

15. Ibid.
16. Ibid.
17. Ibid.
18. Quoted from an interview with Judy Boucher held by Petal Felix and Jacqui Roach, 1987.
19. Ibid.
20. Ibid.
21. Ibid.
22. Ibid.
23. Quoted from the track 'Control' on the LP by Janet Jackson.

10 The Status of Women Working in Film and Television

1. Sarah Benton, 'Patterns of Discrimination Against Women in the Film and Television Industries', *Film and Television Technician*, March 1975.
2. Monica Simms, *Women in BBC Management*, BBC, 1985.
3. Molly Haskell, 'Women Directors: On Toppling the Male Mystique', *American Film*, vol. 1, no. 8, June 1976.
4. Antony Slide, 'Forgotten Early Women Directors', *Films in Review*, vol. 25, no. 3, March 1974.
5. John C. Mahoney, 'Cinema's Women at the Top', *American Cinemeditor*, vol. 25, no. 4, Winter 1975–6.
6. Kevin Brownlow, *The Parade's Gone By*.
7. Nancy Ellen Dowd, 'The Woman Director Through the Years', *Action*, vol. 8, no. 4, July–August 1973.
8. M.P. Fogarty (ed.), Isobel Allen, A. J. Allen and Patricia Walters, *Women in Top Jobs*, p. 152.
9. Sheila MacLeod, 'A Woman's Place', *Action*, Association of Cinematograph, Television and Allied Technicians.
10. Muriel Box, *Odd Woman Out*.
11. Roy Armes, *A Critical History of British Cinema*.
12. Nigel Willmot, 'Who's running Broadcasting?', *Broadcast*, 13 February 1987, pp. 22–3.
13. E. Ann Kaplan, *Women and Film*.

11 Cashing in on the Curse: Advertising and the Menstrual Taboo

1. Tampax, 'Don't be Homebound', *Good Housekeeping*, May 1958.
2. Lil-lets, 'Street-Wise', *Company*, April 1986.
3. Tabu, 'Tabu', *Company*, November 1985.
4. Janice Delaney, Mary Jane Lupton, Emily Toth, *The Curse: A Cultural History of Menstruation*, p. 24.

5. Robin Morgan (ed.), *Sisterhood is Powerful*, p. 162.

6. Paula Weideger, *Female Cycles*, p. 90.

7. Judith Williamson, *Decoding Advertisements: Ideology and Meaning in Advertising*, pp. 25–6.

8. Ibid., p. 99.

9. Roland Barthes, *Mythologies*, p. 116.

10 Ibid., p. 131.

11. Delaney, et al., op. cit., p. 13.

12. Ibid., p. 109.

13. Ibid., pp. 109–13.

14. Dr White's, 'If Men Had Periods', *Elle*, June 1986.

15. Dr White's, 'Cartoon', *Company*, November 1985.

16. Dr White's, 'Deep Blush', *Company*, April 1986.

17. Lil-lets, 'Street-Wise', *Company*, April 1986.

18. Delaney, et al., op. cit., pp. 115, 119.

19. Barbara Christian and Robert Snowden, (eds.), *Patterns and Perceptions of Menstruation: A World Health Organisation International Collaborative Study*, p. 249.

20. Ibid., p. 252.

21. Dr White's, 'Deep Blush', *Company*, April 1986.

22. Weideger, op. cit., p. 12.

23. Mary Douglas, *Implicit Meanings*, pp. 61–2.

24. Weideger, op. cit., p. 12.

25. Ibid., pp. 8–9.

26. Williamson, op. cit., p. 99.

27. Weideger, op. cit., pp. 229–30.

28. Wendy Cooper, 'Menstruation Still Taboo', *Cosmopolitan*, September 1987, p. 154.

29. The Matriarchy Study Group, *Menstrual Taboos*, p. 9.

30. Gloria Steinem, *Outrageous Acts and Everyday Rebellions*, p. 337.

31. Librofem, 'Periods are Part of Being a Woman', *Company*, November 1985.

12 Care to Join Me in an Upwardly Mobile Tango? Postmodernism and the 'New Woman'

1. Editorial comment from the introduction to 'The Age of Confusion', *Elle*, November 1986.

2. J.-F. Lyotard, *The Postmodern Condition: A Report on Knowledge*, p. 37.

3. J.-F. Lyotard, 'Brief Reflections on Popular Culture', in *ICA Documents 4*.

4. Craig Owens, 'The Discourse of Others: Feminists and Post-modernism', in *Postmodern Culture*.

5. Rosa Lee, 'Resisting Amnesia: Feminism, Painting and Post-modernism', *Feminist Review*, no. 26, July 1987.

6. Leah Hertz, 'Cheers for the Capitalist feminist', *Cosmopolitan*, April 1986.

7. Brenda Polan, 'The Age of Confusion', *Elle*, November 1986.

8. Julie Burchill, 'Some Girls Do', *Elle*, October 1987.

13 Feminism and the Politics of Power: Whose Gaze is it Anyway?

1. Lynne Segal, *Is the Future Female? Troubled Thoughts on Contemporary Feminism*, p. 206.

2. Ibid., p. 207.

3. Roszika Parker and Griselda Pollock, 'Fifteen Years of Feminist Action: From Practical Strategies to Strategic Practices' in *Framing Feminism: Art and the Women's Movement 1970–1985*, p. 61.

4. Michèle Barrett, 'Feminism and the Definition of Cultural Politics', in *Feminism, Culture and Politics*, pp. 43–4.

5. Julie Burchill, 'Some Girls Do', *Elle*, October 1987.

6. Stephanie Dowrick, 'Success, Can Women Afford It?', *Spare Rib*, no. 167, June 1986, p. 38: a discussion of the theme of success in Marilyn French, *Beyond Power: On Women, Men and Morals*, Sphere, London, 1986.

7. Grace Evans, 'Feminist Book Fortnight', *Spare Rib*, no. 167, June 1986, p. 23.

8. Michèle Barrett, op. cit., p. 37.

9. Judith Williamson, 'The Problems of being Popular', *New Socialist*, no. 41, September 1986, p. 14.

10. Sheryl Garratt, 'How I learned to stop worrying and love Madonna', in *Women's Review*, no. 5, March 1986.

11. Elizabeth Wilson, *Adorned in Dreams: Fashion and Modernity*, p. 231.

12. Edwina Currie quoted in an interview with Beatrix Campbell, *Marxism Today*, March 1987.

13. Judith Williamson, 'The Making of a Material Girl', *New Socialist*, October 1985.

14. The relationship between conservatism and feminism is discussed by Beatrix Campbell in *The Iron Ladies*.

15. Michèle Barrett and Mary McIntosh, 'Ethnocentrism and Socialist Feminist Theory', *Feminist Review*, no. 20, Summer 1985, p. 25.

204   *The Female Gaze*

16. Roisin Boyd, 'Sisterhood . . . is plain sailing', *Spare Rib*, no. 133, August 1983.
17. Michel Foucault, *The History of Sexuality: An Introduction*, p. 93.
18. Catherine Belsey, *Critical Practice*, p. 5.
19. Michel Foucault, 'Afterword: The Subject and Power', in *Michel Foucault: Beyond Structuralism and Hermeneutics*, p. 211.
20. Michel Foucault, *The History of Sexuality*, p. 100.
21. Michel Foucault, 'Afterword: The Subject and Power', p. 211.
22. Janice Winship, 'A Girl Needs to Get Street Wise: Magazines for the 1980s', *Feminist Review*, no. 21, Winter 1985, p. 46.
23. In the video accompanying Madonna's 1987 single 'Open Your Heart'.
24. Winship, op. cit., p. 46.
25. Wilson, op. cit., p. 231.
26. Angela McRobbie, 'Postmodernism and Popular Culture' in *ICA Documents 4*, p. 55.
27. Craig Owens, 'The Discourse of Others: Feminists and Postmodernism', in *Postmodern Culture*, pp. 61–2.
28. Ibid.
29. For a discussion of feminist uses of the term 'difference' see Michèle Barrett, 'The Concept of "Difference" ', *Feminist Review*, no. 26, July 1987.
30. Rosa Lee, 'Resisting Amnesia: Feminism, Painting and Postmodernism', *Feminist Review*, no. 26, July 1987.
31. G. Bennington, 'The Question of Postmodernism', in *ICA Documents 4*, p. 5.
32. J.-F. Lyotard, *The Postmodern Condition: A Report on Knowledge*, p. 15.
33. Stuart Hall, 'Gramsci and Us', *Marxism Today*, June 1987, p. 19.

Bibliography

Kathy Acker, *Blood and Guts in High School Plus Two*, Pan, London, 1984.

Louis Althusser, *Essays on Ideology*, Verso, London, 1986.

Louis Althusser, *For Marx*, New Left Books, London, 1977.

Ien Ang, *Watching Dallas*, trans. Della Couling, Methuen, London, 1985.

Lisa Appignanesi (ed) *ICA Documents 4*, London, 1986.

Jeffrey Archer, *The Prodigal Daughter*, Hodder & Stoughton, London 1982.

Robyn Archer and Diana Simmonds, *A Star is Torn*, Virago, London, 1986.

Roy Armes, *A Critical History of British Cinema*, Secker & Warburg, London, 1978.

Michèle Barrett, 'Feminism and the Definition of Cultural Politics', in Rosalind Brunt and Caroline Rowan (eds), *Feminism, Culture and Politics*, Lawrence & Wishart, London, 1982.

Roland Barthes, *Mythologies*, Paladin, London, 1973.

Roland Barthes, *The Pleasure of the Text*, Hill & Wang, New York, 1975.

Roland Barthes, *Camera Lucida*, Flamingo, London, 1984.

Lee Baxandall (ed), *Radical Perspectives in the Arts*, Pelican, Baltimore, 1972.

Catherine Belsey, *Critical Practice*, Methuen, London, 1980.

Jessica Benjamin, 'Master and Slave: The Fantasy of Erotic Domination', in Ann Snitow, Christine Stansell and Sharon Thompson (eds), *Desire: The Politics of Sexuality*, Virago, London, 1984.

G. Bennington, 'The Question of Postmodernism', in Lisa Appignanesi (ed), *ICA Documents 4*, 1986.

John Berger, *Ways of Seeing*, BBC and Penguin, London, 1972.

Rosemary Betterton (ed), *Looking On*, Pandora, London, 1987.

Muriel Box, *Odd Woman Out*, Frewin, London, 1975.

Bertholt Brecht, *Mother Courage and Her Children*, trans. John Willett, Methuen, London, 1980.

Kevin Brownlow, *The Parade's Gone By*, Bonanza Books, New York, 1976.

Charlotte Brunsdon (ed), *Films for Women*, BFI, London, 1968.

Rosalind Brunt and Caroline Rowan (eds), *Feminism, Culture and Politics*, Lawrence & Wishart, London, 1982.

Peter Burger, *Theory of the Avant-Garde*, Manchester University Press, Manchester, 1986.

Susan Butler, 'Revising femininity? Review of *Lady: Photographs of Lisa Lyon* by Robert Mapplethorpe', in Rosemary Betterton (ed), *Looking On*, Pandora, London, 1987.

Beatrix Campbell, *The Iron Ladies*, Virago, London, 1987.

Angela Carter, *Heroes and Villains*, Heinemann, London, 1969.

Angela Carter, *The Sadeian Woman*, Virago, London, 1979.

Angela Carter, *The Bloody Chamber*, Penguin, Harmondsworth, 1981.

Angela Carter, *Nothing Sacred*, Virago, London, 1982.

Barbara Christian and Robert Snowden (eds), *Patterns and Perceptions of Menstruation: A World Health Organisation International Collaborative Study*, Croom Helm, London, 1983.

Shirley Conran, *Lace*, Penguin, Harmondsworth, 1982.

Rosalind Coward, *Female Desire: Women's Sexuality Today*, Paladin, London, 1984.

Mary Daly, *Gyn/Ecology*, The Women's Press, London, 1979.

Janice Delaney, Mary Jane Lupton, Emily Toth, *The Curse: A Cultural History of Menstruation*, E. P. Dutton, New York, 1976.

Mary Ann Doane, Patricia Mellencamp and Linda Williams (eds), *Re-Vision*, American Film Institute, Frederick, Maryland, 1984.

Mary Douglas, *Implicit Meanings*, Routledge & Kegan Paul, London, 1975.

Andrea Dworkin, *Pornography: Men Possessing Women*, The Women's Press, London, 1981.

Richard Dyer (ed), *Gays and Films*, Zoetrope, New York, 1984.

Richard Dyer, *Heavenly Bodies*, Macmillan (BFI Cinema Series), London, 1986.

Antony Easthope, *What a Man's Gotta Do: The Masculine Myth in Popular Culture*, Paladin, London, 1986.

B. Ehrenreich, E. Hess and G. Jacobs, *Re-Making Love: The Feminization of Sex*, Fontana, London, 1987.

John Ellis, *Visible Fictions*, Routledge & Kegan Paul, London, 1982.

Ralph Ellison, *Invisible Man*, Penguin, Harmondsworth, 1965.

Frantz Fanon, *The Wretched of the Earth*, trans. Constance Farrington, Penguin, Harmondsworth, 1967.

M. P. Fogarty (ed), Isobel Allen, A. J. Allen and Patricia Walters, *Women in Top Jobs*, Allen & Unwin, London, 1971.

Michel Foucault, *The History of Sexuality: An Introduction*, Penguin, Harmondsworth, 1984.

Michel Foucault, 'Afterword: The Subject and Power', in H. L. Dreyfus and P. Rabinow (eds), *Michel Foucault: Beyond Structuralism and Hermeneutics*, Harvester, Brighton, 1982.

Sigmund Freud, *On Sexuality*, Penguin, Harmondsworth, 1977.

Henry S. Galus, *The Impact of Women*, Monarch Books, Derby, Connecticut, 1964.

Sandra Gilbert and Susan Gubar, *The Madwoman in the Attic*, Yale University Press, Yale, 1979.

Robert Goffee and Richard Scase, *Women in Charge*, Allen & Unwin, London, 1985.

Judith Gould, *Sins*, Futura, London, 1983.

Antonio Gramsci, *Selections from the Prison Notebooks*, edited and translated by Quintin Hoare and Geoffrey Nowell Smith, Lawrence & Wishart, London, 1971.

Molly Haskell, *From Reverence to Rape: The Treatment of Women in the Movies*, Penguin, Harmondsworth, 1973.

Stephen Heath, *The Sexual Fix*, Macmillan, 1982.

Nancy Henley, *Body Politics*, Prentice Hall, Englewood Cliffs, New Jersey, 1977.

Leah Hertz, *The Business Amazons*, Methuen, London, 1986.

Zora Neale Hurston, *I Love Myself When I'm Laughing*, Feminist Press, New York, 1979.

Zora Neale Hurston, *Spunk*, Camden Press, London,1986.

Luce Irigaray, 'When the Goods Get Together', in Elaine Marks and Isabelle de Courtivron (eds), *New French Feminisms*, Harvester, Brighton, 1981.

Rosemary Jackson, *Fantasy: The Literature of Subversion*, Methuen, London, 1981.

Mary Jacobus (ed), *Women Writing and Writing about Women*, Croom Helm, London, 1979.

E. Ann Kaplan (ed), *Women in Film Noir*, BFI, London, 1980.

E. Ann Kaplan, 'Is the Gaze Male?' in Ann Snitow, Christine Stansell and Sharon Thompson (eds), *Desire: The Politics of Sexuality*, Virago, London, 1984.

E. Ann Kaplan, *Women and Film*, Methuen, London, 1983.

E. Ann Kaplan, *Rocking Around the Clock*, Methuen, London, 1987.

Susanne Kappeler, *The Pornography of Representation*, Polity Press, Cambridge, 1986.

Julia Kristeva, *About Chinese Women*, Marion Boyars, London, 1977.

Annette Kuhn, *Women's Pictures: Feminism and Cinema*, Routledge & Kegan Paul, London, 1982.

Annette Kuhn, *The Power of the Image: Essays on Representation and Sexuality*, Routledge & Kegan Paul, London, 1985.

Jacques Lacan, *Ecrits*, trans. Alan Sheridan, Tavistock, London, 1977.

Teresa de Lauretis, *Alice Doesn't: Feminism, Semiotics and Cinema*, Macmillan, London, 1984.

Georg Lukács, 'The Ideology of Modernism', in *The Meaning of Contemporary Realism*, trans. Joan and Necke Mander, Merlin Press, London, 1963.

J.-F. Lyotard, *The Postmodern Condition: A Report on Knowledge*, trans. G. Bennington and B. Massumi, Manchester University Press, Manchester, 1986.

J.-F. Lyotard, 'Brief Reflections on Popular Culture', in Lisa Appignanesi (ed), *ICA Documents 4*, 1986.

Denis McQuail, *Sociology of Mass Communications*, Penguin, Harmondsworth, 1972.

Angela McRobbie, 'Postmodernism and Popular Culture' in Lisa Appignanesi (ed), *ICA Documents 4*, 1986.

Herbert Marcuse, 'Art in the One-Dimensional Society', in Lee Baxandall (ed), *Radical Perspectives in the Arts*, Pelican, Baltimore, 1972.

Elaine Marks and Isabelle de Courtivron (eds), *New French Feminisms*, Harvester, Brighton, 1981.

Karl Marx and Friedrich Engels, *Selected Works*, Progress Publishers, Moscow, 1966.

Matriarchy Study Group, *Menstrual Taboos*, Matriarchy Study Group, London, n.d.

Mandy Merck, '*Lianna* and the Lesbians of Art Cinema', in Charlotte Brunsdon (ed)' *Films for Women*, BFI, London, 1986.

Christian Metz, *Film Language: A Semiotics of the Cinema*, trans. Michael Taylor, Oxford University Press, New York, 1974.

Tania Modleski, *Loving with a Vengeance: Mass Produced Fantasies for Women*, Methuen, London, 1982.

Robin Morgan (ed), *Sisterhood is Powerful*, Vintage Books, New York, 1970.

Anne Ross Muir, *A Woman's Guide to Jobs in Film and Television*, Pandora, London, 1987.

Stephen Neale, *Genre*, BFI, London, 1983.
Stephen Neale, 'Masculinity as Spectacle: Reflections on Men and Mainstream Cinema', *Screen*, vol. 24, no. 6, Nov/Dec 1983.

Open University, *Popular Culture Handbook*, 1984.
Craig Owens, 'The Discourse of Others: Feminists and Postmodernism', in Hal Foster (ed), *Postmodern Culture*, Pluto Press, London, 1985.

Roszika Parker and Griselda Pollock, *Framing Feminism: Art and the Women's Movement 1970–1985*, Pandora, London, 1987.
Marge Piercy, *Woman on the Edge of Time*, The Women's Press, London, 1979.
Janey Place, 'Women in Film Noir', in E. Ann Kaplan (ed), *Women in Film Noir*, BFI, London, 1980.

Adrienne Rich, 'Compulsory Heterosexuality and Lesbian Existence', in Elizabeth Abel and Emily K. Abel (eds), *The Signs Reader: Women, Gender and Scholarship*, University of Chicago Press, Chicago, 1983.
Jacqueline Rose, *Sexuality in the Field of Vision*, Verso, London, 1986.
Robyn Rowland (ed), *Women Who Do and Women Who Don't Join the Women's Movement*, Routledge & Kegan Paul, London, 1984.
Joanna Russ, *The Female Man*, The Women's Press, London, 1985.

Lynne Segal, *Is the Future Female? Troubled Thoughts on Contemporary Feminism*, Virago, London, 1987.
Caroline Sheldon, 'Lesbians and Film: Some Thoughts', in Richard Dyer (ed), *Gays and Film*, Zoetrope, New York, 1984.
Elaine Showalter, 'Towards a Feminist Poetics', in Mary Jacobus (ed), *Women Writing and Writing about Women*, Croom Helm, London, 1979.
Ann Barr Snitow, 'Mass Market Romance: Pornography for Women is Different', in Ann Snitow, Christine Stansell and Sharon Thompson (eds), *Desire: The Politics of Sexuality*, Virago, London, 1984.
Ann Snitow, Christine Stansell and Sharon Thompson (eds), *Desire: The Politics of Sexuality*, Virago, London, 1984.
Susan Sontag, *Against Interpretation*, André Deutsch, London, 196

Michelle Stanworth, *Gender and Schooling*, Hutchinson, London, 1983.

Gloria Steinem, *Outrageous Acts and Everyday Rebellions*, Holt, Reinhart & Winston, New York, 1983.

Barbara Bradford Taylor, *A Woman of Substance*, Grafton Books, London, 1981.

Barbara Bradford Taylor, *Hold the Dream*, Grafton Books, London, 1985.

Tzvetan Todorov, *The Poetics of Prose*, trans. Richard Howard, Basil Blackwell, Oxford, 1977.

J. M. S. Tompkins, *The Popular Novel in England*, Methuen University Press, London, 1932.

Mariana Valverde, *Sex, Power and Pleasure*, The Women's Press, Toronto, 1985.

Hannah Wakefield, *The Price You Pay*, The Women's Press, London, 1987.

Alice Walker, *You Can't Keep a Good Woman Down*, The Women's Press, London, 1982.

Alice Walker, *The Color Purple*, The Women's Press, London, 1983.

Alice Walker, *In Love and Trouble*, The Women's Press, London, 1984.

Alice Walker, *In Search of Our Mothers' Gardens*, The Women's Press, London, 1984.

Alice Walker, *The Third Life of Grange Copeland*, The Women's Press, London, 1985.

Margaret Walters, *The Male Nude: A New Perspective*, Penguin, Harmondsworth, 1979.

Paula Weideger, *Female Cycles*, The Women's Press, London, 1978.

Claire Whitiker, 'Hollywood Transformed: Interviews with Lesbian Viewers', in Peter Staven (ed), *Jump Cut: Hollywood, Politics and Counter Cinema*, Praeger Scientific, New York, 1985.

Judith Williamson, *Decoding Advertisements: Ideology and Meaning in Advertising*, Marion Boyars, London, 1978.

Elizabeth Wilson, *Adorned in Dreams: Fashion and Modernity*, Virago, London, 1985.

Elizabeth Wilson, *Hidden Agendas*, Tavistock, London, 1986.

Mary Wings, *She Came Too Late*, The Women's Press, London, 1987.

Richard Wright, *Black Boy*, Harpers, New York, 1945.

Notes on Contributors

Maggie Anwell is involved in research and teaching in arts education.

Belinda Budge is a freelance publicity and marketing consultant. She is also a founder member of Scarlet Press, a new feminist publishing company.

Petal Felix is a freelance journalist and producer, currently contributing to TV programmes such as *Heart of the Matter*.

Janet Lee is a freelance journalist and radio producer, producing magazine programmes for BBC Radio 4.

Avis Lewallen teaches twentieth century literature for the WEA and is a founder member of Scarlet Press, a new feminist publishing company.

Suzanne Moore is a freelance journalist, film critic for the *New Statesman* and regular columnist for *Marxism Today*.

Anne Ross Muir is a freelance television director, who has worked on a wide variety of productions including news, current affairs, documentaries and docu-dramas, both in this country and in the USA. She is the author of *A Woman's Guide to Jobs in Film and Television* (Pandora, 1987).

Jacqui Roach is a freelance journalist and currently works full time as press and publicity officer at the CAB.

Jackie Stacey teaches women's studies and media studies in the Department of Sociology, University of Lancaster. She is completing her Ph.D. on Hollywood stars and British women audiences at the Department of Cultural Studies, University of Birmingham.

Andrea Stuart has contributed to a collection of essays entitled *Identity*, edited by J Rutherford, Lawrence and Wishart, 1990. She is currently researching a book on the subject of women and performance.

Ann Treneman is a freelance newspaper journalist. She also writes on different aspects of women and the media, and in 1987 received an MA in women's studies from the University of Kent.

Shelagh Young is a freelance journalist. She is also a founder member of Green Eye (an environmental news agency).

Index